ENGLISH THEATRICAL ANECDOTES, 1660–1800

PERFORMING CELEBRITY

Performing Celebrity publishes single-authored monographs and essay collections that explore the dynamics of fame, infamy, and technologies of image-making from the early modern period to the present day. This series of books seeks to add to exciting recent developments in the emerging field of celebrity studies by publishing outstanding works that explore mechanisms of self-fashioning, stardom, and notoriety operating across genres and media in a broad range of historical and national contexts. It focuses on interdisciplinary projects that employ current research and a wide variety of theoretical approaches to performance and celebrity in relation to literature, history, art history, media, fashion, theater, gender(s), sexuality, race, ethnicity, disability, material culture, etc.

Series Titles

Black Celebrity: Contemporary Representations of Postbellum Athletes and Artists, Emily Ruth Rutter

Carrying All before Her: Celebrity Pregnancy and the London Stage, 1689–1800, Chelsea Phillips

Celebrity across the Channel, 1750–1850, edited by Anaïs Pédron and Clare Siviter

ENGLISH THEATRICAL ANECDOTES, 1660–1800

Edited by Heather Ladd
and Leslie Ritchie

UNIVERSITY OF DELAWARE
UNIVERSITY OF DELAWARE PRESS

Newark

Library of Congress Cataloging-in-Publication Data

Names: Ladd, Heather, editor. | Ritchie, Leslie, 1970– editor.
Title: English theatrical anecdotes, 1660–1800/edited by Heather Ladd and Leslie Ritchie.
Description: Newark, Delaware : University of Delaware Press, [2022] | Series: Performing celebrity | Includes bibliographical references and index.
Identifiers: LCCN 2021041118 | ISBN 9781644532607 (paperback) | ISBN 9781644532614 (hardcover) | ISBN 9781644532621 (epub) | ISBN 9781644532638 (pdf)
Subjects: LCSH: Theater—England—Anecdotes. | Theater—England—History—18th century. | Fame—Social aspects—England—History—18th century. | LCGFT: Essays.
Classification: LCC PN2095 .E54 2022 | DDC 792.0942/09033—dc23
LC record available at https://lccn.loc.gov/2021041118

A British Cataloging-in-Publication record for this book is available from the British Library.

♾ The paper used in this publication meets the requirements of the American National Standard for Information Sciences—Permanence of Paper for Printed Library Materials, ANSI Z39.48-1992.

udpress.udel.edu

Distributed worldwide by Rutgers University Press

Manufactured in the United States of America

CONTENTS

ACKNOWLEDGMENTS

The editors would like to thank this volume's contributors for their thoughtful chapters, which have added greatly to the scholarly conversation about anecdotes' form and function. Thanks to Julia Oestreich, director of University of Delaware Press, and Laura Engel, series editor for Performing Celebrity, for their encouragement and guidance. Our gratitude goes out to the anonymous peer reviewers of this volume for their suggestions. We also acknowledge the efforts of Brian Ostrander at Westchester Publishing Services, and the production teams at the University of Delaware Press and Rutgers University Press for their assistance in the publication process. Thank you to Kevin Joel Berland for his work on the index and to our copyeditor, Katherine Woodrow, for her careful editing. Thanks to Carmen Holdsworth-Delgado, Emma Carter, and the Garrick Club, London, for their kind permission to use Johan Zoffany's painting, "Sophia Baddeley, Thomas King, and Robert Baddeley in *The Clandestine Marriage*" as our cover image.

Heather Ladd would like to thank her parents, Gerald and Janet Ladd, her partner, Andrew Robb, and mother-in-law, Catherine Montgomery, for their support over the years. She is also grateful to

Brian Corman from the University of Toronto for sparking her lifelong interest in Restoration and eighteenth-century comedy.

Leslie Ritchie would like to thank the Social Sciences and Humanities Research Council of Canada and Queen's University for supporting her research. Thanks to Brian, Owen, and Alec for their love and for furnishing her with endless anecdotes.

INTRODUCTION

Miniature Stages of Celebrity: English Theatrical Anecdotes, 1600–1800

HEATHER LADD AND LESLIE RITCHIE

Theatrical anecdotes—short, often humorous and titillating, sometimes moralistic tales of theater people, particularly actors and actresses—permeate the literature of the long eighteenth century. Titles from W. R. Chetwood's *General History of the Stage . . . containing many Theatrical Anecdotes* (1749) to William Oxberry's *Anecdotes of the Stage* (1827) show that theatrical anecdotes were marketed as a distinct genre, and consumed with enthusiasm. Despite their referential topicality, anecdotes are anything but ephemeral. Histories of the English stage produced from the eighteenth century onward have depended on anecdotes' revelatory qualities to authenticate their reconstructions of theatrical personnel and performances. Ironically, these ambitious narratives were propelled by anecdotes' salacious properties and fictionality. Anecdotes likewise furnished much of the content of the published memoirs, biographies, and autobiographies of eighteenth-century stage celebrities. David Erskine Baker's *Companion to the Playhouse* (1764), for instance, advertises "a great Number of new Lives and curious Anecdotes never before communicated to the Public" as an incentive to purchase a volume of actors' and dramatic writers' lives.[1] Talk between actors in the green room, that liminal, semipublic, offstage theatrical space, is imagined for readers in such volumes as *The Theatrical Jester: or Green-Room Witticisms* (1795) and *The Theatrical Olio: Or, Thespian Jester* (1798) in a manner reminiscent of the secret history.[2]

While each individual anecdote is self-contained, brief, and singular, when considered as a genre, theatrical anecdotes resist formal containment and display a magnetic tendency toward accretion, collection, and performative recirculation. Malina Stefanovska aptly connects "striking" anecdotes with the contents of cabinets of curiosities, illuminating the similarity between material and textual collection in her suggestion that both are "governed by the pleasure principle which allows for repetition, accumulation, and exhibition."[3] Repetition of theatrical anecdotes, like repetition in the theatrical repertoire, is an important index of taste. As anecdotes are amassed into collections or subsumed into larger texts, including novels, diaries, and periodical essays, they afford complex, sometimes contradictory, testaments to theatrical evolution, such as the apparent trends in the eighteenth century toward more naturalistic acting, the professionalization of acting, and the construction of celebrity.

For eighteenth-century readers, theatrical anecdotes promised a mode of sociability predicated on the retailing of compressed, often comic, insider information that could enhance their reputation for possessing theatrical intelligence. A typical green room exchange, humorous and conflictual, involved English comedian Charles Bannister mocking actor-singer Charles Dignum for his costume as Cymon. Dignum thought he was looking rather well and was begging for compliments, but was met with this rebuff: "—No, replied Charles, you look more like a hog than a cimon—Alluding to the cant name for a shilling and sixpence."[4] Readers could cite this incident, or use it as inspiration to create a similar low pun themselves, modeling their own discourse on actors' green room wit. Anecdotes were acknowledged to possess "a kind of *creative* power, generating their like, and even happily effecting a salutary change in the predisposition of the reader's mind,"[5] dispensing their happy affect as they were read or replicated. Cheering anecdotes were intended to lift the spirits; much like popular song, they were "pills to purge melancholy."[6]

Anecdotes' perceived value was not confined to their comic effect. Adjectives preceding "anecdote" in eighteenth- and nineteenth-century publications insistently speak to anecdotes' purpose and value: they are not only "droll,"[7] "pleasant," and "remarkable"[8]; they are also "very extraordinary" and "authentic,"[9] "singular,"[10] "characteristic," and "curious"[11]; anecdotes, the reader is advised, are "real."[12] Such claims are often made simultaneously with no apparent sense of contradiction. After recounting an extended tale detailing the rivalry between Robert Wilks and George Powell, Colley Cibber excused his own liberal use of anecdotal storytelling by arguing for its usefulness to other stage performers as well as its entertainment value to laypeople: "However trifling these Theatrical anecdotes may seem, to a sensible Reader, yet, as the different Conduct of these rival Actors may be of use, to others of the same Profession, and from thence may contribute to the Pleasure of the Public; let that be my Excuse, for pursuing them."[13] Cibber's defense points to the complexities of the theatrical anecdote as a literary form closely linked to the stage and its celebrity culture. This collection surveys the varied, often surprising cultural work theatrical anecdotes performed during the eighteenth century, and considers, too, their role in current theater scholarship.

Orality and Theatrical Anecdote

The theatrical anecdote shares with jests and bon mots an intimate relationship with the spoken word; speaking and listening are the central actions of countless theatrical anecdotes, and many anecdotes appear or claim to have been first transmitted orally before being transcribed and printed for further recirculation in conversation. As scholars like Paula McDowell and Dianne Dugaw have explicated, the relationship between literacy and orality is a complicated one. McDowell, in her work on the "unruly orality" of *A Journal of the Plague Year* (1722), argues that although eighteenth-century authors like Daniel Defoe "attempted to make print more credible by modelling it as separate from certain types of orality," print and orality were messily entwined.[14] Theatrical anecdotes likewise show orality and print as "media forms that are in reality copresent and interdependent," but authors and compilers of these stories are far less likely than Defoe to insist on a hierarchy of media forms that privileges print.[15] McDowell's model of media elements in competition works well for journalistic fiction, but less so for published theatrical anecdotes, which usually embrace rather than try to elide or denigrate the element of orality upon which they are so frequently contingent. Dugaw's work on orality in James Boswell's autobiographical writing stresses "mixing" rather than competition; she describes Boswell's diaries, which incorporate allusions to popular songs and song culture, as "a privately rendered staging of moments of orally-enacted social intercourse."[16] Theatrical anecdotes likewise stage such moments but do so for a public audience, and in ways that explicitly present orality as authority.

Early paradramatic works like theatrical biographies, miscellanies, and histories show the transmission of theater lore has often occurred through speech acts that make their circuitous way into print. Thomas Davies's *Dramatic Miscellanies* (1783–1784) praises a minor actor, Nat[haniel] Clarke (the original Filch in *The Beggar's Opera*), as "the chronicle of the theatre," one who "knew the whole history of the players, and made himself acceptable to busy enquirers after theatric matters by communicating to them many a laughable anecdote."[17] Davies—himself a busy enquirer after theatric matters—no sooner establishes Clarke's authority than he deploys his access to Clarke's authentic green room orature to relay an anecdote about Clarke and the famous Harlequin John Rich. Rich is punched in the stomach by an angry audience member who mistakes him for Clarke, his under-Harlequin. This "whimsical accident," also related in William Cooke's *Memoirs of Charles Macklin, Comedian* (1804), is chalked up to the "similarity of form" that made Clarke an ideal stand-in for Rich on stage.[18] The juxtaposition of Davies's description of Clarke's stature as an oral historian of the theater with this amusing anecdote of the misdirected punch leads the reader to assume that Davies is relating a reliable eyewitness account, and gives the reader a pleasing sense of participating in the conversational chain of anecdote initiated by Clarke and Davies.

Anecdotes frequently incorporate dialogue, with quotation marks indicating reported speech attributed to an individual, or with more oblique linguistic discourse markers. Many titles personified these anecdote collections as convivial companions offering improving conversation. *The Complete London Jester* (1765) offers would-be wits all the humor "which has lately flowed from the Two Universities, from the Two Theatres," the Bedford Coffee House, and theatrical spouting clubs, the better to "improve the Wit, create Mirth, [and] entertain Company" and teach "the agreeable Art of

Story-telling" by "furnishing Pieces of Wit for the Amusement and Improvement of both Sexes."[19] Rather than rendering it questionable, reference to orality generally authenticates and authorizes theatrical anecdote.

As Simon Dickie's study of eighteenth-century humor *Cruelty and Laughter* confirms, there is significant overlap between the theatrical anecdote and the joke. Several eighteenth-century jestbooks comprised of highly condensed comic tales and witty exchanges are credited to celebrated performer-wits, including such titles as *Nancy Dawson's Jests* (1761), *Quin's Jests* (1766), *Colley Cibber's Jests* (1761), *Spiller's Jests* (1730), *Garrick's Complete Jester* (1779), and the long-enduring *Joe Miller's Jests, or the Wits Vade-Mecum* (1739). Dickie's study is more concerned with the enduring topoi of jests than with jests' changing attributions to particular speakers. The chapters in this volume, however, approach primary texts with an eye to their celebrity references and (re)packaging, attending to the ways in which bon mots, jests, and other forms of theatrical anecdote have shaped and modeled discourse about the theater. At first glance, many theatrical anecdotes afford only light entertainment. *English Jests and Anecdotes (Nuggets for Travellers)* (1886)[20] includes a brief story about Garrick, dressed as Ranger from *The Suspicious Husband* (1747), dining out in the "beef-stake room at Covent Garden" before a show. The actor is late to the theater thanks to a carriage jam on Russell Street. Dr. Ford, one of the theater patentees, chides his lateness and reminds him that given the "stake you and I have in this theatre, you might pay more attention to its business." Garrick punningly rejoins: "I should have been in good time; but I was thinking of my *steak* in the other."[21] Yet this groaner of a "Joe Miller"[22] also underlines Garrick's status as a gentleman-player who enjoys fine meals and good society, and who travels by carriage. Theatrical anecdotes, unlike jests, are not always comical, and unlike bon mots, they are not simply "pointed axioms and acute replies" that "fly loose about the world,"[23] valued more for their witty formulation than their origins. A theatrical anecdote offers a moment of recognition and confirmation as its reader or listener realizes the anecdote's referential claims upon real persons and places.

Anecdotes and Their Referents

Joel Fineman, in his seminal study of the genre's history, introduces the anecdote as being "understood as a specific literary genre, with peculiar literary properties."[24] Fineman, aware of the anecdote's slippage between fiction and nonfiction, qualifies this assessment with the observation that "the anecdote, however literary, is nevertheless directly pointed towards or rooted in the real—[this] allows us to think of the anecdote, given its formal if not its actual brevity, as a *historeme*, i.e., as the smallest minimal unit of the historiographic fact."[25] More recently, Virginia Scott has acknowledged anecdotes' relation to history as "troublesome," but nonetheless worthy of study "because history without anecdotal evidence loses its focus on human behaviour" and because, at bottom, the stage is a testing ground for what makes us human.[26]

Eighteenth-century writers concerned with the theater also expressed ambivalence about anecdotes' relation with history, sometimes characterizing their inclusion of anecdotes as a temptation into indulgence or fiction. In his *Original Anecdotes Respecting the Stage, and the Actors of the Old School, with Remarks on Mr. Murphy's "Life of Garrick"* (1805), Tate Wilkinson introduces a charming story with the confession, "*I cannot resist a little* anecdote here, that I believe is not known, but which is, however, an indisputable fact."[27] He relates that Garrick has another performer swear to secrecy, not on a Bible, but on a volume of Shakespeare, solemnly kissed. This anecdote contributes to Garrick's reputation; it underlines his sense of honor, essential to his identity as a genteel actor, and his "reputation as a man of letters . . . [and] authority on all things Shakespearean."[28] Wilkinson transitions between this gently comic Garrick anecdote and one about Susannah Cibber playing Juliet in Garrick's Shakespearean adaptation with the remark, "How apt the relation of one anecdote is to remind us of another,"[29] signaling the anecdote's tendency toward casual, thematic, or even nonlinear accretion. Anecdotes create a kind of additive narrative rhythm that often precludes more than the most cursory of transitions, pursuing associative thematic cascades rather than strict chronologies. In part, it is this quality of anecdote—its distracting sideways tug at history's chronology—that leads some theater historians to temper their inclusion of anecdotes with apologies.

Identifying the anecdote *as* anecdote allows historians who view anecdote as unreliable or quasi-fictional to have it both ways. The popular historian Liza Picard, for example, gives her book on Restoration London the subtitle "Engaging Anecdotes and Tantalizing Trivia from the Most Magnificent and Renowned City of Europe," which encapsulates this usage.[30] Other historians view anecdote as an essential complement to history. The editor of the *Encyclopaedia of Anecdote* (ca. 1800) argues, "*Memoirs* and *Anecdotes* are the co-aids of *history*: minute details, traits of character, and reflections on events, are generally passed over in historical works; but, like interior machinery, those latent movers direct the whole of the proceedings."[31] The history of the theater would be very thin indeed without either memoir or anecdote, both of which play a key role in the curating and archiving of stage celebrity.

Theatrical Anecdotes and Liveness

Theater, born of bodies in motion, is the art of the singular, the production of unduplicatable, imperfect artistic events. Within the current of variant performances, each itself potentially worthy of comment, theatrical mishaps and other remarkable events erupt like sharp rocks in a stream, reinforcing the immediacy and singularity of the theatrical event. Historians accord anecdotes of the stage a special ability to transfix and transcend theatrical ephemerality, each one offering a moment of stasis that paradoxically calls attention to theater's liveness. With a practitioner's eye for detail, Tate Wilkinson describes how the actress Susanna Cibber, unable to locate Juliet's dagger, was forced to mime her heroine's tragic suicide: "At last, evidently much distressed, she held up her delicate fist (which was really so) and ideally plunged the weapon to her heart. The audience did not laugh, but applauded, from respect to her talents: but the instant the curtain dropt, laughter prevailed about the theatre; and from that night, I believe, Juliet has ever trusted to her own care that necessary plaything, the dagger."[32] Wilkinson ends the story by supposing this particular "unlucky mistake" to be the source of this "custom" among actresses playing Juliet.[33] Anecdotes like this one were used by early theater historians to illustrate stage practices, giving audiences a privileged glimpse into the workings of the playhouse and exciting confirmation of theater's "liveness."

Another such anecdote features rival actors David Garrick and James Quin appearing onstage together in Shakespeare's *Henry IV, Part 1* in their 1746–1747 season at Covent Garden. Quin, as Falstaff, carries the body of Hotspur, played by Garrick. While they head offstage, Quin asks Garrick, in earshot of the audience, "Where shall we sup?" In speaking to a character ostensibly dead, Quin compromises the audience's suspension of disbelief, reminding theatergoers that this is a performance by actors very much alive (and hungry). Both Quin and Falstaff are "convivial" men of appetite, and the actor (a noted gourmand) "seemed born to play" Shakespeare's edacious knight.[34] Peter Thomson, noting the actors' difference in stature, observes that "in stage silhouette, they would have looked more like Laurel and Hardy than serious rivals for the dramatic crown."[35] This frequently retailed anecdote underlines the actors' physical presence, and transforms a tragic moment into a comic one. Anecdote intervenes and disrupts our presuppositions of dramatic texts' affect, reminding us of the vast compass of interpretive possibilities and accidents theater's liveness offers.

Theatrical Anecdotes and/as Literature

Stefanovska situates anecdotes within a nexus of related narrative forms and genres, from popular histories to imaginative fictions, proposing that "when heavily amplified and elaborated, they are still at the root of the literary short story and the novel."[36] The eighteenth-century English novel, episodic from its beginnings with Daniel Defoe, is also a vessel for striking micronarratives. Sometimes, as in Frances Burney's *Evelina* (1778), novels' episodes retell, echo, or otherwise resemble theatrical anecdotes. The young heroine's feeling response to the opera she watches is juxtaposed against the insensitivity of her vulgar London relatives, the Branghtons, who mock her for enjoying the performance.[37] Elsewhere, Evelina gushes in a letter to her guardian about Garrick, whose dramatic powers she has witnessed firsthand. In Frances Brooke's *The Excursion* (1777), the aspiring writer-heroine Miss Villiers arranges to have her play introduced to a theater manager (tacitly modeled on Garrick) by Mr. Hammond, who is unsuccessful in his "very friendly interposition in favour of her tragedy."[38] Such moments offer testament not only to the novel's heterogeneity but also to theatrical anecdotes' appeal and reach, and the two genres' common interest in verisimilitude.

Anecdotes intersected with the growing body of life-writing and "life"-writing (fictional and quasi-fictional autobiographical works) published in eighteenth-century England. This connection is rendered explicit in a title like *Anecdotes & Biography: Including Many Modern Characters in the Circles of Fashionable and Official Life, Selected from the Portfolios of a Distinguished Literary and Political Character Lately Deceased, Alphabetically Arranged* (1799). Eighteenth-century publishers clearly possessed commercial confidence in the anecdote. Yet anecdotes were not simply championed for their market value, but for their capacity to represent character. Samuel Johnson and James Boswell, the great biographer and "the biographer to the great biographer," are pioneering figures in the theory and practice of eighteenth-century anecdotal biography.[39] Both valued particularity in biographical writing, and even spoke and acted in ways conducive to provoking anecdote. Dugaw terms this Boswell's "histrionic personality," and stresses that her subject is a product of a theatrical culture: "The omnipresent sway of drama as a ready cultural forum encouraged the theatricality, oral artfulness, and performance orientation of even the most private and informal personal exchanges."[40] By that token, all eighteenth-century anecdote is theatrical and performative. While Johnson himself did not go this far, he did vindicate the anecdotal method of biography and the biographer's investment in character and appreciation of individuality. Famously, Johnson made a case in *The Rambler* No. 60 for the biographer's inclusion of "minute details," arguing that "more knowledge may be gained of a man's real character, by a short conversation with one of his servants, than from a formal and studied narrative."[41] Johnson changed the face of biography with his monumental achievement, *Prefaces, Biographical and Critical, to the Works of the English Poets* (1779–81). Popularly referred to as *The Lives of the Poets*, this work melded literary criticism with the anecdotal detail that we now take for granted as part of commercialized celebrity culture, literary and dramatic. Johnson's own preeminent biographer famously perfected this intimate method of composing biography, as Helen Deutsch observes in her analysis of "Boswell's art of the anecdote" with its revelatory particularities, often gleaned by oral exchange.[42]

In keeping with the period's commercial and artistic belief in the anecdote's centrality to biography, anecdotal content was regularly advertised on the title pages of theatrical biographies and autobiographies, such as James Boaden's biography of the great comic actress of the eighteenth century, Dorothy Jordan: *The Life of Mrs. Jordan: Including Original Private Correspondence, and Numerous Anecdotes of Her Contemporaries* (1831).[43] Stefanovska, focusing more on the French tradition of anecdotal narratives, mentions "the extremely popular '*—ana*' consisted of compiled anecdotes, scholarly observations, and witticisms published under the name of the man of letters who uttered them."[44] This tradition is also applicable to eighteenth-century actors. The comic impresario Samuel Foote, for instance, was posthumously honored with several collections of his celebrated sayings and antics. *Aristophanes, being a Classic Collection of true Attic Wit, containing the Jests, Gibes, Bon-mots, Witticisms, and most Extraordinary Anecdotes of Samuel Foote, Esq.* (1778) is but one of the best-known examples of collections of table talk, bon mots, and vignettes by performers known for their wit, both on- and offstage.[45]

In terms of their formal structure, theatrical anecdotes might be described productively as "microcomedies" and "microtragedies" to highlight the genre's affinities with dramatic literature. As Lionel Gossman remarked, "What most people would consider the classic anecdote is a highly concentrated . . . three-act structure consisting of situation or exposition, encounter or crisis, and resolution—the last usually marked by a 'pointe' or clinching remark, often a 'bon mot.'"[46] To expand upon Gossman's discussion of form, we might venture to say that anecdote is an inherently dramatic genre. Anecdotes may not always have authors, but they do always have actors—real human bodies from whom the anecdote's action originates. Building on the work of Joseph Roach, Elaine McGirr avers that "images and anecdotes enable celebrity by testifying to corporality, to realness: even apocryphal stories can be traced back to real bodies."[47] Theatrical anecdotes, in which the agents of the anecdotal action are generally professional actors, perhaps represent the most complex expression of the genre, referring as they do to persons noted for performing fictive actions, speaking words that do not belong to them, and portraying sundry characters on- and offstage. As Joseph Haslewood's *Secret History of the Green Room* (1792) puts it, theatrical anecdotes' "zest" derives from the fact that "Heroes and Heroines of the Buskin, in their *real*, as well as their *assumed* characters, experience that vicissitude and adventure to which the unvaried tenor of mechanical industry is a stranger. Their life teems with incident which almost seems destined to realize the fictions they represent."[48] If anecdotes in general are troubling in their conflicted allegiances to literariness and to history, to the representation of real bodies and of characters, theatrical anecdotes are even more so. After all, theatrical anecdotes *are* a kind of theatre.

Anecdotes and Celebrity

Anecdotes are part of the process by which theatrical celebrities are both mythologized and humanized. In the mid- to late eighteenth century, these entertaining microhistories of the stage piqued, fed, and sustained interest in stage celebrities, sharing as they do the essential quality of celebrity itself, described by Emrys D. Jones and Victoria Joule as "the meeting point of public appearance and private desire."[49] Commercial and critical success entwined with the commodified individualization of both the star and the fan in celebrity culture. As David Giles, Leslie Ritchie, Chris Rojek, and others have theorized, eighteenth-century celebrity was generated in large part by media.[50] Theatrical anecdotes formed a considerable part of that media environment, recounting in print both career-changing events and day-to-day incidents within celebrities' professional and personal lives. Rendered a commodity by the entertainment industry, the actor was given a visible private life within print culture, although that constructed interiority, or "public intimacy" as Felicity Nussbaum terms it, could be considered another mode of commodification.[51]

William Woodfall's newspaper, *The Morning Chronicle*, ran a regular column entitled "Theatrical Anecdotes," and the column for April 12, 1774, vividly illustrates the intersection of celebrity and commodification in the media, dishing up news of devious offstage benefit-season maneuvers. "Miss Y—e" of Drury Lane, hearing that the comedian Tom Weston was ill, sent him a doctor, who found the actor drinking punch, "not really, but politically ill." In revenge for this discovery, when told that Miss Y—e was indisposed just as she should be playing for his benefit, Weston sent her a doctor with an empiric for a "certain fashionable disorder," implying that she caught an intimate disease from him, upon which Miss Y—e reportedly threw the doctor downstairs. Two days later, Weston took out a card in the *Chronicle*, offering to meet with the author of the column and correct him and his anecdote, "for Tom hates a liar." Without ever stating which part of the anecdote was a lie (if any), Weston's intervention in the media realigned his image with the public's understanding of his persona as a merry man of honor with whom they were on a familiar, first-name basis.

As the Y[oung]e–Weston anecdote hints, such intimate views need not be as glamorous as the ubiquitous anecdote of Lavinia Fenton's ascendancy from the role of Polly Peachum to that of Duchess of Bolton; accidents onstage and in private life humanized and endeared actors to their audiences.[52] Playwright John Gay had an enormous stage hit with *The Beggar's Opera* (1728), which ran for an astonishing sixty-two nights. An anecdote about the writer's awkward encounter with royalty in the years before his ballad opera was produced subtly softens the glare of this triumph. Benjamin Victor, in *The History of the Theatres of London and Dublin, From the Year 1730 to the Present Time* (1731), relates that when Gay brought a manuscript of his tragedy *The Captives* (1724) to Leicester House to read to the Princess of Wales (the future Queen Caroline), he tripped over a low footstool and fell into a screen, which he toppled. Victor uses this story to pay a compliment to the monarch, concluding, "Her Royal Highness's great Goodness soon reconciled this whimsical Accident, but the unlucky Author was not so soon clear of his Confusion."[53] This farcical anecdote is suggestive of Gay's facility for comedy, and a humbling reminder that comedy was his true métier (*The Captives*, which ran a respectable seven nights, was his only tragic play). The range of theatrical anecdotes tends toward extremes, from appealingly intimate, humbling follies to aggrandizing moments of dramatic or musical prowess, but to the same end: the moment of recognition that constitutes celebrity.

Anecdotes, both makers and breakers of theatrical reputations, are crucial in elevating certain actors above others as they confirm the singularity of the actor's dramatic skill and admirable character, offstage and on. Garrick's talents as an actor have been immortalized in countless anecdotes that illustrate the impact of his acting on not only playgoers but also other performers. Garrick, playing Macbeth, "exclaimed to the murderer in the banquet scene, 'There's blood upon thy face' with such power that the man replied, 'Is there, by God?'"[54] This unexpected off-script moment humorously reinforces Garrick's ability to make stage fictions seem real, even to fellow players.[55] Stories about how audiences responded to Garrick form another significant grouping of theatrical anecdotes about the mid-eighteenth-century stage. James Roose-Evans recounts a story involving the king of Denmark attending a performance of *The Suspicious Husband* with Garrick in the role of Ranger: "When Garrick appeared, the audience roared with applause and the king rose, assuming it was for him, and Garrick had to wait until he sat down."[56] This anecdote speaks to Garrick's popularity, but also to the actor's respectful professionalism and social refinement in the face of the king's faux pas.

The preponderance of Garrickian anecdotes in this introduction and throughout this collection illustrates the fact that certain performers attracted more anecdotal activity than others. Considerations of an actor's talent, power within the theatrical community, market influence, and personal eccentricities offer only partial answers as to why this is so. As the chapters in this volume show, the most frequent subjects of theatrical anecdotes sometimes actively courted attention by encouraging the transmission of stories about themselves. Others deliberately structured their encounters with the public in ways that translated easily into this genre. For example, the comedian Jo. Haines wrote and subsequently delivered an epilogue while mounted on an ass, a marketable moment that was captured and recirculated in prints.[57] Epilogues, like anecdotes themselves, were an entryway into the performer's persona, and presented a curated caricature for theatergoers to enjoy. Offstage, Georgian actress Mary Wells engaged in "wild public performances" that promoted her notoriety.[58] One anecdote features Wells chasing King George III in a rented yacht, belting out "God Save the King" while riding a deck gun.[59] Anecdote immortalizes theater manager and performer John Rich's idiosyncratic persona as a cat fancier: in a description of Irish actress Peg Woffington's first meeting with him, Rich is portrayed surrounded by his many cats, one of whom is even eating from his plate.[60] Robert D. Hume relates this charming anecdote with cautions concerning its disreputable source (a pornographic text purporting to be the actress's autobiography) and questions concerning what it supposedly proves about Rich: "Whether Rich was innately eccentric or cultivating eccentricity is hard to say," muses Hume.[61] Mapping concentrations of anecdote around certain theater personnel, and considering the reasons for such concentrations, is one of this collection's ambitions.

Anecdote's Moral and Gendered Dimensions

Like parables or fables, anecdotes frequently possess a moral, though it is often implied rather than overt, masked by the genre's comic tang and entwined with other social and cultural assumptions. Actresses, as many scholars have observed, are even more likely than their male counterparts to be associated with and to generate anecdotes testifying to their moral character. Diana Solomon analyzes a "factually unverifiable" story about Restoration actress Anne Bracegirdle that "confirms Bracegirdle's enduring celebrity persona as the virgin actress,"[62] in which aristocratic men, unlikely patrons of purity, drink to Bracegirdle's virtue and then send a generous sum with their compliments to the performer. This anecdote's perfectly crafted exemplarity demonstrates the Bracegirdle brand in just a few lines, and accomplishes what Stefanovska, drawing on the ideas of Roland Barthes, sums up as anecdote's gift: an ability to "effectively capture the real by way of condensation."[63] The sheer number of anecdotes in this vein (i.e., extraordinary demonstrations of appreciation) shows the extent to which microhistories of the stage construct and sustain lasting fame for both actresses and actors. However, this anecdote's condensation of gendered behavior expectations along with its affirmation of an actress's talent is revealing.

Stories of female creative collaboration, mentorship, friendship, and mutual professional support seem to have been less represented in the media and in collections of anecdotes than reports of sexual misconduct and backstage and onstage catfighting.[64] Solomon warns against the uncritical deployment of anecdote in regard to gender and sexuality,[65] cautioning that anecdote can help "recover a more inclusive history," but negligently repeated, has the "potential to reinscribe non-inclusive cultural narratives, such as the discrediting of female agency and the erasure of theatre history."[66] As many feminist theater historians have underscored, the corpus of anecdotes reiterated about actresses differs significantly from the stories told and retold about actors, not because actors and actresses conducted their lives and careers differently, but because actresses were perceived, judged, and hence represented differently. Actresses were (and continue to be) persistently sexualized in the cultural imagination. Problematically, some scholars still reproduce anecdotes of actresses as a form of titillating gossip, which "either reinscribes gendered behaviour or alludes to sexual at the expense of professional activity."[67] A consideration of how anecdotes are used toward moral ends in past or current scholarship can reveal the obsessions, anxieties, and prejudices of a historical period.

Some anecdotes are used by theater historians to disprove particular rumors or rehabilitate the reputations of specific theater people. In *Oxberry's Anecdotes of the Stage*, playwright Thomas Otway is given an end more dignified than being "choked by a morsel of roll, which he was eagerly eating after having long suffered from extreme hunger."[68] The anecdote about Otway dying in a baker's shop after begging for money was first told in Theophilus Cibber's *Lives of the Poets of Great Britain and Ireland* (1753). Instead, Oxberry claims that Otway actually "fell a victim to the warmth of his friendship," attempting to revenge the murder of a friend by following the assassin to France, where Otway was stricken with a fever[69]—a demise appropriate to a writer of tragedies like *Venice Preserv'd, or, A Plot Discover'd* (1682). Oxberry's corrective anecdote implicitly aligns Otway's fate with his creative output, but does not overwrite Cibber's tale of the Restoration writer's ignominious accident.[70]

This book considers theatrical anecdotes about theater people who were professionally active between 1660 and 1800. Our contributors, continuing the revisionist work of theater and literary historians, analyze the cultural work done by theatrical anecdotes in the evolving celebrity culture of the time. The first grouping of chapters in this collection, "Acting Badly: Misbehaving Performers," considers anecdotes that tell stories that police theater practitioners' behavior, and examines anecdotes that behave badly or function counter to expectation. In "Killing Delane; or, Mimickry and the *Anecdota obscura*," Leslie Ritchie addresses the accusations that David Garrick murdered the Irish actor Dennis Delane in what may well be the only recorded instance of death by mimicry. Subsequent use of the anecdote by Garrick's biographers paradoxically erased the purported subject of the anecdote, Delane. Máire MacNeill's chapter, "Violent Afterlives: The Anecdote in Eighteenth-Century Theater Biographies," examines anecdotes of violence in the theatrical community in memoirs by and about actors. MacNeill demonstrates that while violent acts by actors, including Robert Wilks, Charles Macklin, and James Quin, underwent careful modulation in biographers' hands as conceptions of masculinity changed, similar violent acts by actresses such as George Anne Bellamy and Margaret Woffington were likely to be rendered as farcical by biographers. Heather Ladd's chapter, "Samuel Foote, Esq.: Caricature, Class, and the Comic Theatrical Anecdote," considers humorous anecdotes about Georgian actor, playwright, and theater manager Samuel Foote as metatheatric, often socially conservative microcomedies about the theater and London society as *theatrum mundi*. Anecdotes of Foote's elitist interactions address the professionalization of actors and authors during this period and the growing influence of the celebrity performer, and enact a form of social and cultural policing of labor that speaks to the rise of the profession as well as to concerns about performance and class.

The second section of this collection focuses on "Anecdotal Bodies," with three chapters that examine the female body as the site/sight of theatrical anecdotes. Chelsea Phillips's "Pregnancy and the Late Stuart Stage, 1661–1702" interprets anecdotes relating to actresses' pregnancies on the late Stuart stage, taking Elizabeth Farley, known as Mrs. Weaver—the first actress known to have encountered conflicts between her reproductive and professional life—as the primary example. Reading an anecdote claiming that Weaver "turned in all her parts" and refused to act during her pregnancy against other contemporary sources and practices, Phillips reveals the biases and assumptions we often bring to our readings of anecdotes. Nevena

Martinović considers the way that anecdotes treat the aging actress's body in her chapter, "'A High Treat to the Anecdote Hunters!': The Body of Mrs. Sophia Baddeley." Comparing Baddeley's obituaries with earlier anecdotes that pair accounts of moral transgressions with descriptions of her body as prematurely aged, Martinović explains this dichotomy; the publication of those anecdotes in newspapers and other sources suggests the public's desire for a cautionary tale that shows how immoral behavior results in punishments inflicted on the aging female body. Michael Burden's chapter, "A Bellyful of Nightingales: Seven Stories of Seven Singers," examines the tales of singers featured in a curious collection entitled *Green Room Gossip; or, Gravity Galliniput* (1809), describing how the circulation of anecdotes about female singers from Francesca Cuzzoni to Kitty Clive affected public perception of these musicians. Using the ambiguities and peculiarities of these tales as a starting point, Burden then fruitfully appraises the complex interplay between the performers, anecdotes, and their biographies.

The third group of chapters in this volume, "Acting Careers and the Professional Anecdote," considers anecdotes that speak about acting as a profession and that define what counted as professional behavior on London and provincial stages. Fiona Ritchie's chapter, "Anecdote and the Regional Actress: A History of the Farren Family in Several Anecdotes," explores the use of anecdote as a means of writing regional theater history, analyzing as a case study the anecdotes about the actresses of the Farren family. Stories about Mrs. Farren and her three daughters, Betsey, Kitty, and Peggy are recorded by R. J. Broadbent in his *Annals of the Manchester Stage*. Ritchie employs anecdote as a form of microhistory that constitutes a productive source and indeed a methodology that can increase our understanding of regional theater and the overlooked role of regional actresses in eighteenth-century Britain. In "Neither Confirmed nor Refuted: The Anecdotal Elizabeth Barry," Seth Wilson turns his attention to anecdotes' role at the moment when actresses were first introduced to English public stages, and reads denigrating anecdotes of Elizabeth Barry as exemplary of a larger discursive formula for vilifying actresses. These anecdotes of Barry have survived precisely because their unverifiable and salacious nature made them useful in painting Barry as a mercurial deviant rather than a nascent professional.

The final section of this collection, "Anecdotes' Afterlives: Scholarly Encounters," features chapters that focus on how modern theater scholars employ the anecdote, and to what effects. Elaine McGirr's chapter, "Anecdotal Origin Stories: Mary Ann Yates's Trip to Drury Lane," examines a persistent but inaccurate origin story that claims that the actress-manageress Mary Ann Graham Yates was inspired to act after viewing Susannah Cibber's performance as Juliet. McGirr theorizes the cultural work of origin anecdotes in erasing theatrical conflict and making celebrity appear natural and inevitable. Amanda Weldy Boyd's chapter, "The Vanishing Subject in 'Anecdotal' Abridgments of Theatrical Biographies," considers anecdote's relation to life-writing by examining two serialized actor biographies. Weldy Boyd argues that, in Thomas Davies's *Memoirs of the Life of David Garrick* (1780), serialized and abridged for the *Universal Magazine* in mid-1780 as "Anecdotes of the Late David Garrick, Esq.," and Thomas Kirkman's 1799 biography of Charles Macklin, serialized in the *Edinburgh Magazine* as the "Anecdotes of Charles Macklin," the anecdotes that formed a cornerstone of celebrity worship also distracted readers from contemplation of the supposed central figure, with profound effects upon life-writing practices. Danielle Bobker's chapter, "Queering Roxane from Davenant to Richardson," complements existing scholarship on a Restoration sex scandal. Whereas Katie Trumpener, Ros Ballaster, and Felicity Nussbaum have variously argued that in eighteenth-century England and France, a composite Eastern queen figure whom they call "Roxane" became a key signifier of women's strategic participation in the dominant patriarchal sexual economy, Bobker reads this figure as subversive; a close reading of a particular theatrical anecdote with a clear homoerotic subtext in Anthony Hamilton's influential early eighteenth-century memoir of the Restoration court highlights this figure's value as a signifier of the complexity and intensity of relationships between women.

Without sufficient contextualization and analysis, anecdotes remain spicy trivia rather than valuable tools for exploring the attitudes that shape histories of English theater. Anecdote is not just a textual container for the excesses associated with celebrity; anecdotes are also a discursive social formation, and studying their production, circulation, and consumption is vital to ongoing scholarship concerning actors' biographies, celebrity, and theater history. We hope that these chapters model analyses of theatrical anecdotes that recognize the risks and potential in examining anecdotes in theater scholarship.

Notes

1. David Erskine Baker, *The Companion to the Playhouse: or, An Historical Account of all of the Dramatic Writers (and their Works) that have appeared in Great Britain and Ireland, from the Commencement of our Theatrical Exhibitions, down to the Present Year 1764*, 2 vols. (London: T. Becket and P. A. DeHondt, C. Henderson, T. Davies, 1764).

2. The secret history, often comprising scandal among aristocratic courtiers, is both predecessor of and coextensive with the theatrical anecdote. As the center of culture shifted from the royal court to public spaces like the playhouse, powerful theater managers like John Rich and David Garrick were akin to monarchs as focal points of gossip; voyeuristic reports about what went on behind the scenes gave theatrical anecdotes the glamour of court secrets. For more on the secret history, see Rachel K. Carnell, *The Secret History in Literature, 1660–1820* (Cambridge: Cambridge University Press, 2017).

3. Malina Stefanovska, "Exemplary or Singular? The Anecdote in Historical Narrative," *SubStance* 38, no. 1 (2009): 27.

4. *The Theatrical Olio: Or, Thespian Jester. Being an Entertaining Selection of Droll Anecdotes, Pleasing Stories, Funny Jokes, Bon Mots, Epigrams, Whimsical Adventures, &c. &c. Related by Several Eminent Performers* (Southwark: W. Kemmish, [1798]), 5.

5. Anonymous, *The Encyclopaedia of Anecdote* (Dublin: T. Jackson, [ca. 1800]), 9.

6. Thomas D'Urfey, *Wit and Mirth; or, Tom D'Urfey's Pills to Purge Melancholy: A Selection of his Best Songs into One Volume. With an Account of the Author's Life* (London: William Holland, 1791).

7. *The Theatrical Olio*, title page.

8. Benjamin Victor, *The History of the Theatres of London and Dublin, From the Year 1730 to the present Time*, 2 vols. (London: T. Davies, 1761), 1:215, 1:29.

9. William Granger, *The New Wonderful Museum, and Extraordinary Magazine: Being a Complete Repository of All the Wonders, Curiosities, and Rarities of Nature and Art, from the Beginning of the World to the Present Year* (London: Alex Hogg, 1807), 2583, 2323.

10. George Anne Bellamy, *An Apology for the Life of George Anne Bellamy, late of Covent-Garden Theatre. Written by herself*, 5 vols. (London: J. Bell, 1785), 1:37.

11. Jacob Larwood, *Anecdotes of the Clergy: Or, The Antiquities, Humours, and Eccentricities of "The Cloth"* (London: Chatto & Windus, 1890), 286, 38, 206.

12. John Genest, *Some Account of the English Stage, from the Restoration in 1660 to 1830*, vol. 6 (Bath: Printed by H. E. Carrington, 1832), 325.

13. Colley Cibber, *An Apology for the Life of Mr. Colley Cibber, Comedian* (London: John Watts, 1740), 139.

14. Paula McDowell, "Defoe and the Contagion of the Oral: Modeling Media Shift in *A Journal of the Plague Year*," *PMLA: Publications of the Modern Language Association of America* 121, no. 1 (2006): 104.

15. McDowell, "Defoe and the Contagion of the Oral," 104.

16. Dianne Dugaw, "Theorizing Orality and Performance in Literary Anecdote and History: Boswell's Diaries," *Oral Tradition* 24, no. 2 (2009): 418.

17. Thomas Davies, *Dramatic Miscellanies: Consisting of Critical Observations on Several Plays of Shakspeare: With a Review of his Principal Characters, and Those of Various Eminent Writers, as Represented by Mr. Garrick, and Other Celebrated Comedians*, 3 vols. (London: Printed for the author, 1783–1784), 1:192–193.

18. William Cooke, *Memoirs of Charles Macklin, Comedian* (London: James Asperne, 1804), 49–50.

19. *The Complete London Jester, or Wit's Companion*, 2nd ed. (London: T. Lownds, 1765).

20. *English Jests and Anecdotes (Nuggets for Travellers)* (Edinburgh: William Patterson, 1886).

21. *English Jests and Anecdotes*, 60.

22. A "Joe Miller" is a stale, repeated joke, or a joke that reappears in several collections. It takes its name from the actor credited in the title of the jestbook *Joe Miller's Jests*. See "Joe, n.2," *OED Online*, Oxford University Press, accessed January 17, 2020, https://www-oed-com.proxy.queensu.ca/view/Entry/101472?redirected From=Joe+Miller.

23. Samuel Johnson, "Life of Waller," in *The Lives of the English Poets*, 3 vols. (London: Thomas Tegg, 1824), 1:257.

24. Joel Fineman, "The History of the Anecdote," in *The New Historicism*, ed. H. Aram Veeser (Abington, UK: Routledge, 2013), 50.

25. Fineman, "The History of the Anecdote," 57.

26. Virginia Scott, *Women on the Stage in Early Modern France, 1540–1750* (Cambridge: Cambridge University Press, 2010), 15.

27. Tate Wilkinson, *Original Anecdotes Respecting the Stage, and the Actors of the Old School, with Remarks on Mr. Murphy's "Life of Garrick"* (London: J. Wright, [1805]), 18, our italics.

28. Vanessa Cunningham, *Shakespeare and Garrick* (Cambridge: Cambridge University Press, 2008), 76.

29. Wilkinson, *Original Anecdotes*, 18.

30. Liza Picard, *Restoration London: Engaging Anecdotes and Tantalizing Trivia from the Most Magnificent and Renowned City of Europe* (London: Harper Perennial, 2000).

31. Anonymous, *The Encyclopaedia of Anecdote*, 21.

32. Anonymous, *The Encyclopaedia of Anecdote*, 21.

33. Anonymous, *The Encyclopaedia of Anecdote*, 21.

34. Charles Robert Leslie and Tom Taylor, *Life and Times of Sir Joshua Reynolds: With Notices of Some of His Contemporaries*, 2 vols. (London: John Murray, 1865), 2:248.

35. Peter Thomson, "Celebrity and Rivalry: David [Garrick] and Goliath [Quin]," in *Theatre and Celebrity in Britain, 1660–2000*, ed. Mary Luckhurst and Jane Moody (Basingstoke, UK: Palgrave Macmillan, 2005), 133.

36. Stefanovska, "Exemplary or Singular?," 17.

37. Frances Burney, *Evelina: or, A Young Lady's Entrance into the World. In a Series of Letters*, ed. Susan Kubica Howard (1778; Peterborough, ON: Broadview Press, 2000), 196.

38. Frances Brooke, *The Excursion*, ed. Paula R. Backscheider (1777; Lexington: University Press of Kentucky, 2015), 85.

39. Celia Barnes, "'A Morbid Oblivion': Samuel Johnson, James Boswell, and Remembering Not to Forget," *The Age of Johnson* 23 (2015): 57.

40. Dugaw, "Theorizing Orality and Performance," 422.

41. Samuel Johnson, *The Major Works*, ed. Donald Greene (1984; Oxford: Oxford University Press, 2008), 206.

42. Helen Deutsch, *Loving Dr. Johnson* (Chicago: University of Chicago Press, 2005), 73.

43. James Boaden, *The Life of Mrs. Jordan: Including Original Private Correspondence, and Numerous Anecdotes of Her Contemporaries* (London: E. Bull, 1831).

44. Stefanovska, "Exemplary or Singular?," 17.

45. A Gentleman, *Aristophanes, Being a Classic Collection of True Attic Wit, Containing the Jests, Gibes, Bon-mots, Witticisms, and most Extraordinary Anecdotes of Samuel Foote, Esq.* (London: Robert Baldwin, 1778).

46. Lionel Gossman, "Anecdote and History," *History and Theory* 42 (May 2003): 149.

47. Elaine McGirr, "Nell Gwyn's Breasts and Colley Cibber's Shirts: Celebrity Actors and Their Famous 'Parts,'" in *Intimacy and Celebrity in Eighteenth-Century Literary Culture: Public Interiors*, ed. Emrys D. Jones and Victoria Joule (Cham, Switzerland: Springer, 2018), 18.

48. Joseph Haslewood, *The Secret History of the Green Room: Containing Authentic and Entertaining Memoirs of the Actors and Actresses in the Three Theatres Royal*, 2nd ed., 2 vols. (London: J. Owen, 1792), 1:vi.

49. Jones and Joule, introduction to *Intimacy and Celebrity in Eighteenth-Century Literary Culture*, 2.

50. See Chris Rojek, *Celebrity* (London: Reaktion, 2001); Leslie Ritchie, *David Garrick and the Mediation of Celebrity* (Cambridge: Cambridge University Press, 2019); David Giles, *Illusions of Immortality: A Psychology of Fame and Celebrity* (London: Macmillan, 2000).

51. Felicity Nussbaum, *Rival Queens: Actresses, Performance, and the Eighteenth-Century British Theater* (Philadelphia: University of Pennsylvania Press, 2010), 45.

52. For one instance of this anecdote, see Petronius Arbiter, Esq., *Memoirs of the Present Countess of Derby, (Late Miss Farren); Including Anecdotes of Several Distinguished Persons* (London: Symonds, [ca. 1797]), 5, where the anecdote is used to introduce the similar social rise of Elizabeth Farren.

53. Benjamin Victor, *The History of the Theatres of London and Dublin, From the Year 1730 to the Present Time. To Which Is Added, An Annual Register Of all the Plays, &c. Performed at the Theatres-Royal in London, from the Year 1712* (London: T. Davies, 1761), 157.

54. Harold Hobson, *Theatre* (London: Burke Publishing, 1953), 114. This anecdote is also told with different actors in place of Garrick—what might be termed "Garrickian drift."

55. Hobson, *Theatre*, 116.

56. James Roose-Evans, *London Theatre: From the Globe to the National* (Oxford: Phaidon, 1977), 64.

57. See Diana Solomon, *Prologues and Epilogues of Restoration Theater: Gender and Comedy, Performance and Print* (Newark: University of Delaware Press, 2013), 62.

58. Elizabeth Savage, "Making Mary: Imitation and Infamy in the Eighteenth-Century Theater," *Restoration and Eighteenth-Century Theatre Research* 30, no. 1 (Summer 2015): 77.

59. See also Laura Engel, "Notorious Celebrity: Mary Wells, Madness and Theatricality," in *The English Malady: Enabling and Disabling Fictions*, ed. Glen Colburn (Cambridge: Cambridge Scholars Publishing, 2009), 276–277.

60. A print titled *Portrait of Margaret ('Peg') Woffington and John Rich* depicting this anecdote is housed in the University of Illinois Theatrical Print Collection in Urbana, Illinois.

61. Robert D. Hume, "John Rich as Manager and Entrepreneur," in *The Stage's Glory: John Rich (1692–1761)*, ed. Berta Joncus and Jeremy Barlow (Newark: University of Delaware, 2011), 34.

62. Diana Solomon, "Anecdotes and Restoration Actresses: The Cases of Elizabeth Barry and Anne Bracegirdle," *Restoration and Eighteenth-Century Theatre Research* 31, no. 2 (2016): 30.

63. Stefanovska, "Exemplary or Singular?," 24.

64. Solomon, "Anecdotes and Restoration Actresses," 31.

65. Solomon, "Anecdotes and Restoration Actresses," 20.

66. Solomon, "Anecdotes and Restoration Actresses," 19.

67. Solomon, "Anecdotes and Restoration Actresses," 23.

68. William Oxberry, ed., *Oxberry's Anecdotes of the Stage, &c. &c.* (London: G. Virtue, 1827), 6.

69. Oxberry, *Oxberry's Anecdotes of the Stage*.

70. As Jessica Munns observes, Otway's end is obscured by competing anecdotes: "Most accounts agree that Otway died in Tower Hill on 14 April 1685, probably in extreme poverty. Theophilus Cibber paints a pathetic picture of Otway choking to death on a roll bought with money he had begged (T. Cibber, *Lives of the Poets of Great Britain*, 2 vols., 1753, 2.334). Other accounts have Otway dying after pursuing the murderer of a friend (*Works*, 1.31; Ham, 214–15). John Dennis simply states that Otway died in an 'Alehouse . . . in Adversity unpitied, and dy'd unlamented' (J. Dennis, *Remarks upon Mr. Pope's Translation of Homer*, 1717, 5–6)." Jessica Munns, "Otway, Thomas (1652–1685), playwright and poet," *Oxford Dictionary of National Biography*, September 23, 2004, accessed February 19, 2020.

PART I
ACTING BADLY
Misbehaving Performers

I
KILLING DELANE; OR, MIMICKRY AND THE *ANECDOTA OBSCURA*

LESLIE RITCHIE

> Who has not heard of the thousand little tricks he [Garrick] has used to bury Genius in obscurity, to damp its generous powers, and turn it aside from the road to Fame? For this it was that he exposed the simple *inadvertencies* of some to scorn, dextrously turning the public laugh against them, or (as the theatrical phrase emphatically expresses it) *took them off* with such accumulated mimickry, that they retired from the stage either disgusted or terrified. For this it was too, that he doomed others to such a low walk of characters as they were always superior to.
>
> —*The Green-Room*, No. XII

What is lost—and what is taken—when one actor imitates another? Is "taking someone off" a euphemism for an act of forgery, theft, slander, or even murder? Accusations that David Garrick had done the Irish actor Dennis Delane to death began early, and were eagerly repeated. As David Williams wrote, Garrick's "personal caricatura's" were no less than "a species of robbery on the reputation of actors," and his imitation of Delane was of such injurious "effect on the mind of poor *Delane* . . . that it absolutely occasioned his death."[1] Francis Gentleman more subtly accused Garrick of theatrical character assassination: "Mr. DELANE, an actor of great merit, and a valuable member of society, had two peculiarities on the stage, which Mr. GARRICK took off, and rendered him so ridiculous, that he was constantly laughed at; having generous, though week [*sic*] feelings, Mr. DELANE took to drinking, and in reality broke his heart."[2]

The anecdote enshrining Delane's death by mimicry is set in the ideal spot for such a surreal crime: a metadramatic rehearsal play. In early career performances as the playwright Bayes in the Duke of Buckingham's play *The Rehearsal* (1671), Garrick altered the play's original object of satire from a faulty writer (John Dryden) to faulty players, adding an extra layer of metatheatricality to the metadrama by taking off several well-known actors, including Delane.[3] Garrick, writes his biographer Thomas Davies, did Delane "no service, by mimicking him in the famous simile of the boar and sow in the Rehearsal. His voice and manner were so exactly imitated, that the audience enjoyed the representation by repeated applause."[4] By the time Charles Dibdin's *Complete History of the Stage* appeared in 1800, Delane's twenty-one-year stage career had been compressed, brutally, into that single anecdote: "DELANE was considered as a sound good actor of a respectable but by no means of a first rate description. He was particular and GARRICK successfully mimicked him in the *Rehearsal*."[5] In the case of Dennis Delane, anecdote eclipsed the actor it purported to commemorate.

It is this anecdote's misbehavior, its perverse success in obscuring its alleged subject, which makes it an interesting text for thinking about the work theatrical anecdotes perform. Joel Fineman's often-cited musings on the nature of anecdote recognize it as a form that "however literary, is nevertheless pointed towards or rooted in the real"; it is, he posits, "a *historeme* . . . the smallest minimal unit of the historiographic fact."[6] While Malina Stefanovska draws our attention to anecdotes' suspect association with "rumor, legend, lack of rigor or evidence" and their "fascination with singularity and with aesthetic form, lawlessness, contamination with fiction, and subjectivity,"[7] other theater historians, including Jacky Bratton and Jonathan Bate, have demonstrated the anecdote's capacity to portray representative or symbolic truths, even in the absence of verifiable fact.

The anecdote of Garrick killing Delane, however, is a peculiar example of the form, even beyond its entertainingly bizarre premise. Anecdotes promise to reveal secret histories,[8] but there is nothing secret or private about publicly mocking another performer on stage. Indeed, mimicry depends upon communal knowledge of the imitated object, which affords audiences the pleasure of recognition. The act of mimicry to which this anecdote refers does gesture at the real, citing Delane as the person imitated by Garrick, but the work of the anecdote is quite different: it forces a misrecognition on the reader. The shared reality to which the anecdote refers is evanescent and malleable, consisting of a series of variously remembered mimical performances, condensed into the anecdote's single, singular event. This anecdote conceals more than it reveals. I propose that the anecdote, that entertaining and instructive historical morsel, is a genre that has spawned a shady subspecies, the *Anecdota obscura*: the anecdote applied by theater historians and biographers such that it capitalizes on and misdirects the anecdote's entertainment value, provides a deceptive sense of representation, or uses the anecdote's structure and obsession with singularity and telling detail to distract from its misbehavior as a false witness to history.

Dennis Delane Restored

Dennis Delane enjoyed a considerable reputation as an actor in England and Ireland before Garrick's allegedly fatal imitation. To appreciate the extent of that imitation and demonstrate what the anecdote of his death by mimicry obscures, it is necessary to recover Delane's pre-anecdotal persona and compare it briefly with the familiar contours of Garrick's biography.

Delane was born in Ireland and educated at Trinity College, Dublin. He held property in Ireland: estates in Counties Roscommon and Galway are referred to in his will, while the Irish Records of Deeds record a number of leaseholds and transactions throughout the 1730s.[9] He appears to have had sufficient reason to style himself "a Gentleman" and "Esquire" in the occasional poetry miscellanies and classical translations to which he subscribed.[10] The very definition of clubbable, Delane was one of the original members of the Sublime Society of Beefsteaks.[11] He enjoyed the social position of literary country gentleman to which Garrick aspired, and later purchased with his Hampton estate, numerous literary subscriptions, and assiduous cultivation of genteel social connections.

Delane commenced his theatric career at Smock Alley Theatre in Dublin in 1729, and began there to create an impressive suite of roles: Chamont in *The Orphan*; Brutus in *Julius Caesar*; Lothario in *The Fair Penitent*; Tamerlane, Macbeth, Lear, Cato, and Richard III; as well as comic parts, such as Bevil in *The Conscious Lovers* and Aimwell in *The Beaux' Stratagem.*[12] Delane aimed at variety in representation, and his impressive pre-anecdote performance record indicates a success in achieving breadth that contrasts vividly with posthumous reviews of his ability and range by writers including Thomas Davies and John Hill.

Perhaps with knowledge of his genteel background, Davies remarked in one such review that Delane's "easy and polite" manner was better suited to playing fine gentlemen, such as Bevil, than the tragic heroes like Alexander that "pushed him into notice."[13] By contrast, Hill argued that Delane's reputation would have "unquestionably have been much higher than it was" if he had been confined to such characters as Alexander and Hotspur, to which his "strength of voice and dignity of figure" were proper.[14] These divergent opinions in one sense concur: Delane's attempts at variety—a concept closely associated with Garrick by the time Hill and Davies were writing[15]—far from impressing critics with wonder at his range, occasioned their uneasy sense that Delane had never settled into a productive walk of characters. The mobile variety hailed as the pinnacle of acting when claimed by Garrick read, in Delane's case, as a disturbing lack of direction, dilettantism, or even a moral failing; as a writer in the *European Magazine* put it, his "merits were lost in indolent indulgence."[16]

Delane's English career began with an engagement in Henry Giffard's company at Goodman's Fields in 1731 (as did Garrick's career, ten years later); and much as Garrick did before becoming a patentee, Delane pursued a cross-Channel career.[17] He played summer seasons in Dublin most years throughout the 1730s,[18] and debuted at Covent Garden on October 25, 1735, as Alexander in *The Rival Queens*, consolidating his reputation as the "young Tragedian from *Dublin*"[19] during the remainder of that decade. Theophilus Cibber's *Apology*, published in 1740, proclaims Delane as at the head of his profession: "*Quin* at *Drury-Lane* House, and *Delane* at *Covent-Garden*, are the *Personae Dramatis* which are without Competitors: They both play the chief Characters in the same Cast."[20]

There are no reliably identified images of Delane extant,[21] but W. R. Chetwood records Delane's "Person and excellent Voice" as meritorious,[22] and Cibber describes him as a handsome man and a precocious talent:

> Novelty, Youth, a handsome Figure, *&c.* took off from any severe Criticism on his Elocution and Action . . . though so far from the polite End of the Town, he drew to him several polite Audiences, and became in such a Degree of Repute, that Comparisons were made between him and *Quin*; nor was he without Admirers of both Sexes who gave him the Preference . . . in two or three Years on the Stage [Delane] gain'd that Station on it which most of the other Actors could not in many Years attain to.[23]

Delane's youthful good looks, natural ability, and star draw to the unfashionable end of town uncannily presaged Garrick's London debut, memorialized in nearly identical terms by Davies and other biographers.[24]

Theophilus Cibber also captures the features of Delane's performance style that Garrick was to mimic: a drawling monotone, punctuated with eruptions of shouting to express violent passions. Cibber writes that Delane "has a Sameness of Tone and Expression, and drawls out his Lines to a displeasing Length: But that loud Violence of Voice is useful to him when Anger, Indignation, or such enrag'd Passions are to be express'd; for the shrill Loudness marks the Passion. . . . In such Parts, especially *Alexander, Delane* pleases many; for the Million, as C.[olley]C.[ibber] says, are apt to be transported when the Drum of the Ear is soundly rattled."[25] These caveats aside, Delane's pre-anecdotal reputation indicates that he was "a bright theatric star,"[26] and as Tate Wilkinson proclaimed, "an actor of the first rank."[27] In the theatrical season of 1741–1742, these two young actors, Delane and Garrick, were engaged in close competition with one another and with Quin; indeed, some saw Delane, not Quin, as Garrick's "only competitor."[28] Garrick himself privately figured their relationship as competitive, writing from Dublin to his brother, "Delane has play'd against Me, but wanting allies has quitted ye field."[29] The anecdote of Delane's death conceals one motive for Garrick's imitation—competition—by positioning Delane as always already an outmoded declaimer, on the losing side of Garrick's supposed invention of natural acting.

With knowledge of Delane's professional stature before Garrick's mimicry, the anecdote of Garrick imitating Delane in *The Rehearsal* appears a sleight of hand, distracting not only from the competition that framed Garrick's entry into the market for theatric fame but from Garrick's imitation of other aspects of Delane's persona, including his social status, conspicuous literary patronage, theatrical range, and appeal to novelty. As a mimic's audience, writes Jacky Bratton, we are "impressed by the clever observation, selection and reproduction of characteristic traits—a cleverness in which we share, via our recognition of the subject performed"; yet we are also "disturbed or excited" as our "comfortable sense of the unique fixity of individuality is challenged and upset."[30] Garrick's mimicry of Delane may have felt especially disturbing to its subject and impressive to the theatrical public, as it certainly exceeded an imitation of Delane's performance of one theatric role. If, as proposed by Jonathan Bate, that "the point of the anecdote is not its factual but its representative truth,"[31] then the first truth represented by the anecdote stating that Garrick's mimicry killed Delane is that this anecdote's synecdoche (one imitation standing in for many) misleadingly contributes to the narrative of Garrick's instant originality and stardom by obscuring the extent of Garrick's imitations of Delane.

Killing Delane's Character

Delane had established a measure of cultural authority not just through acting tragic leads but also some of his comic roles, most importantly, in the underrated part of Smith in *The Rehearsal.* To separate the work of mimicry from the work of anecdote, the particulars of the performance, from performance records to the potentialities of the script, are outlined below. Garrick's imitation obliterated Delane's reputation largely because he chose to imitate Delane within that particular play, effectively killing Delane's ability to play Smith ever again.

Frank Smith is a country fellow come to town—the commonsensical straight man to Johnson, a sophisticated London critic. Johnson introduces Smith to the playwright Bayes, who invites the men to his new play's dress rehearsal. Smith's lines tend to exposition, repetition, and amplification of Bayes's follies ("Elevate and surprise! prithee make me understand the meaning of that").[32] Yet the role is not so flat or echoic as that description portends. Smith and Johnson are whips, whose reactions tell the audience when and how to laugh at Bayes. Smith is neither fool nor booby: "I find the Author will be very much oblig'd to the Players, if they can make any sense out of this," he retorts upon hearing Bayes's cockamamie theories of playwriting.[33] An author who has written "a great many fine things already,"[34] Smith is no barren critic, but a theatrical practitioner. As the play progresses, Smith appears as an authoritative cultural arbiter, turning Bayes's own words against him: "I never did before this see anything in Nature, and all that, (as *Bayes* says) so foolish," he pronounces after the play's inaudible exposition in whispers.[35] While Johnson's buttered flattery prods the prideful playwright to ever more ludicrous flights, Smith prefers ironic praise, though he occasionally joins Johnson in baiting Bayes.[36] The role is comic, with short, responsive lines, and not as physically demanding as that of Bayes (who must dance, fall down and break his nose, etc.). Smith ridicules, but is not ridiculous himself.

The role accommodated Delane's strengths by minimizing action and providing a reason for the occasional violent expostulation. Delane's flat drawl could play as skepticism, intellectual superiority, irony, or (if amplified) even belligerent refusal to partake of Bayes's snip-snap aesthetic.[37] Playing Smith, the knowledgeable critic of bad drama, was a rewarding night's work for Delane; it kept him before the public in an easy comic part possessed of sufficient dignity that it did not undermine his ability to play tragic heroes. Newspaper advertisements confirm Smith as an important role, as it is one of only three named parts advertised, and Delane's name is repeatedly associated with the part in print.[38] The play's continuing popularity in the repertoire solidified Delane's position within the company and profession. Performance records reveal that Delane played the sensible Smith to Colley Cibber's foppish Bayes at Covent Garden at least twenty-seven times in the 1739–1740 season and at least seven times in the 1740–1741 season.[39] When in 1741–1742 Delane moved to the Drury Lane company, he took along this valuable role, and appeared with Colley's son, Theophilus Cibber, as his Bayes eight times. Delane's polished, laconic Smith was nicely congruent with his offstage identity as a genteel literary patron.

Both Covent Garden and Drury Lane theaters ran productions of *The Rehearsal* in 1741–1742, preparing the theatrical public for mimicry by familiarizing them with the play and its usual players. On February 3, 1742, Garrick began to play Bayes at the theater in Goodman's Fields, appearing sixteen times in the role before his last performance there in May. "I have ye Greatest Success imaginable in ye Part of Bayes, & instead of clapping Me they huzza wch is very uncommon approbation—& tho The Town has been quite tir'd out with ye Play at ye Other End of ye Town Yet I have ye Great Satisfaction to See crowded Audiences to It Every Night," Garrick wrote triumphantly to his brother.[40] Garrick's mimicry of Delane began sometime during this run. Davies's telling of the anecdote states that Garrick imitated not just Delane but also Hale, Ryan, and Bridgwater (who played, respectively, Prince Prettyman, Johnson, and Thunder in the Covent Garden production), as well as Giffard, who appeared alongside Garrick as Johnson at Goodman's Fields. The reference to mimicry nearest the event, Henry Fielding's *Champion* No. 455, reprinted in the *Gentleman's Magazine* for October 1742, excuses the mimicry as a novelty draw, executed at Giffard's request: "Some have been offended at his [Garrick] mimicking the Players; . . . it was done first at *Goodman's-Fields*, to excite the Curiosity, and serve the Proprietor, and cannot perhaps be easily omitted; that the Characters of some of our best Actors are too well establish'd to be hurt that Way; that the most excellent Actor has, and must have, some peculiar Criterion which may be ingeniously hit off."[41] Garrick was not just taking aim at rival actors, but rival productions, Fielding suggests, and this mimicry was instigated and continued as a commercial opportunity, devoid of personal animus.

Garrick's mimicry was perceived by Fielding, and subsequently by Garrick's biographers, to have a diffusing effect, as if having multiple targets diminished the mimicry's impact on each actor, whose reputation and ability would afford a protective carapace. The multiple target theory's proponents also consider Garrick's mimicry a critique of bad acting, rather than a series of malicious attacks upon particular persons. Arthur Murphy contextualizes his relation of the Delane anecdote like this: "The best performers of the day had recourse to strutting, mouthing, and bellowing. This was altogether repugnant to Garrick's school of acting . . . he selected some of the most eminent performers of the time, and by his wonderful powers of mimickry, was able to assume the air, the manner and the deportment of each in turn. . . . In this manner he exposed the fashionable errors of the time, and, of course, made way for his own just and correct idea of dramatic imitation."[42] Anecdotes are sometimes "told and retold as markers of change, of the coming of new inspiration" or the "triumphant overturning of traditional performance practice,"[43] Bratton writes. Garrick's biographers and theater historians employ the anecdote in this way, so that it becomes less the story of the death of Delane and more the death of declamatory acting. The anecdote redirects affect, shuttling from passing sympathy for the victims of mimicry to admiration at Garrick's intervention. The anecdote thereby recasts an act consistently figured by contemporary theater critics as "low"—the imitation of private or personal foibles on stage—as a high-minded historic reform of acting technique.[44] The *Anecdota obscura* first invokes, then betrays, anecdote's usual obsessive singularity to exemplarity and the projection of a large cultural shift.

That Garrick's imitation of Delane was but one of many did not lessen, but rather increased its efficacy. Jane Moody contends that "imitations fuelled performers' fears about the commercial value and the vulnerability of their public faces. For imitations challenged the presumption of originality by demonstrating just how easily that originality could be reproduced."[45] The overt theatricality of Garrick's chameleonlike transmutations before the audience fragmented Delane, reducing his characteristic motions and declamatory lilt to jetsam. In recognizing Garrick's fractured Delane, the audience now also recognized the elements that made up Delane's renowned technique as poor stuff, easily reproduced, and Delane as comparable to the other second-rate actors whom Garrick likewise atomized and thereby dismissed.

It is probable that Garrick imitated Delane and other actors multiple times during February 1742, and that the anecdote condenses many acts of mimicry into a single, shattering extinction event. However, it is just possible that the anecdote refers to one cataclysmic imitation, capping all the mimicry that had transpired to date.

Garrick's first performance at Drury Lane Theatre, just two days after quitting the stage at Goodman's Fields, was as Bayes. A solitary news clipping records that this was also Delane's final performance as Smith. As both men were now in the same company, Garrick would have had the opportunity to imitate Delane to his face:

> Drury Lane Theatre. W. May 26. 1742. The Rehearsal.
>
> The part of Bayes to be performed by Mr. Garrick. "Delane is listed as playing the part of Mr. Smith; Mr. Mills plays Johnson. Boxes 5 / Pit 3 / First Gallery 2/."[46]

After this performance, Delane never played the role of Smith again; in fact, Delane did not appear on a single cast list for *The Rehearsal* for the rest of his life. Delane had indeed been "taken off" the bill.

Mimicking Delane within a play that accorded him cultural authority, in a role that blurred metatheatrically into his offstage persona, was a devastating maneuver. Garrick can be acquitted of theft, for he did not steal Delane's role directly; nonetheless, his mimicry cost Delane a considerable part of his theatric property. The anecdote takes on an exculpatory role: it explains the outcome of two actors fighting for first-rank parts at Drury Lane as a tale of mastery. Garrick imitated Delane; therefore, like a large fish consuming a smaller one, Garrick was greater than Delane and more deserving of prime roles. By referring to the multiple targets of mimicry, retailers of the anecdote suggest Garrick's motivations for mimicry were ideological, not tactical arson.[47] Burning down Delane's reputation and making this role too hot to touch were all in the noble service of eradicating declamatory acting.

Killing the "Young Tragedian"

A premise of the anecdote is that it affords unique, particular information that is best conveyed in a narrative concerning a single action. The anecdote sings the singular. Garrick's imitation of Delane is conveyed in an anecdote we might refer to as "the one about the boar and the sow," and this particularity offers another revelatory, representative truth: the speech Garrick selected as the grounds for his imitation efficiently attacked Delane's reputation as a tragedian.

Villiers's famous simile of the boar and sow originally ridiculed Dryden's overwritten pathetic fallacy in his heroic tragedy, *The Conquest of Granada*,[48] replacing Dryden's chaste turtledoves separated by an oncoming storm with a pair of pigs loudly consummating their love in the muck. Garrick, famously a proponent of Shakespeare, was less sanguine concerning Augustan heroic tragedy. Garrick's delivery combined with *The Rehearsal*'s burlesque of heroic tragedy to skewer Delane's dignity. The cadence of Villiers's mock-heroic couplets undoubtedly summoned the audience's memory of Delane in his best-known tragic lead, Alexander, in Nathaniel Lee's *The Rival Queens*.[49] Garrick never played this part, but delighted in disparaging the taste of those who did. He continued to nourish a grudge against the "detestable" part of Alexander years after Delane's death, writing, "Every Genius must despise it, because [it] . . . is ye bane of true merit—If a Man can act it well, I mean to please ye People, he has something in him that a good actor shd not have . . . Delane was once a fine Alexander—damn ye Part."[50] To be a fine Alexander was to be a poor actor, and Delane was a fine Alexander. The anecdote validates Garrick's taste in tragedy by representing heroic tragedy itself as outmoded by means of its association with *The Rehearsal*, which mocked the genre, and by extension with a declaimer like Delane, who had succeeded in that genre.

Garrick's imitation of Delane mocked not just heroic tragedy but also the "young Tragedian." His mimicry of Delane was a miniature set piece, unfolding over six lines, and its brevity made a callous point: the actor was not worth extended consideration. John Genest's account, which cites Murphy's biography, states that Garrick's imitation extended to Delane's attitudes as well as his characteristic vocal delivery: "Delane, who was at the head of his profession, was tall and comely, had a clear and strong voice, but was a mere declaimer; Garrick . . . retired to the upper part of the stage, and drawing his left arm across his breast rested his right elbow upon it, raising a finger to his nose, he then came forward in a stately gait, nodding his head as he advanced, and in the exact tone of Delane spoke the famous Simile of the boar and sow."[51] The entertaining effect of Garrick's multivalent burlesque is perhaps best grasped by comparison. Cathy Berberian's famous take on the Beatles's song

"Ticket to Ride," rendered "as it might be sung by a Handel oratorio singer in the provinces,"[52] similarly exploits the humorous distance between a low subject (a popular song) and its mannered, florid performance, rendered with high seriousness in an imitation that simultaneously serves as a satiric correction of pernicious vocal faults. Berberian, however, does not mimic a particular individual: her audience's pleasure is derived from recognizing the familiar tune under a barrage of inappropriate ornamentation and a deliberately overblown delivery, not from recognizing a particular performer's vocal liabilities. Garrick's mimicry likewise layers funny on funny, piling mimicry on mock-heroic verse on dramatic burlesque, but the audience's pleasure hinges on their recognition of Delane the serious tragedian as the object of caricature.

Terry Threadgold writes that "performance always involves the labour of making the self, a muscular, emotional labour, a labour of constructing memories for the body, which 'brands' the materiality of the body and leaves its corporeal traces in the text of performance."[53] In imitating another actor's performance, one purloins that labor by stealing that actor's motions and emotions, bereft of the material and emotional memories that form it. Theatric mimicry is akin to standing behind an image of a muscled weight lifter with the face cut out: the stance of the actor peeping through the represented identity is one of mockery of the original's ambitions, mastery of his motions, and smirking, half-ironic self-promotion. Although theatric mimicry is a form of imitation, it is imitation with a difference.[54] If "taking someone off" is a crime, Garrick may be acquitted of forgery at least, for the aim of forgery is to pass as current, and Garrick had no wish to pass as Delane. The anecdote misdirects us yet again, from poor Delane to the skill with which Garrick caricatures him, declaiming with nodding head, stately gait, and finger to nose, each telling detail moving the reader further away from the anecdote's supposed subject.

Garrick's biographers and the period's theater historians, with the exception of Tate Wilkinson (himself a noted mimic), portray mimicry as a low art, a first step toward developing an acting technique that depicts universal human behaviors and emotions rather than one that imitates particular persons. Both Murphy and Davies refer to the young Garrick performing imitations in taverns as a preparation for the stage, and Genest characterizes Garrick's later turn from mimicry as a reluctant moral reformation brought on as a response to "taking off" Delane: "Delane was somewhat hurt in the estimation of the town by Garrick's imitation of him. . . . Some years after this, Garrick at the solicitation of his friends, the remonstrances of the actors, and from full conviction that his own merit required not such an aid as Mimickry, which was but a trifling feather in his cap of fame, for once in his life (as Wilkinson expresses it) did a generous action and gave up what he no longer wanted."[55] If taking off Delane was a crime, it was a youthful infraction, and Garrick reformed after his early temptations to mimicry: instead of imitating particular persons, he imitated nature with his perfected technique, his contemporary biographers suggest. Read in the context of this developmental narrative, the anecdote of Delane's death by mimicry represents a kind of emotional truth. It feels true because, like Garrick, the anecdote's reader must overcome a moral failing: that squirm of conscience or guilty pleasure, as reading of the mimicry's success and precision—even its allegedly deadly result—engenders a respectful awe for the imitator and a fleeting moue of amused sympathy for the imitated. There is some leaven of malice in all comic imitations, and the idea that Garrick murdered Delane with mimicry generates considerable emotional resonance.

The biographers' developmental narratives also obscure the fact that Garrick did *not* give up mimicry. Closely following a pathetic invocation of Delane, David Williams's *Letter to David Garrick* (1772) tells of Garrick's continued use of mimicry as a managerial instrument of correction in the 1770s, more than twenty years after Delane's death[56]:

> Whenever a brother of the buskin or sock has the ill-luck to be mentioned with commendation for his public talents, or with esteem for his private virtues, his figure, his gestures, his face, his voice are stretched on the rack of ridicule; his private character is stabbed by a misrepresented anecdote, or an exaggerated foible. Hence the distorted views we have had of Mrs. Yates, Mr. Woodward, Mr. Smith, and other performers of great excellence. Nay, such a foe are you [Garrick] to merit in others, that it hurts even your interest: how else can we account for your having made Mr. and Mrs. Barry, Mr. King, Mrs. Abingdon,

> Mr. Moody, Mr. Aickin, Mrs. Baddely, Mr. Brereton, performers of great merit on your own theatre, the objects of your severest ridicule?[57]

Williams's account reveals an arsenal of ridicule that extends from the rack of bodily stage mimicry to weaponized anecdote. His pamphlet's larger purpose is to argue that Garrick has purchased shares in newspapers to control the public image of himself and his theater. Mimicry, Williams suggests, has become but one of Garrick's modes of shaping other actors' reputations, for now Garrick's acts of ridicule feed the newspapers in which he has a proprietary interest with carefully planted anecdotes.

While it remains speculative to propose that Garrick's imitation of Dennis Delane in the "boar and sow" speech of *The Rehearsal* intimidated or infuriated Delane to such an extent that he was no longer willing to be associated with a play in which he had been so memorably mocked, it does seem a credible explanation for Delane's sudden relinquishing of a comic role for which he was both well suited and well known. The anecdote of the "boar and sow" imitation enshrines Garrick's versatility and variety (key components of his personal brand) even as it obscures Delane's similar, earlier achievement of range. The anecdote reduces Garrick's competitor for theatric fame to an easily reproduced object; in anecdote, Delane becomes a thing acted upon, rather than an actor. Garrick's mimicry was assuredly not the kind of reverential, community-building passing on of faithful resemblances or what Bratton calls "a history of performance"[58] via one actor's imitation of another; rather, it was a demonstration of Garrick's virtuosic mobility that used the audience's communal knowledge of players' foibles against his colleagues to enhance his own commercial value. The particularity of Garrick's mimicry of Delane, built upon mock-heroic couplets in a play that was itself a metadramatic burlesque of heroic tragedy, derided Delane's stature as a tragedian of the first rank as something risible. This anecdote of Delane's death by mimicry most frequently surfaces in Garrickian biographies, where it serves as a false witness to Garrick's supposed abandonment of mimicry to pursue the imitation of nature. Garrick's mimicry reframed the acting techniques of his day, rehearsing Delane's faults so that they read as Garrickian mastery, and theater historians' and biographers' rehearsing of this *Anecdota obscura*,[59] which conceals as much as it reveals, annihilated Dennis Delane.

Notes

Epigraph: The Green-Room, No. XII; newspaper clipping in Forster Collection file FL4-3312, Victoria & Albert Museum, London.

1. [David Williams], *A Letter to David Garrick, Esq. On His Conduct as Principal Manager and Actor at Drury Lane* (London: S. Bladon, 1772), 10–11.

2. Sir Nicholas Nipclose [pseud. Francis Gentleman], *The Theatres. A Poetical Dissection* (London: John Bell and C. Etherington, 1772), 9.

3. Davies identifies Dennis Delane, Lacy Ryan, Roger Bridgwater, Henry Giffard, and Sacheverel Hale as the actors imitated by Garrick in the part of Bayes. Hale, Davies reports, laughed heartily at Garrick's imitations of others, but when the theatre erupted in "loud laughter and thundering applause" at an impression of his own manner, "Hale was shocked at the mortifying scene, and felt the folly and injustice of approving that ridicule of others which he could not bear himself." Thomas Davies, *Dramatic Miscellanies: Consisting of Critical Observations on Several Plays of Shakspeare: With a Review of His Principal Characters, and Those of Various Eminent Writers, as Represented by Mr. Garrick, and Other Celebrated Comedians*, 3 vols. (London: Printed for the author, 1783–1784), 1:7. Jean Benedetti notes the importance of the role of Bayes to Garrick's career, and describes the difference between his early and late career representations of the part thus: "*The Rehearsal* was essential to Garrick. He played it ninety-one times in the course of his career, more than Richard III. He developed and deepened his performance. He initially played Bayes in contemporary costume, recognizable as Garrick, settling scores. Later, following his own logic of characterisation, he particularised the appearance of the part more fully, dressing it in the full-bottomed wig and the clothes of an earlier generation, thus marking a certain distance. This was essential, for, more than anything he wrote, this play became the medium through which he expressed his views on acting. The criticism, however, was now generalised, not personalised." Benedetti, *David Garrick and the Birth of Modern Theatre* (London: Methuen, 2001), 66.

4. Davies, *Dramatic Miscellanies*, 2:299.

5. Charles Dibdin, *A Complete History of the Stage*, 5 vols. (London: C. Dibdin, [1800]), 5:202.

6. Joel Fineman, "The History of the Anecdote: Fiction and Fiction," in *The New Historicism*, ed. H. Aram Veeser (London: Routledge, 1989), 56–57.

7. Malina Stefanovska, "Exemplary or Singular? The Anecdote in Historical Narrative," *SubStance* 118, vol. 38, no. 1 (2009): 16.

8. Samuel Johnson's definition of anecdote is succinct: "Something yet unpublished; secret history." Johnson, in *A Dictionary of the English Language: in which The Words are deduced from their Originals, and Illustrated in their Different Significations by Examples from the best Writers* (London: W. Strahan, for J. Knapton; C. Hitch and L. Hawes; A. Millar; R. and J. Dodsley; and M. and T. Longman, 1756).

9. For Delane's will, see PROB 11/778/81. See also W. R. Chetwood, *A General History of the Stage; (More Particularly the Irish Theatre) from Its Origin in Greece Down to the Present Time* (Dublin: E. Rider, 1749), 133.

10. For instance, Delane takes the title "Esq." in the subscribers' list for Henry Jones's *Poems on Several Occasions*. See Henry Jones, *Poems on Several Occasions* (London: R. Dodsley, 1749).

11. Roberta Mock, "Dennis Delane [Delany], (1694/5?–1750)," in *Oxford Dictionary of National Biography*, ed. David Cannadine (Oxford: Oxford University Press, 2004), 1. The Sublime Society of Beefsteaks was a dining club founded by theater manager John Rich in 1735 for the purposes of conviviality and eating beefsteaks in a room above Covent Garden Theatre.

12. Philip H. Highfill Jr., Kalman A. Burnim, and Edward A. Langhans, eds., "Delane, Dennis," *A Biographical Dictionary of Actors, Actresses, Musicians, Dancers, Managers & Other Stage Personnel in London, 1660–1800*, 16 vols. (Carbondale: Southern Illinois University Press, 1975), 4:286.

13. Thomas Davies, *Memoirs of the Life of David Garrick, Esq., Interspersed with Characters and Anecdotes of His Theatrical Contemporaries*, 3rd ed., 2 vols. (London: The author, 1780), 1:27.

14. John Hill, *The Actor: Or, a Treatise on the Art of Playing* (London: R. Griffiths, 1755), 322.

15. For more on Garrick's association with variety, see chapter 3 of Leslie Ritchie, *David Garrick and the Mediation of Celebrity* (Cambridge: Cambridge University Press, 2019), 72–116.

16. "Account of Mr. James Quin," *The European Magazine, and London Review* 22 (1792): 50.

17. For information concerning Garrick's work in Dublin, see Robert D. Hume, "Garrick in Dublin in 1745–46," *Philological Quarterly* 93, no. 4 (2014): 507–540.

18. See Garrick's June 23 [1742] letter from Dublin to his brother Peter for an instance of cross-Channel rivalry, cited later in this article. David Garrick, *The Letters of David Garrick*, ed. David M. Little, George M. Kahrl, and Phoebe deK. Wilson, 3 vols. (Cambridge, MA: Harvard University Press, 1963), 1:40.

19. Theophilus Cibber, *An Apology for the Life of Mr. The' Cibber, Comedian. Being a Proper Sequel to the Apology for the Life of Mr. Colley Cibber, Comedian, with an Historical View of the Stage to the Present Year* (Dublin: George Faulkner, 1741), 171.

20. Cibber, *An Apology*, 170.

21. One illustration in the Folger Shakespeare Library of a handsome young man dressed as Comus from Milton's entertainment of that name is hand-inscribed "Delane." If this is Delane, it is a cruel irony that he, an alcoholic, should be remembered solely as the specious sorcerer who commands a train of Bacchanals, and portrayed with glass in hand, in garb wound around with grapes. The identification is plausible, as Delane did play Comus; see the *London Daily Post and General Advertiser* for April 9, 1743. For this image, see PN2598.G3F5 Copy 3, extra-illustrated, opposite 1:250, Folger Shakespeare Library, Washington, D.C.

22. Chetwood, *A General History of the Stage*, 132.

23. Cibber, *An Apology*, 171.

24. Of Garrick's first run at Goodman's Fields, Davies reports, "Such was the universal approbation that followed our young actor, that the more established theatres of Drury-lane and Covent-garden were deserted; Mr. Garrick drew after him the inhabitants of the most polite parts of the town; Goodman's-fields was full of the splendor of St. James's and Grosvenor-square; the coaches of the nobility filled up the space from Temple-bar to Whitechapel." Davies raves of the actor's instant accomplishment and maturity: "Mr. Garrick shone forth like a theatrical Newton; he threw new light on elocution and action; he banished ranting, bombast, and grimace; and restored nature, ease, simplicity, and genuine humour." Davies, *Memoirs of the Life of David Garrick*, 1:42–43.

25. Cibber, *An Apology*, 172.

26. Nipclose, *The Theatres*, 5.

27. Wilkinson condemns Garrick's mimicry of Delane: "The peculiarities of Mr. Delane, an actor of the first rank, were so severely pointed out by Mr. Garrick, in the character of Bayes, that it is said to have actually occasioned Mr. Delane's flying to the bottle for relief to his hurt mind; he continued to use it with such excess that he never was himself again." Tate Wilkinson, *Memoirs of His Own Life, by Tate Wilkinson, Patentee of the Theatres-Royal, York & Hull*, vol. 1 (York: Printed for the Author by Wilson, Spence, and Mawman, 1790), 83.

28. Anonymous, *The Life of Mr. James Quin, Comedian* (London: S. Bladon, 1766), 79.

29. Garrick, *The Letters of David Garrick*, 1:40.

30. Jacky Bratton, "Anecdote and Mimicry as History," in *New Readings in Theatre History* (Cambridge: Cambridge University Press, 2003), 106.

31. Jonathan Bate, as quoted in Bratton, "Anecdote and Mimicry as History," 103.

32. George [Villiers], Duke of Buckingham, *The Rehearsal: As It Is Now Acted at the Theatre-Royal . . . To Which Is Added, a Key, or Critical View of the Authors, and Their Writings, Expos'd in This Play*, 13th ed. (London: W. Feales, R. Wellington, J. Wellington; A. Bettesworth, and F. Clay, 1735), 18, 8. All references are to this edition.

33. Villiers, *The Rehearsal*, 15.

34. Villiers, *The Rehearsal*, 24.

35. Villiers, *The Rehearsal*, 26.

36. Villiers, *The Rehearsal*, 32.

37. Bayes mistakes a galloping tempo for wit, telling Smith that he shall see the players "come in upon one another snip-snap, hit for hit, as fast as can be. First one speaks, then presently t'other's upon him slap, with a Repartee . . . and so eternally, eternally, I'gad, till they go quite off the Stage." Villiers, *The Rehearsal*, 35.

38. For an instance of Delane advertised as Smith in the production (one of the three named parts), see the *London Daily Post, and General Advertiser* of November 8, 1739.

39. And possibly in seven more performances for which the cast was not listed; see *The London Stage* part 3, vol. 2, 825–850.

40. Letter to Peter Garrick of February 6, 1741 [dated 1742 (Old Style) in letter]. Garrick, *The Letters of David Garrick*, 1:37.

41. Henry Fielding's *Champion* no. 455, reprinted in *Gentleman's Magazine* 12 (October 1742): 527.

42. Arthur Murphy, *The Life of David Garrick, Esq.*, 2 vols., vol. 1 (London: J. Wright, J. F. Foot, 1801), 52–53, 56.

43. Bratton, "Anecdote and Mimicry as History," 119.

44. Here is one of many examples of contemporary theater critics figuring personal imitations as low, addressed to Garrick: "The introducing private characters upon a stage can never be justified; and I am afraid least of all in you, whose great success should place you above those freedoms which disgrace a theatre, and which offend humanity. I do not know by what authority the master of a company of comedians should take into his hand the punishment of the guilty; but when the unoffending are condemned to this severe repeated execution the fault is violently exaggerated. . . . Whatever joy the meaner part of an audience may find in such representations, they are offensive to the rest." Anonymous, "A Letter to Mr. Garrick on the Opening of the Theatre, with Observations on the Conduct of Managers, to Actors, Authors, and Audiences: And Particularly to New-Performers" (London: J. Coote, 1758), 17.

45. Mary Luckhurst and Jane Moody, *Theatre and Celebrity in Britain, 1660–2000* (New York: Palgrave Macmillan, 2005), 71.

46. Charles Burney, "Burney Collection, the Life and Work of David Garrick, ed. British Library (British Library 1741–1747), Microfilm 939.D.1-9." This newspaper clipping looks similar to advertisements in the *London Daily Post*, but the source cannot be confirmed. Neither the British Library nor the electronic *17th–18th Century Burney Collection Newspapers* retains issues of the 1742 *London Daily Post*, which is accessible only through isolated clippings; see Arthur Hawley Scouten, ed. *The London Stage, 1660–1800; a Calendar of Plays, Entertainments & Afterpieces, Together with Casts, Box-Receipts and Contemporary Comment, Part 3: 1729–1747*, 2 vols. (Carbondale: Southern Illinois University Press, 1961), 2:924, 2:996.

47. "Vandalism" was not yet a word in general use: the *OED* identifies its earliest usage as 1793, "from the French *vandalisme*, first used by Henri Grégoire, Bishop of Blois, *c*1793." "vandalism, n.," *OED Online*, June 2019, Oxford University Press, accessed June 13, 2019. Arson, however, had a well-established legal definition that, like murder, used malice as a determinant.

48. This aspect of literary parody was still available to audiences in Delane's day via the "Key" to *The Rehearsal*, printed with contemporary editions of the play. Villiers, *The Rehearsal*, 8, 93.

49. There are numerous resonances between *The Rehearsal* and *The Rival Queens*, including each play's obsession with doublings, and Alexander's reference to Lysimachus and Clytus as his Thunder and Lightning, but the ponderous pace and elevated diction of the iambic lines would surely have been the most obvious: "And now methinks I stand like the dread God, / Who while his Priests and I quaff'd sacred Blood, / Acknowledg'd me his Son." Nathaniel Lee, *The Rival Queens: Or, the Death of Alexander the Great* (London: W. Feales, 1677; 1736), 28.

50. See Garrick's letters to Colman of April 11, 1764, and June 12, 1764: "damn Alexander—O horrible horrible &c!—Delane got credit by that Stuff—damn it, I say again—." Garrick, *The Letters of David Garrick*, 1:411, 1:416–417.

51. John Genest, ed., *Some Account of the English Stage, from the Restoration in 1660 to 1830*, 10 vols. (New York: Burt Franklin, 1832; 1965), 4:21. See also Murphy, *The Life of David Garrick*, vol. 1, 53.

52. A video of Cathy Berberian's performance of "Ticket to Ride," introduced by Berberian, is available on YouTube at https://www.youtube.com/watch?v=WLqVioiDldc.

53. Terry Threadgold, *Feminist Poetics: Poiesis, Performance, Histories* (London: Routledge, 1997), 132–133.

54. See Linda Hutcheon's definition of parody as "imitation with critical difference," which is itself inspired by Gilles Deleuze's *Différence et répétition* (1968). Linda Hutcheon, *A Theory of Parody: The Teachings of Twentieth-Century Art Forms* (Urbana: University of Illinois Press, 1985, 2000), 6, 36.

55. Genest, *Some Account of the English Stage*, 4:22.

56. Delane died March 31, 1750, probably as the result of alcohol-related illness. His last years were not pleasant: he suffered the death of an infant daughter, and presumably considerable stress after leaving Drury Lane for Covent Garden Theatre in 1748 following another disagreement with Garrick. See Mock, "Dennis Delane [Delany]."

57. Williams, "A Letter to David Garrick, Esq.," 11–12.

58. Bratton, "Anecdote and Mimicry as History," 115.

59. This chapter has traced one *Anecdota obscura* in considerable detail; other examples of this subspecies of theatrical anecdote abound. To give another instance of an "anecdote applied by theater historians and biographers such that it capitalizes on and misdirects the anecdote's entertainment value, provides a deceptive sense of representation, or uses the anecdote's structure and obsession with singularity and telling detail to distract from its misbehavior as a false witness to history," to cite my earlier definition, one might consider the letter to the printer of the *St. James's Chronicle* of November 11–13, 1777. This letter seeks to correct one circulating theatrical anecdote about the actor West Digges and the riot that occurred in the Smock Alley Theatre in 1754. After Digges refused to repeat a speech from the play *Mahomet* that had contemporary political overtones, the theater was destroyed, and Digges allegedly never played in Ireland again. While Digges is a rascal whose talent grows "like a Cow's Tait, downward," the letter writer "Veritas" states, it is not true that this riot caused Digges to leave the Irish stage, and "Veritas" cites dates in proof of this. Here, the *Anecdota obscura* is a false witness that attempts to erase Digges's continuing peripatetic cross-Channel career. Further, as Chris Mounsey observes in his analysis of the riot, benefit performances were held a mere two weeks after the riot in Smock Alley Theatre, which makes this theatrical anecdote doubly deceptive. See Chris Mounsey, "Thomas Sheridan and the Second Smock Alley Theatre Riot, 1754," *New Hibernia Review / Iris Éireannach Nua* 4, no. 3 (2000): 65–77.

2

VIOLENT AFTERLIVES

The Anecdote in Eighteenth-Century Theater Biographies

MÁIRE MACNEILL

On the evening of the tenth of May 1735, the actor Charles Macklin launched a violent attack on his colleague Thomas Hallam in the green room at the Theatre Royal, Drury Lane. The two men had fallen into a dispute over a wig that was to be worn in the farce being staged that evening, until "at last Mekelin took up a small Crab-tree Stick, and made a Lunge at Hallam with such Force, that he run him thro' the Eye into the Brain."[1] Hallam languished until early the next morning, when he died from his wounds, while Macklin managed to escape. This bare-bones description is a fair summation of the reports published in the London newspapers over the following week, with each offering its own additional details. The *General Evening Post* told its readers that "Mr. Mechlin made his Escape from the top of the House thro' the upper Gallery, and went off unobserved with the Crowd,"[2] while the *Daily Journal* noted that "after he had committed this cruel Action, [Macklin] went on the Stage, and acted his Part, but in a great Confusion."[3] The news that the coroner's jury had reached a verdict of "wilful murder" brought about additional commentary. The *General Evening Post* now drew a grim parallel to an earlier case, in which a young law student, irate at being taunted by a criminal being driven to Tyburn, drew his cane and stabbed his heckler through the eye, killing him. The law student was subsequently tried for murder, found guilty, and executed.[4] The *Weekly Miscellany* took the opportunity to provide social commentary to the reading public by comparing Macklin's fatal skirmish to an aristocratic duel, making the cynical observation that if the actor could "procure his Pardon, he will probably make the better Figure for this Accident, among those eminent ones, who have each taken upon themselves the Satisfaction of Gentlemen, and had the Glory of killing his Man."[5] Compared (coolly) to a convicted murderer and (caustically) to a duelist, Macklin was grouped with other violent perpetrators unwelcome in society.

After a week of reports and speculation, the newspapers abandoned the story; despite the unusual circumstances underpinning the episode, neither actor was a major star, and there were other news items to interest the public. The case received sporadic updates throughout the year, with the disputed wig emphasized in these accounts, reminding readers of the triviality of the argument: "Mr. Mechlin, the Comedian, surrenders, to make his Tryal for the Murder of Mr. Hallam, on a sudden Quarrel at Drury-Lane Theatre, about the wearing of a Wig," one typical notice ran.[6] Yet after it went to trial at the Old Bailey the following autumn—and Macklin was found guilty of manslaughter and sentenced to be burned on the hand—the incident largely fell out of mention in print until the end of the century. It re-emerged after Macklin's death in 1797, by which time his celebrity had grown and those authoring accounts of his life (published in memoirs and obituaries) were forced to contend with the problem of how to explain their subject's violent actions sixty years earlier.

Mercurial attitudes toward actors during the eighteenth century meant that the representation of theatrical anecdotes relating to violence shifted depending on both the medium in which they appeared and the reputation and gender of the subject. While newspaper reports published immediately following a violent incident gave what information they could, they rarely provided the context for their stories, often leaving out details about the actor's life and career. Some of these reports also contained obvious mistakes or inconsistencies; for example, Macklin's name was given variously as "Mecklin," "Mekelin," "Mechlin," and "Macloughlin" in the week after his attack on Hallam. Conversely, theatrical biographies (usually published later in an actor's career or after his or her death, when any violent incidents were at a distance) wove anecdotes about their subjects' duels and tussles in among the other events in their lives. Biographers trumpeted their narratives as accurate and definitive, claims that could not always be justified. These biographies often had a picaresque quality to them, with actors' lives told through a series of loosely connected events that could be rearranged or eliminated according to the biographer's fancy, to help shape or reinforce the popular image of a particular performer.

This chapter analyzes acts of physical violence that occurred between actors in accounts that were told and retold throughout the century to examine how biographers variously styled anecdotes about violence as vindications, apologias, or exposés. Actors made intriguing biographical subjects for a celebrity-hungry readership—as prominent public figures they had "the potential to symbolise politeness and to propagate its modes of expression"[7]—but the violent incidents that peppered the lives of these stage heroes and heroines were difficult to reconcile with a society increasingly beholden to the idea that both men and women should learn to curb their anger.[8] By examining descriptions of scuffles on and off the stage, as well as duels provoked by professional disputes, we can learn how biographers attempted to translate the suspect or embarrassing episodes in their subjects' histories for new generations of audiences. However, the disparate sympathies of different biographers meant that anecdotes and the morals drawn from them could conflict across different sources. Likewise, there is a significant gender divide in how male and female violence was represented. As we shall see, while Macklin and James Quin (who were both convicted of manslaughter) often had their emotional drives elevated and rationalized by their biographers, violent encounters between women (including Faustina Bordoni and Francesca Cuzzoni, Elizabeth Barry and Elizabeth Bowtell, and George Anne Bellamy and Margaret Woffington) were remembered as farce. Violent anecdotes were revised and restructured, and sometimes eliminated from an actor's life altogether; an analysis of how these anecdotes were utilized in the construction of theatrical lives demonstrates how biographers could manipulate their subjects' histories to forward their own narrative ambitions.

Violent Afterlives

If Macklin's career had ended after his trial in December 1735, then Hallam's death may have been remembered simply as the consequence of a gory encounter that illustrated the vanity of two minor actors. Yet, as the *Weekly Miscellany* had predicted, Macklin escaped with a manslaughter conviction and did not suffer serious ill consequences, social or professional, in the aftermath of the incident. In 1741, after a fifteen-year presence on the London stage, he found stardom in his interpretation of Shylock in a new production of *The Merchant of Venice*. This performance was widely acknowledged as one of the touchstones of the naturalistic style of acting of the 1740s, and Macklin would continue to act this role sporadically for almost half a century. His subsequent career solidified his legacy: he engaged in playwriting—*Love à la Mode* (1759) and *The Man of the World* (1781) were both successful within his lifetime—and provided acting instruction for younger performers and, briefly, a school of oratory for the public.[9] After his death in 1797, newspaper obituaries produced sympathetic portraits of the "Father of the Stage." The *Morning Herald* included a description of Hallam's death (inaccurately dated to 1733) but concluded by characterizing Macklin as "humane, courteous, chearful, and convivial, though somewhat warm in argument."[10] The *Whitehall Evening Post* noted: "The consciousness . . . of having been the occasion of the death of a fellow creature, made a strong impression upon Macklin, and almost disposed him to look with disgust upon a profession which had led to such a lamentable event."[11] Shifting the blame for the incident to the acting profession as a whole, the author invites his readers to query the conscience-stricken performer's culpability in the affair—perhaps even to the point of casting him as another victim.

These sympathetic retellings of the event are reinforced in the *Memoirs of the Life of Charles Macklin, Esq.* (1799), in which James Kirkman retells the anecdote over an expansive sixteen pages, which includes additional commentary and a long quotation from the trial's published transcription from 1736.[12] This enables him to include significantly more information than the original newspaper reports, including the lurid detail that after being stabbed, Hallam "sat down, and said to *Mr. Arne's* son, (who was dressed in woman's cloaths) 'Whip up your clothes, you little b—h, and urine in my eye.'"[13] Kirkman's use of the trial's transcription also meant that he could present the verdict of manslaughter as the definitive interpretation of the event, parsing it as an "impartial relation,"[14] objective and therefore accurate. Thus construed, he can offer Macklin far more leniency than the newspapers of 1735 allowed, with Hallam (already debased through the inclusion of his vulgar speech to young Arne) sharing equal responsibility for the event: "There were faults on one side, as well as on the other," Kirkman writes, giving the event a moral ambiguity absent in the newspaper reports.[15] Likewise, while Kirkman is conscious that downplaying the seriousness of the incident might not be beneficial to either his subject or his narrative (for "the public might accuse us of an attempt to conceal what we know"), he is nevertheless anxious to plead Macklin's case, writing that otherwise the actor "might, in a very important point of view, be censured and condemned to an extent beyond what the whole circumstances of the case, taken together, will warrant or allow."[16] He concludes his retelling of this chapter in Macklin's life with the words: "Mr. Macklin's long and honourable life justified this verdict of the Jury; and his conduct as a father, an husband, a friend, and a member of society, ranks among the first, for tenderness, affection, friendship, and honesty."[17] For Kirkman, Macklin's life after the event is that of family man, friend, and honest citizen, and he appears not as a career-driven public figure drawn to petty disputes but rather as a paradigm of respectable, middle-class domesticity.

Other authors writing after Macklin's death were more circumspect in their use of the anecdote. Throughout his life Macklin maintained a reputation for being earthy and even boorish, a counternarrative to the reputation he had cultivated as a learned authority on oratorial technique. He was dogged by accusations of illiteracy,[18] commonly represented as a man "without any education except what he had acquired through regular industry," and who had given the star actor James Quin a "drubbing" in the green room at Drury Lane.[19] One obituary from 1797 urged readers to remember Macklin for his behavior *offstage* as much as his talent *on* it, writing: "His excellence as a Comedian was not greater than his irascibility of temper, which perpetually involved him in quarrels."[20] When Francis

Congreve came to recount Hallam's death in his *Authentic Memoirs of the Late Mr. Charles Macklin, Comedian* (1798), he was likewise critical of his subject's inability to resolve arguments without the use of violence. Although his account of the incident is only briefly relayed over two pages, he creates a narrative of violence by pairing it with Macklin's fight with Quin the following year, linking the two anecdotes thusly: "Although his recent delivery and bare escape from condemnation might have warned him to suppress the natural irritability of his temper, yet it appears to have had little weight with him."[21] Contrary to the obituary in the *Whitehall Evening Post*, Macklin was remarkable for his *failure* to reflect upon or seriously regret his attack on Hallam, and it was this lack of contrition which drew him into further acts of violence.

These diverse interpretations of Hallam's death show the essential rift in how Macklin's biographers sought to represent him, exemplifying the rival "rogue and gentleman" dichotomy defined by Cheryl Wanko.[22] Was Macklin a talented performer and family man, devoted to "enlarging and enriching his mind" through independent study,[23] who was drawn into a fight in which he accidentally killed his opponent, to his everlasting regret? Or was he an illiterate hothead, known for his quick temper, and who was "in argument . . . always desirous of obtaining victory"?[24] The opposing uses of this anecdote demonstrate the ease with which the actor's reputation could shift depending on the narrator's intent. Some biographers avoided mention of Macklin's violent actions altogether and emerge just as anxious to represent him as nonviolent as those who attempted to write in his defense. In the third *Memoirs* of Macklin, published in 1804, William Cooke omits the Hallam anecdote and describes the tussle with Quin as a "quarrel," a verbal subterfuge that implies a nonphysical dispute.[25] Cooke gives far more space to a description of Macklin and Quin's reconciliation over a bottle of alcohol, representing his subject as a man who resolves disputes through conviviality rather than violence. But whether critical or sympathetic of Macklin, later accounts were unanimous in their shift from the farcical undertones of the original story. The wig, prominent in the earliest newspaper reports, declines in importance, and Macklin's actions are blamed on "a momentary, and instantaneous gust of passion," or a "hasty fit of passion."[26] For late eighteenth-century biographers informed by the literature of sensibility, male acts of violence needed to be codified through emotions, not objects.

Actionable Words and Self-Defense

Quin, whose backstage brawl with Macklin provoked disagreement between Congreve and Cooke at the end of the century, was a difficult subject for his own biographers, as he fought at least two duels during his lifetime. Swordplay, long a marker of genteel masculinity, was increasingly problematized during the eighteenth century as social reformers promoted a masculine discourse founded on diplomacy rather than dueling.[27] Exceptions primarily rested on self-defense; for example, the fencing master William Hope concluded his critique of dueling by allowing that a man might fight without compromising his moral code if he had repeatedly tried and failed to reason with his challenger.[28] Nevertheless, as Jason Solinger has argued, throughout the century, "older facets of masculine comportment are strategically incorporated, rather than swept aside, by emergent paradigms of masculinity,"[29] and men who had both the skill and dexterity to control a sword and the integrity and backbone to control their emotions were widely admired. For example, the actor Robert Wilks "understood the *Small Sword* as well as any Man, yet he had not an Occasion to use it in any Quarrel, for his Behaviour was such that he never had any Cause to send or to receive a Quarrel."[30] This ideal, a balancing of the skilled swordsman–rational man dichotomy, was to direct how Quin's biographers wrote about their subject.

In April 1718, Quin fought a duel with the actor William Bowen after an argument in a tavern "about which of them two was the honestest Man."[31] Unlike the editorializing that accompanied reports of Macklin's attack on Hallam, the few newspaper notices of Quin's duel with Bowen were merely perfunctory.[32] Although the court depositions later appeared in a volume of *Remarkable Tryals,* the story lacked a narrative hook like Macklin's wig that might have helped it sustain a stronger presence in the press.[33] Quin was mostly absent from the stage between the time of the duel and the end of his murder trial in July 1718, but his career thereafter seems to have continued unaffected: by September of that year, he was acting his old parts again, as well as new title roles in *Macbeth* and *The Double Dealer*. Although he fought another duel in 1739 against Theophilus Cibber, which resulted in only minor injuries, the newspapers again published few notices of the incident. Quin's duels do not appear to have damaged his career significantly. Most public criticisms of him referred to his monotonous acting style rather than his checkered private life, and after his death in 1766, these fights were not mentioned in his newspaper obituaries.[34] The *London Chronicle*, for example, remembered him as a favorite star of the stage, a gourmand, and a noted wit.[35] Others reported that he had left one thousand pounds to the hospital in Bath, his city of residence in his later years.[36] Skating over Quin's duels, the newspapers preferred to remember the dead icon as a frank speaking and generous Roger de Coverley figure for the mid-eighteenth century.

Unlike the newspaper biographies, the anonymous *Life of Quin*, published the year of his death, does not dispute its subject's violent past, but does manage to both mitigate and muddle it. Ignoring the duel with Bowen, the author instead details a different duel that sparked from an affront that took place during a performance of *Cato* at Drury Lane. The slight occurred when an actor called Williams, playing the part of the messenger, spoke the line, "Caesar sends health to Cato," and mispronounced the last word as "Keeto."[37] Quin ad-libbed a response: "Would he had sent a better messenger."[38] Outraged, Williams followed Quin off the stage into the green room, began to argue with him for "making him appear ridiculous in the eyes of the audience, and thereby hurting him in his profession," and demanded satisfaction. Quin refused but Williams ambushed him outside later that evening; unluckily for Williams, Quin managed to draw his sword and kill him.[39] The author concludes: "Quin was tried for this affair at the Old Bailey, and it was brought in manslaughter, to the entire satisfaction of the court, and to all who were acquainted with the origin and progress of the quarrel."[40] Much like Kirkman in his biography of Macklin, Quin's biographer concludes that moral as much as legal justice was carried out in court. However, it is unclear when this duel might have occurred.[41] The author assigns it no year but places it narratively between an anecdote about Quin's acting the lead in *Macbeth* (from November 1718) and the premiere of *The Beggar's Opera* (January 1728), dates when Quin was at Lincoln's Inn Fields rather than Drury Lane. Additionally, there is no record of Quin playing the lead in *Cato* before January 1734. The fact that the *Life of Quin* is the first source for this duel, thirty years or more after it must have taken place, casts further doubt on whether it really happened.

Veracity aside, the anecdote is significant because it advances the idea that Quin was forced to fight; indeed, the biographer writes that his subject had attempted to refuse the duel "with his usual philosophy and humour."[42] The author's erasure of the Bowen duel, an event emerging from a drunken dispute, in favor of one invented or embellished with Williams, in which Quin is more clearly provoked into defending himself, suggests that the author was offering a narrative that diminished the subject's culpability. Likewise, where the trial document of the Quin–Bowen duel suggests a rambling alehouse squabble over acting ability, honesty, and politics, Quin's biographer offers a clearer narrative of a professional quarrel between actors and the fatal consequences. Like the early obituaries of Macklin, the emphasis on the theater as a tempestuous arena for inspiring a duel shifts the blame away from Quin. Indeed, the author is keen to imply a divide between public masks and private selves: Quin's testy reputation masked his true self, the author suggests, for "notwithstanding the rough fantastic manner which so much characterized him, no one was of a more humane disposition, or less addicted to revenge."[43] It was both Williams's failure to recognize this divide and his anger over Quin's extempore speech onstage that triggered the fight.

The duel with Bowen re-emerges in the *New and General Biographical Dictionary* in 1798. This work takes a more redemptive approach to the duel, not significantly downplaying Quin's part but concluding the anecdote with the reflection that although the "unhappy incident was not calculated to impress a favourable opinion of Quin on the public mind . . . Whatever effect it had at the time, he lived to erase the impression it had made by many acts of benevolence."[44] Although less anxious to clear Quin of wrongdoing than the *Life*, the author here filters his subject's biography through the lens of celebrity and public face: if Quin "lived to erase the impression" left by his duel with Bowen, we might interpret his philanthropic spirit as driven by consciousness of his reputation as much as genuine desire to atone. Yet ultimately the author remains forgiving of his subject, ending with a quotation from one of Quin's friends which "approaches more nearly to truth than any other": although there was a "sediment of brutality in him, when you shook the bottle; but he made you ample amends, by his pleasantry & good sense when he was sober."[45] Quin, like Macklin, was never regarded as truly genteel—the references to his love of eating and drinking throughout his memoirs and obituaries indicate that he was identified with Falstaff off the stage as much as on it—but his later biographers attempted to marry his dueling, a historic signifier of upper-class masculinity, with its newer equivalents of rationalism, philanthropy, and conviviality.

Rival Queens

If most biographers were inclined to fuss over the violent behavior of their male subjects, they were less anxious to interrogate anecdotes about violence between women. Public expressions of anger could compromise a woman's femininity, according to Elizabeth Foyster, and public fights between actresses were pictured as variously scandalous or ridiculous.[46] The rivalry between opera stars Faustina Bordoni and Francesca Cuzzoni was noted in the press in June 1727 when the two had an encounter onstage during Giovanni Bononcini's *Astianatte* that caused the performance to end prematurely. Although the details of the incident are unclear (Suzanne Aspden writes that all descriptions of the event are drawn from contemporary satirical pamphlets, and must therefore be read with caution), the event was to inform the subsequent reputation of both women in England.[47] John Arbuthnot gave it a satirical treatment in the immediate aftermath, describing it as a "horrid and bloody BATTLE" that should be decided by a prizefight for their public with the male opera singers Boschi and Palmerini acting as their seconds.[48] An anonymous farce, *The Contre Temps*, burlesqued the incident the following month. Later versions of the story saw a shift in tone from satire to reproof. When Faustina's biography appeared in John Hawkins's *General History of the Science and Practice of Music* (1776), three of the four pages on her life were devoted to her rivalry with Cuzzoni and their onstage tussle: "Private slander and public abuse were deemed weapons too innoxious in this warfare, blows were made use of in the prosecution of it, and, shame to tell! the two Signoras fought."[49] For Hawkins, the women's shame is emblematic of a toxic operatic culture in the 1720s; special blame is meted out to the supporters of each singer, particularly women such as the Countess of Pembroke, who "encouraged" the singers' rivalry. Although Hawkins does not provide details of the fight, he depicts the atmosphere before and afterward as one of "jealousy, hatred, and malice,"[50] and thus succeeds in amplifying the event to become the most significant incident in either woman's career, suggesting a reluctance to forgive women for their acts of violence.

Other authors utilized violent encounters between actresses to weave a humorous anecdote into a longer narrative. In his *History of the English Stage* (1741), Edmund Curll describes an early production of *The Rival Queens*, in which Elizabeth Barry and Elizabeth Bowtell played the lead roles of Roxana and Statira. The two actresses quarreled over who should wear a certain veil in the performance, and at the height of the argument, when Roxana (Barry) came to murder Statira (Bowtell) on the stage, Barry "struck with such Force, that tho' the Point of the Dagger was blunted, it made way through Mrs. *Boutel*'s Stayes, and entered about a Quarter of an Inch in the Flesh."[51] Curll continues by repeating contemporary gossip about the incident, that "Mrs. *Barry* was jealous of Mrs. *Boutel* and Lord *Rochester*," and that the town believed that she stabbed Bowtell "with Design to destroy her."[52] After this narrative diversion, however, he concludes that "on the strictest Examination of both Parties," it was determined that the veil *was* the true source of the dispute.[53] Barry's penalty (whether inflicted by the courts, her theater, or her public) is not mentioned, if she received any at all. Like the Williams duel in the *Life of Quin*, it is unclear if this incident really occurred (Curll seems to be the earliest source), but here the anecdote works to both actresses' disadvantage, for it is framed as fundamentally about clothes and gossip. The veil is at the story's centerpiece, undermining the emotional charge of both the scene and the actresses' careers, while the reference to Barry's jealousy over rumors about an affair between Bowtell and Rochester only serves to remind the reader of Barry's own relationship with the earl: her status as a mistress is as important to Curll's story as her status as a professional actress. In representing Barry and Bowtell as clotheshorses and mistresses who willingly stage their private disagreement in the midst of a public performance, Curll undermines his heroines' status as professional performers.

The Rival Queens was once again the setting for a display of violence between two actresses in January 1756, when George Anne Bellamy and Margaret Woffington argued over their clothes in a production of the play at Covent Garden, like Barry and Bowtell before them. In this anecdote, recounted in Bellamy's memoir, *An Apology for the Life of George Anne Bellamy* (ghostwritten in 1785), Woffington was costumed in a straw-colored dress, which, although formerly the possession of the Dowager Princess of Wales, looked soiled next to Bellamy's yellow and purple finery. Woffington, the senior of the two actresses, ordered Bellamy to never wear her costume again, and so the following night Bellamy wore one that was even more beautiful. Woffington was furious and, in Bellamy's words, "Oh! dire to tell! she drove me off the carpet, and gave me the *coup-de-grace* almost behind the scenes."[54] The audience, who were able to see most of the attack, hissed their disapproval of Woffington, and the incident proved inspiration for a farce several months later, Samuel Foote's *The Green-room Squabble* (1756). Bellamy's anecdote concludes on a moment of comic triumph after the two women had been separated: "Though I despise revenge, I do not dislike retaliation. I therefore put on my yellow and purple once more."[55]

This last anecdote differs somewhat from the others we have discussed, in that Bellamy is (nominally at least) the author of a work in which she herself is the victim of an assault, and she, more than any of our other authors, might have cause to castigate her attacker. Despite this, she recalls the event with a tone of comic bemusement rather than outrage. The distance of almost twenty years may simply have softened the incident for her; Wanko has argued that Bellamy creates a victimhood narrative in her *Apology*, and the idea of being assaulted onstage may be one way that this is extended.[56] However, it is also possible that, conscious of both her celebrity and her gender, she shapes a violent memory to make it comical (and therefore harmless) for her readership. If Williams came under fire from the author of the *Life of Quin* for confusing onstage and offstage emotions, Bellamy further blurs the distinction between actress and character by (like Barry and Bowtell before) having Roxana/Woffington attack

Statira/Bellamy in the same instant. Bellamy, in her own autobiographical mythmaking, erases the public–private divide and invites her reader to regard her onstage actions as offstage fact.

Perhaps because their violent encounters were rarely as dangerous as those of their male colleagues, actresses' physical fights were documented as farcical performances. The tragicomic tone of Bellamy's writing undermines the possibility of any emotional gravitas; the reader cannot comprehend Bellamy or Woffington as plausible combatants in a serious fight because Bellamy herself cannot parse them as such. As they were not dogged by the weighty consequences of their violent actions, actresses were instead characterized as driven by jealousy or shallow competition and remembered less for the force of their emotions than for petty rivalries, gossip, and showiness. The public nature of violent encounters between actresses may have contributed to how they were subsequently represented; whereas Macklin and Quin restricted their violent encounters to the backstage rooms or spaces outside of the theater in relative seclusion, women's disputes spilled into their professional work, in front of their publics. As such, the biographic anecdote typically depicts fights between women as less momentous (and therefore easier to laugh at) than those of men. These women were supposedly quick to resort to violence, and their failure to regulate their responses to insult, or in the case of Bellamy, to regret their reactions later, further underscores their inadequate emotional depth. The jealous rivalry over a beautiful costume, present in both *Rival Queens* anecdotes, has its counterpart in the wig that drove Macklin to stab Hallam in the eye—but while Macklin's wig sunk in prominence in his theatrical afterlife, actresses' costumes continued to carry the momentum of the anecdotes. Unlike Macklin, whose biographers emphasized the force of his passion, or Quin, whose biographers suggested he was a man of wit who was only driven to fight at the incitement of others, violent anecdotes about actresses primarily served to reinforce popular ideas about the triviality of women's concerns and emotions.

Examining actor biographies suggests a mixed—and indeed, specifically gendered—attitude toward those who performed acts of violence. Macklin and Quin were both found guilty of manslaughter as young men, but neither saw their crime and conviction seriously impede their careers. When their biographers placed earlier anecdotes of their subjects' violent acts within the broader narrative of their lives, they often minimized culpability, suggesting that acts of violence were out of their male subjects' control, whether due to a momentary lapse in emotional discipline or from the provocation of another. Authors who placed more blame on their subject, such as some of Macklin's biographers who were more resistant to excusing his violent past, used anecdotes about male violence as cautionary tales, emphasizing the importance of male self-control under aggravation. Conversely, Barry and Bowtell, and Bellamy and Woffington, were granted less emotional understanding of their own violence; they were instead represented as the comical icons of female vanity by the import they placed on fine clothing and their inability to distinguish between their real and theatrical personas. In these disparate ways, as violent acts occurred on and off the stage, theatrical biographers attempted to reconcile their subjects' historic actions to a public increasingly antipathic to violent behavior.

Notes

1. *Daily Journal*, Tuesday, May 13, 1735, issue 4469. All newspaper citations are taken from the *Seventeenth and Eighteenth Century Burney Newspapers Collection*.
2. *General Evening Post*, May 10, 1735–May 13, 1735, issue 252.
3. *Daily Journal*, Tuesday, May 13, 1735, issue 4469.
4. *General Evening Post*, May 13, 1735–May 15, 1735, issue 253. This observation was reprinted in the *Weekly Journal or British Gazetteer*, Saturday, May 17, 1735, issue 528.
5. *Weekly Miscellany*, Saturday, May 17, 1735, issue 127.
6. *London Daily Post and General Advertiser*, Friday, December 12, 1735, issue 347.
7. Paul Goring, *The Rhetoric of Sensibility in Eighteenth-Century Culture* (Cambridge: Cambridge University Press, 2004), 9.
8. Robert Shoemaker, *The London Mob: Violence and Disorder in Eighteenth-Century England* (London: A&C Black, 2004), 292–293.
9. This school, called the British Inquisition, was held in Covent Garden between 1754 and 1755. A description of Macklin's style of acting tuition appears in John O'Keeffe, *Recollections of the Life of John O'Keeffe, Written by Himself*, 2 vols. (London: Henry Colburn, 1826), 1:285–286.
10. *Morning Herald*, Wednesday, July 19, 1797, issue 5708.
11. *Whitehall Evening Post*, July 18, 1797–July 20, 1797, issue 7906.
12. James Kirkman, *Memoirs of the Life of Charles Macklin, Esq.*, 2 vols. (London: Lackington, Allen, and Co., 1799), 1:188–204.
13. Kirkman, *Memoirs*, 202.
14. Kirkman, *Memoirs*, 188.

15. Kirkman, *Memoirs*, 190.

16. Kirkman, *Memoirs*, 188–189.

17. Kirkman, *Memoirs*, 204.

18. For example, see "Macklin, Charles," in *A Biographical Dictionary of Actors, Actresses, Musicians, Dancers, Managers & Other Stage Personnel in London, 1660–1800*, ed. Philip H. Highfill Jr., Kalman A. Burnim, and Edward A. Langhans, vol. 10, *M'Intosh to Nash* (Carbondale: Southern Illinois University Press, 1983), 25. Shortly after Macklin's death, the *St. James's Chronicle* claimed that it was a well-known fact that he had been illiterate until the age of forty (July 13, 1797–July 15, 1797, issue 6173).

19. *True Briton*, Thursday, July 13, 1797, issue 1420.

20. *Oracle and Public Advertiser*, Friday, July 14, 1797, issue 19 674.

21. Francis Aspry Congreve, *Authentic Memoirs of the Late Mr. Charles Macklin, Comedian* (London: J. Barker, 1798), 15–17.

22. Cheryl Wanko, *Roles of Authority: Thespian Biography and Celebrity in Eighteenth-Century Britain* (Lubbock: Texas Tech University Press, 2003), 23–50.

23. Kirkman, *Memoirs*, 1:45.

24. Congreve, *Authentic Memoirs*, 60.

25. William Cooke, *Memoirs of Charles Macklin, Comedian* (London: Printed for J. Asperne by T. Maiden, 1804), 17–19.

26. Kirkman, *Memoirs*, 1:189; Congreve, *Authentic Memoirs*, 16.

27. Robert B. Shoemaker, "The Taming of the Duel: Masculinity, Honour and Ritual Violence in London, 1660–1800," *The Historical Journal* 45, no. 3 (2002): 538–540.

28. William Hope, *A Vindication of the True Art of Self-Defence* (Edinburgh: William Brown and Company, 1724), 37–41.

29. Jason Solinger, *Becoming the Gentleman: British Literature and the Invention of Modern Masculinity, 1660–1815* (New York: Palgrave Macmillan, 2012), 5–6.

30. Daniel O'Bryan, *Authentic Memoirs or, the Life and Character Of that most Celebrated Comedian, Mr. Robert Wilks* (London: S. Slow, 1732), 29.

31. *Weekly Journal or British Gazetteer*, Saturday, April 26, 1718.

32. Cf. *Weekly Journal or Saturday's Post*, Saturday, April 26, 1718, issue 72.

33. *A Compleat Collection of Remarkable Tryals of the Most Notorious Malefactors, at the Sessions-House in the Old Baily*, vol. 4 (London: J. Philips, 1721), 252.

34. For a selection of criticisms of Quin's acting, see *A Biographical Dictionary*, vol. 12, *Pinner to Rizzo* (Carbondale: Southern Illinois University Press, 1987), 235–240.

35. *London Chronicle*, February 1, 1766–February 4, 1766, issue 1424.

36. Cf. *St. James's Chronicle or the British Evening Post*, January 30, 1766–February 1, 1766, issue 767, and *London Evening Post*, February 1, 1766–February 4, 1766, issue 5962.

37. *The Life of Mr. James Quin, Comedian* (London: S. Bladon, 1766), 37.

38. *The Life of Mr. James Quin*.

39. *The Life of Mr. James Quin*, 37–38.

40. *The Life of Mr. James Quin*, 38.

41. Quin's entry in *A Biographical Dictionary*, vol. 12, *Pinner to Rizzo*, 228–229, offers 1717 as a possible date, as Quin did not perform at Drury Lane after that year until 1734, but also speculates "whether the Williams anecdote might not have grown out of the Bowen incident."

42. *The Life of Mr. James Quin*, 36–37.

43. *The Life of Mr. James Quin*, 36–37.

44. William Tooke, Robert Nares, and William Beloe, eds., *A New and General Biographical Dictionary*, vol. 12 (London: G. G. and J. Robinson et al., 1798), 449.

45. Tooke, Nares, and Beloe, *A New and General Biographical Dictionary*, 461.

46. Elizabeth Foyster, "Boys Will Be Boys? Manhood and Aggression, 1660–1800," in *English Masculinities, 1660–1800*, ed. Tim Hitchcock and Michele Cohen (London: Longman, 1999), 157–158.

47. Suzanne Aspden, *The Rival Sirens: Performance and Identity on Handel's Operatic Stage* (Cambridge: Cambridge University Press, 2013), 5–6.

48. John Arbuthnot, *The Devil to Pay at St. James's: Or, a Full and True Account of a Most Horrid and Bloody Battle between Madam Faustina and Madam Cuzzoni* (London: A. Moore, 1727), 3–6.

49. John Hawkins, *A General History of the Science and Practice of Music: Volume the Fifth* (London, 1776), 312.

50. Hawkins, *A General History*.

51. Edmund Curll, *The History of the English Stage, from the Restauration to the Present Time* (London: E. Curll, 1741), 21.

52. Curll, *The History of the English Stage*, 22.

53. Curll, *The History of the English Stage*.

54. George Anne Bellamy, *An Apology for the Life of George Anne Bellamy. Late of Covent-Garden Theatre*, vol. 1 (Dublin, 1785), 250.

55. Bellamy, *An Apology*, 250.

56. Wanko, *Roles of Authority*, 85.

3
SAMUEL FOOTE, ESQ.
Caricature, Class, and the Comic Theatrical Anecdote

HEATHER LADD

A significant proportion of eighteenth-century theatrical anecdotes are intentionally funny, functioning as small-scale comic texts designed to make readers laugh with and at their favorite stage personalities. Many of these comic anecdotes, published long into the nineteenth century, starred England's principal comedians and captured their ability to think on their feet, to offer up pithy, humorous takedowns and insouciant comebacks in different situations. These anecdotes did not just mythologize improvisational skills on and off the footlighted boards; other theater people were often the butt of the comedian's jokes in these metatheatrical vignettes, which performed the ideological work of social and cultural policing. Particularly through their punchlines, anecdotes served to reinforce social, moral, and theatrical hierarchies, distinguishing good acting from bad, high art from low, and gentlemen from rogues and mechanics.

Foote, Footeisms, and Footean Drift

Actor, theater manager, and playwright Samuel Foote (1720–1777) features prominently in this enormous body of anecdotes that regale with entertaining antics and clever remarks. Foote's fulsome afterlife in anecdote presents a fitting extension of his anecdote-driven satire, which relentlessly mocks the public figures he singles out as upstarts. In comedies including *The Minor* (1760), *The Commissary* (1765), and *The Nabob* (1772), Foote demonstrates attitudes, particularly toward other performers, that are replicated in the anecdotal record. Also, like an editor of a collection of theatrical anecdotes himself, he worked in the anecdotal mode, his dramatic writing and stage performances involving gathering and presenting amusing topical ephemera. *A Biographical Dictionary of Actors, Actresses, Musicians, Dancers, Managers & Other Stage Personnel in London, 1660–1800* makes a casual, but telling, connection between anecdotes about Foote and his self-authored roles, noting: "Soon after Foote's death biographical sketches, anecdotes, and collections of *bon mots* and witticisms began to appear in profusion. Most of them were as exaggerated in truth as were the zestful theatrical caricatures created by Foote himself."[1] Jane Moody unpacks the identity-borrowing of Foote's caricatures, his appropriation through mimicry of the identifying quirks of known public figures, arguing that "Foote used the celebrity of other people as the artistic raw material for the creation of his own fame."[2] As a playwright-performer, he constructed roles to undermine recognizable public figures as his social, moral, and artistic inferiors.

Foote was not just a parasite feeding on celebrity but a celebrity in his own right. He developed a distinctive brand identity that was desired and copied by others. "Celebrity," as Jane Wessel succinctly puts it, "relies at once on singularity and reproduction," also calling cards of the anecdote itself as a genre.[3] Footeisms, comic anecdotes featuring Foote's sharp-tongued wit, reproduced his attitudes as a comedian and extended the public's appreciation of his satiric gifts beyond the playhouse walls. Most biographical treatments of Foote contain a selection of humorous stories about—as well as witticisms purportedly said by—the "English Aristophanes." Many are likely apocryphal. Even if Foote had no direct hand in writing these anecdotes about himself, he created the comic templates undergirding these anecdotal fabrications. Nigel Rees, who has edited several modern books of quotations, coined the term "Churchillian drift" to describe the misattribution of commanding statements to Churchill.[4] A similar trend of "Footean drift" has occurred with the waggish performer in eighteenth-century theatrical anecdotes. While Churchill gets credited with stentorian bravery, Foote gets credited with bold humor—blunt insults and otherwise risqué punchlines. On closer inspection, however, the comedian is surprisingly conservative about class relations and identities, both on the playhouse stage and, as he is endlessly reiterated in Footeisms, on the print stage of theatrical anecdote.

This chapter has two major intersecting themes: Foote's class-conscious anecdotal identity and the distinct vein of classism that runs through his oeuvre and reverberates in the body of extant anecdotes about him. Theatrical anecdotes about this Georgian comedian, I argue, echo Foote's own particular branding as a celebrity writer-performer (established in his comedies) and assert a hierarchy that concretizes concerns about social mobility and the rise of the professional actor from the ranks of the middle class. Strategically occupying the position of gentleman-clown during his career as a satirist, Foote presents a unique figure within and against the backdrop of growing thespian professionalism for the striking centrality of the anecdote to his social and artistic practices.

Samuel Foote, Esquire

Anecdotes are the very building blocks of Samuel Foote's fame, constituent parts of a public—and very much performed—identity that demands both the elevation and degradation of the self. Significantly, Foote's first initiation into Georgian notoriety was as the author of an anecdote writ large in a lurid pamphlet detailing the murder of one of his maternal uncles by another: *A Genuine Account of the Murder of Sir John Dineley Goodere* (1741). Here, and subsequently, Foote engages in a "strikingly modern form of celebrity," what Ruth Scobie describes as the "commodified oscillation between concealment and exhibition."[5] His printed exploitation of family tragedy reveals both gentility and criminality among his relations and hides his own mercenary authorial motives, rhetorically setting himself apart from the "persons [who] have made their advantage of this circumstance."[6] Instead, in purporting to set the record straight, he exercises the class privilege that informs his later dramatic satire.

Although Foote himself possessed no titles, he was born into a prominent Cornwall family, the son of a baronet's daughter who had married a well-regarded man who held several public offices. Foote's early biographers and the comedian himself emphasized his pedigree.

Aristophanes: Being a Classic Collection of True Attic Wit (1778), "collected," according to the title page, "by a Gentleman," relates: "His father was member for Tiverton in Devonshire, and his mother the heiress of the Dinely [*sic*] and Goodere families, of which he always spoke with much pleasure, and kept the tree of pedigree and genealogy hung up on the stair-case, which he would frequently produce to prove the origin of the family, and the honour of his lineage."[7] Foote was educated and socialized as a gentleman: he attended Oxford, traveled the continent, and exhausted several inheritances.[8] Despite the fact that Foote left university without a degree, his biographers often mention his learning and intelligence. A sketch of his life in the nineteenth-century periodical *The Living Age* praises "the always ready scholarship of Foote," and the author compares Foote with his wide-ranging knowledge and mental dexterity to the less elitely educated David Garrick.[9]

Foote himself showcased his learning in his writing, notably in *The Roman and English Comedy Consider'd and Compar'd. With Remarks on "The Suspicious Husband"* (1747). This work of dramatic criticism, like his published self-defense of his controversial comedy *The Minor, A Letter From Mr. Foote to the Reverend Author of the Remarks, Critical and Christian, on "The Minor"* (1760), is signed "Samuel Foote, Esq." "Esquire" self-identifies Foote as a gentleman, but by the mid- to late eighteenth century, many upwardly mobile professional men appended "Esq." to their surnames, even if they did not have the right to a coat of arms, its original denotation. Foote's establishment of his class and learning acted as the legitimizing structure for later biographers' assertion of his social importance. Remarks on his rank and genius appear frequently in biographies, anecdotes, and anecdotal biographies about the comedian, functioning to establish his place within a theatrical hierarchy. Foote's recent biographer Ian Kelly carefully attends to the performer's background, writing that "he announced himself in London as being 'descended from some of the most illustrious Families in this kingdom' and frequently boasted when he was verbally assaulted as a mere comic, a drunken one at that, that he was as good 'as any Lord.'"[10]

As in other biographies, and specifically theatrical biographies, the extraordinary subject's rise to fame is presaged by anecdotes—here, tales of early irreverent comic genius and inborn gentility.

Foote's persona as a witty gentleman rogue, intellectually and socially licensed to misbehave, is confirmed in an anecdote set during his university days that emphasizes both the performer's gift for improvisation in concert with an innate genteel panache that cannot be unseated by poverty. The impecunious Foote is wearing boots with no stockings about town, but after visiting his bookseller to get paid, pops into a stocking shop where he purchases this missing article of clothing. Two other Oxford students shame him after glimpsing his naked legs. Foote's response is a masterful extemporization that neatly bandies back the insult, preserves his dignity, and gives himself the upper hand socially: "He coolly replied, with all the *sang-froid* of *ung apprentif de la ley*, that it was 'very true; but his practice was to wear none until he dressed for the afternoon, taking the precaution to carry a pair in his pocket (producing them), lest he should meet with impertinent persons, who might wish to cast a slur upon his gentility.'"[11] The key stage property of this scene, the pair of stockings, is revealed at the perfect moment, and Foote is preserved as a master of comic timing as well as a gentleman above his materially oriented detractors. His nonchalance here looks forward to his successful celebrity career, which demanded a measure of verbal adroitness outside the playhouse.

Foote asserted his nobility through a skill with words, what Erin Mackie identifies as the aristocratic rake's "heavily performative and rhetorical claims to prestige," an acuity that is recorded by his contemporaries and perpetuated by later admirers.[12] He was a skilled anecdotalist; James Boswell drew on Foote for anecdotes about his biographical subject Johnson, and, describing Foote's conversation in his *Life of Johnson* (1791), recollects that he "entertained us with stories that were not true; but that, indeed, it was properly not as narratives that Foote's stories pleased us, but as collections of ludicrous images."[13] Boswell also imparts a story that illustrates Foote's ability to charm and persuade, set when the comedian partnered with a brewer whose product "was so bad the servants resolved not to drink it."[14] The servants sent a boy to Foote with the message of their refusal, but after speaking to the comedian, the boy announced: "This is the finest man I have ever seen. I will not deliver your message. I will drink his small beer."[15] This story is regularly reprinted and embroidered well into the nineteenth century. In a later version, the punchline becomes: "Verily, the man whose brilliancy can give sparkle to bad beer must indeed be a bit of a genius."[16] As it is retold by William Cooke in *Memoirs of Samuel Foote, Esq: With a Collection of His Genuine Bon-mots, Anecdotes, Opinions, &c* (1805), this same exchange serves as "natural proof of the superior powers of his conversation."[17] An ordinary, quotidian setting becomes an impromptu stage for the clever Foote to showcase his verbal dexterity and a rhetorical power that reasserted his gentility in the face of possible degradation through commerce. Foote's formula for preserving both his own celebrity and class status seems to have been a combination of expensive consumption and self-conscious slumming; Matthew Kinservik appositely refers to his "unique brand of social privilege and irreverent humour."[18] After Foote moved on from the brewery venture, newspapers reported that he had been able to conjure up a "vogue" for this small beer, which "he puffed off so well to the nobility."[19] Instead of hiding his link to this coarse commodity, he paraded it, and, motivated by self-interest, even attempted to rebrand small beer as a genteel beverage. Significantly, he preserved gentility as a social quality evidenced by his own wit(s)—supposedly a natural outgrowth of his birth and breeding—rather than by money.

Foote's performance of gentility veered into self-caricature when he embraced aristocratic excess and indulgence, which was often. As a young man, he cultivated expensive tastes: "His college life, like his subsequent career, was marked by extravagance."[20] Multiple anecdotes feature the adult Foote enjoying the high life: riding in coaches, eating haute cuisine, and wearing expensive clothing. In a recurrent comic anecdote, Foote is pictured riding in his own carriage, "drawn by four duns [i.e., tan-colored horses with dark points]," and a punning exchange ensues about this status symbol, as dun is also a word for creditor.[21] A gentleman on a first-name basis with the comedian says: "I am glad to see, Sam, that you drive the duns," and Foote responds, "And so am I, for they have driven me a long time."[22] Although Foote was constantly one step away from debtors' prison (he had several stints in the Fleet), he retained the appearance and accoutrements of a gentleman, which included wit and nonchalant self-dramatization.

While stage celebrity offered a ticket to the bon ton for leading performers, Foote, having a better pedigree than most actors, had greater access to spaces where he could build upon aristocratic relationships. The career-making event of Foote's life—his "depeditation," as Johnson puts it[23]—was frequently truncated into a sensational anecdote, no less sensational for occurring in royal company. In 1766, Foote was severely injured in a riding accident in the company of the Duke of York and had to have one leg amputated to the knee.[24] Like so many eighteenth-century jokes and anecdotes, this affair involved a pun: Foote losing his foot. In recompense (for the injury, not the pun), the duke secured for the maimed comedian the Haymarket Theatre's royal patent for London's summer season, which broadened Foote's opportunities for celebrity networking.[25]

Theatrical anecdotes published in the eighteenth and nineteenth centuries charted Foote's impressive connections, made both before and after he became the manager of a royally sanctioned London theater. *The Cyclopedia of Anecdotes of Literature and the Fine Arts* (1851) observes that Foote and James Quin "associated with the best company, and were also distinguished for a certain contempt for a portion of the society they courted, viz, the more noble, but less intelligent."[26] A place in high life represented some protection against lingering prejudices against stage performers in a time when they were gaining in sociocultural capital.[27] Anecdotes supposedly recording Foote's interactions with named and unnamed aristocrats and even royals circulated in print well after his death. Henry Wilson's *Wonderful Characters: Comprising Memoirs and Anecdotes of the Most Remarkable Persons of Every Age and Nation* (1826), like other works of its kind, shows Foote as hand in glove with aristocratic men, mentioning that he "lived with habits of intimacy with Lord Kellie" and enjoyed an "uninterrupted friendship with Sir Francis Blake Delaval."[28] Many anecdotes in that vein involve the jokester abusing men and women above his station, which is less subversive than it sounds. An anecdote in *English Jests and Anecdotes (Nuggets for Travelers)* (1886) presents Foote as a satiric moralist and advisor to the great; he chides the Duke of Norfolk for excessive drinking by suggesting he go to a masquerade sober, which would be "a new character" for the nobleman.[29] Foote scolds aristocrats in both his comedies and the comic anecdotes that collect around him, but only does so when members of the ruling class fail to embody the moral and intellectual superiority expected of them. The Duke of

Cumberland is teased by Foote in a green room anecdote set backstage in the Haymarket Theatre; this titled visitor is presumably Prince Henry, Duke of Cumberland and Strathearn (1745–1790) because of the clarification "the *foolish* Duke."[30] Unlike the previous Duke of Cumberland, a respected war hero, this one secretly disobeyed the king by marrying a commoner. The exchange, which begins with the duke complimenting Foote, unfolds as follows: "'Well, Foote,' said he, 'here I am, ready as usual to swallow all your good things.' 'Really,' replied Foote, 'your Royal Highness must have an excellent digestion, for you never bring any up again.'"[31] Foote levels the duke, his better socially, implying his own superiority over this obtuse nobleman who so ill-plays his princely part. On the night King George III and Queen Charlotte attended Thomas Francklin's *The Contract* (1776) at the Haymarket, Foote gives a tongue-in-cheek reply when the monarch asks who wrote the play: "'By one of your Majesty's chaplains,' said Foote, unable to suppress his wit, 'and dull enough to have been written by a bishop.'"[32] Foote's witticism about tedious plays and boring bishops is not exactly groundbreaking, especially as it centers on criticizing another playwright. Under scrutiny, anecdotes showcasing Foote's proximity to power only play at a social role reversal, and prove to be ideologically conservative, invested as they are in self-aggrandizement and upholding the status quo.

Foote's identification with the ruling class is aggregated in anecdotal exchanges where the entitled comedian insists on being treated as quality or asserts dominance over other performers. In an example of the former, Foote rebukes a beggar with a lesson he accompanies with a shilling: "Whenever you see a gentleman like myself, never offend him by asking for a half-penny."[33] When convenient for him, money and gentility operated as separate categories for Foote. He exercised lavish generosity when he had the means to perform aristocratic largesse, but when he was cash-strapped, he took care to distinguish his inability to foot the bill from the stereotypically middle-class parsimony attached to actor David Garrick. Foote made his first appearance on the stage just two years after Garrick, and their careers ran parallel—occasionally intersecting in marvelously anecdote-begetting ways. Collections of Footeisms almost always include stories of Foote targeting Garrick's habits and character, especially his reputed stinginess. Scholarly biographer Alan Kendall characterizes the "lovers of anecdote" as those "who need all the nuances to be heightened and exaggerated," observing that "even in his lifetime Garrick suffered from his own reputation, and the wealth of anecdotes had already begun to obscure the real person."[34] Many Foote–Garrick anecdotes participate in this process, an egregious example involving Foote at a coffeehouse with his friends passing the hat "for the relief of a poor player." [35] An absent Garrick is insulted in the anecdote's punchline: "'If Garrick hears of this,' exclaimed Foote, 'he will send *his* hat.'"[36] Jokes like these overshadowed Garrick's proven philanthropical bent and positioned Foote as the superior gentleman.[37]

Attacking the Upstart

Foote's comedy, and the anecdotes it spawned, was intent on knocking others down who had risen in the world, and operated on exclusionary principles. Social climbers, hypocrites, and parvenus were common types that were put in their place within both farces and Footeisms. *The Nabob* (1772) is a scathing portrait of an arriviste, Sir Matthew Mite (played by Foote), who has returned to England with a fortune. As he is described by a character from an "ancient" family, Sir John: "Sir Matthew Mite, from the Indies, came thundering amongst us; and, profusely scattering the spoils of ruined provinces, corrupted the virtue and alienated the affections of all the old friends to the family."[38] Sir Matthew is shown adopting "macaroni" (i.e., foppishly Italianate) dress and paying for gambling lessons, desiring "to throw the dice with a grace."[39] But his hastily acquired gentility is a farce, his performances of refinement unmasked as just that: performances. The Foote of theatrical anecdotes—which participate in what Walter Ernst Schäfer sees as the anecdote's "dependence, like the drama, on stereotypes and shared assumption"[40]—and the Foote of other historiographical sources share a propensity to confirm their own social and artistic belonging in ways that are also problematically exclusionary. *The Treasury of Modern Anecdote* (1881) relates a typical and much-repeated anecdotal encounter between Foote and "a pompous person, who had made a large fortune as a builder, [and] was holding forth on the mutability of the world."[41] Responding to the intellectual pretensions of this contractor-cum-philosopher, the comedian reminds him of his trade by speculating that the "world was built by contract." [42] Similarly, Foote cuts a "mercantile man" who had penned a poem; the aspiring author recites the poem's first line—"Hear me, O Phoebus, and ye Muses nine!"—but Foote appears distracted. [43] When the merchant-poet asks him to attend to his verses, Foote wittily reassures him: "I am . . . nine and one are ten. Go on!"[44] Foote's retort reduces the other man's poetry to numbers, sending him the message that he cannot transcend his identity as a merchant, for whom calculation is central. Whether or not this punchline is authentic, such anecdotes enshrine and recirculate the spontaneous sprezzatura that Foote cultivated as part of his brand of disruptive wit and show their propinquity to classism.

Foote excluded other performers from so performing gentility, preferring to be the only actor in a room of aristocrats. Anecdotally, the comedian mocks an actor for mispronouncing a Greek word and runs down Charles Macklin for daring to use Latin. The source of the latter story is an anecdote-laden autobiography by John Taylor, who cites his father for this firsthand story about Foote's biting snobbery: "[The author's father] said Foote expressed his surprise that Macklin should have had a Latin quotation in his advertisement,—'but I have it,' said he: 'when he was a footman to a wild, extravagant student at the university, and carried his master's books to the pawnbroker's, he probably picked up this quotation on the way.' After a pause, Foote added, 'No, that could not be, for the fellow could not read at the time.'"[45]

Foote's persistent mockery of other thespians' ambitions to gentility also appears in anecdotes concerning the vexed topic of instruction in oratory and elocution. A common anecdote features Foote variously interrupting one of Macklin's lectures held at the Irish actor's "Magnificent Coffee-Room and School of Oratory." Foote's early biographer William Cooke declines to repeat the well-worn details, but generalizes that this establishment "called out the talents of Foote, who constantly attended the lectures, and who equally perplexed the orator and delighted the audience by his repeated sallies of wit and humor."[46] Foote's mockery of these efforts extended into his playwriting, namely *The Orators* (1762) and *The Mayor of*

Garratt (1764), which burlesques Thomas Sheridan's contributions to this field.[47] Paula McDowell, recognizing how works like Sheridan's *A Course of Lectures on Elocution* (1762) offer up an antidote to the linguistic exclusivity of polite society, notes that "Foote satirized the class implications of Sheridan's proposal."[48] Although nineteenth-century writers and editors foreground Foote's wit and panache in these stories, classism centered on education forms an undeniable strand within the subgenre of comic theatrical anecdotes. Appearing as himself, Foote delivers a lengthy lecture about oratory in which he recommends "the art of reading" to prospective orators and facetiously declares literacy is optional for actors: "With the regard to *the professors of the stage*, though reading is undoubtably useful, yet, as the performer is to repeat, and not to read, the deficiency may but be supplied by the introduction of a third agent, *viz.* a person to read to him till the words are rooted in his memory. This expedient, though tedious, I have known frequently practiced with good success: little blunders will now and then unavoidably arise."[49] In keeping with his ambivalent, if not negative, attitude toward acting in his comedies, Foote is frequently depicted in anecdotes as running down players or offering only weak ripostes to attacks on the profession. For example, "A person abusing the players in general" claims that actors have no gratitude.[50] Although Foote's reply begins promisingly, "you are too severe upon the profession," it progresses into a joke about money-hungry players; his punchline: "There are no people more distressed at *benefits forgotten*."[51] Painting other actors with a broad brush, this anecdotal Foote characterizes them as unduly fixated on the profits to be gained from a benefit night. He, on the other hand, aristocratically pursues pleasure for pleasure's sake.

Other anecdotes feature the impresario mocking prominent theater people who use their newfound wealth to (awkwardly) adopt aristocratic diversions—mockery that subtly underlines Foote's own superior gentility. These stories reveal efforts to hastily acquire wit and grace through education and other means that confer gentility as laughable. For example, Foote makes fun of an unnamed manager of Covent Garden Theatre who "went to Dijon, to learn riding and French at fifty years of age."[52] While these skills would normally be acquired by a young gentleman, their belated acquisition by an aging theater manager who grew up in the playhouse is ripe for mockery. When this manager has trouble learning the language, Foote recommends that he self-medicate with a concoction of broth mixed with "Boyer's [French–English] Dictionary" as a "glister," or enema.[53] The aging would-be beau's efforts are rendered ridiculous by this vulgar punchline, which substitutes a low quack treatment for a gentleman's education.

Classism centered on education fuels multiple other Footeisms, including one concerning John Rich, famous for his performances as Harlequin. Although his pantomime was superb, not so his education, for "his language was vulgar and ungrammatical."[54] Rich calls everyone, including Foote, just "Mister," and irritated by this, Foote schools Rich on his bad manners. Rich responds with the admission that he sometimes forgets his own name, but Foote is implacable and calls Rich illiterate: "For though I knew you could not write it, I did not suppose that you could forget it."[55] Foote's insult was perhaps motivated by cultural prejudices against Rich's commercialized brand of performance as the harlequin Lun, a persona that "kept returning [Harlequin] to his marginalized status as a low, fairground creature oscillating between the two poles of physicality and make-believe."[56] Foote's put-down reasserts a long-standing hierarchy of theatrical genres and artistic expression that places verbal wit over Lun's mute clowning antics.

Comic anecdotes likewise engage in the social policing of class relations, and performers who actively court their betters are caricatured, their "achieved celebrity" rendered grotesque under the harsh light of satire.[57] In one such anecdote, Foote is told that when Garrick visits elegant country houses, he bestows complimentary verses on his hosts. Garrick even published some of these verses, thereby showing off his access to these spaces of privilege. Foote, considering himself above such boasting and toadying to the great, burlesques his social-climbing counterpart with his own spontaneous verses:

Whenever Garrick dines or sleeps,
He drops a doggerel rhyme;
The snail thus marks the road she creeps,
By slobb'ring sordid slime.[58]

Mocking Garrick's strategic ingratiation, the insulting poetic punchline confirms Foote as a force of oppositional conservatism and social discipline.

Actors or Mechanics? Enforcing Theatrical Hierarchies

Much within the repertory of anecdotes about Foote seems to highlight the precarious respectability of eighteenth-century entertainers. A number of these anecdotes read like "playlets," miniature farces that perform the friction between differing conceptions of theater professionals within Foote's society. Although Joel Fineman argues for the "essentially disruptive" character of the anecdote, which he claims is rooted in the real rather than the literary, Footeisms frequently seem wary of—or even resistant to—social change.[59] They respond to the changing status of acting in the eighteenth century, using humor to underscore rather than elide the junctures between the playhouse and other commercial activity, between acting and other, more mechanical trades that likewise depend on bodies and things. One such anecdote involves a cook-turned-comedian who reportedly "fought a duel with a gentleman of the theatre."[60] Foote's rejoinder: "Yes, damn him for an ungrateful fellow, 'twas I took the spit from the fire, put it by his side, and made him a gentleman [i.e., a sword-carrying man on the boards]."[61] This anecdotal Foote draws attention to the cook's social rise as a fantasy facilitated by the theater manager; the arriviste actor takes his social climbing too far, aping real sword-wearing gentlemen.

By all accounts, Foote appeared to delight in drawing attention to the material side of performance: the physical tools of the trade rather than the higher affordances of poetic and musical art. This insistence on the material is his way of undercutting pretensions to gentility among his contemporaries. He modeled "Dr. Catgut," an unpleasant character in *The Commissary*, after the well-known composer Thomas Arne; this crass sobriquet associates him with the animal innards used to make instrument strings rather than with the elegant theater music he produced for the London stage. Foote's scathing caricature may have something to do with Arne's irregular background: although educated at Eton College, he came from a family of upholsterers, and as a Roman Catholic, Arne was shut out from musical opportunities within the Anglican Church. In Foote's comedy, Catgut vulgarly boasts of satisfying his audience's appetites, announcing: "I have just given the public a taste, but there's a belly-full for them in my larder at home."[62] Depicted with a rhyming dictionary in his pocket, his songwriting is likewise reduced to a hack's tricks. Catgut's lascivious comment, "The *muses*—you know I was always fond of the ladies,"[63] foregrounds Arne's reputation for womanizing rather than his claims to artistic inspiration.[64] The anecdotal record reproduces the playwright's insolence toward Arne in *The Commissary*, an anecdote of Foote further mocking the composer in an involved practical joke: the comedian spots an "inferior person in the street" who resembles Arne and arranges to have this imposter dress in the clothes and wig that distinguish the musician.[65] Foote has the Arne double appear on stage in a menial capacity, carrying music books and otherwise serving the Commissary, the government official after whom Foote titles his play. Similarly, Foote's metatheatrical mimicry—widely referenced in theatrical anecdotes, biographies and autobiographies, reviews, and other sources concerning the Georgian stage—reinforced his own superior gentility by enacting classist caricatures of those he satirized. In the role of Puzzle in his *Diversions of the Morning* (1747), Foote put (supposedly) overrated actors in their place: "Suiting his own voice and manner to those of the person represented, he either mimicked him (or her) in one of his *worst scenes*, or whimsically assigned to him some degrading station in life—as a beggar-man—watchman—razor-grinder, &c."[66]

The Foote of anecdote likewise exerts his conservative wit upon the ambitious rising star Charles Holland, whom he links with the material side of things on several occasions. In one metatheatrical tale, a gentleman asks Foote his opinion on a particular actor on the Drury Lane stage. At a loss for the name of the performer in question, Foote asks and is told "Holland, Sir," to which the comedian retorts: "No . . . it's Dowlas, by G—d."[67] In other words, this actor is inferior, as dowlas, a coarse linen fabric, is inferior to its finer counterpart: holland. The use of commercial materials in this critical assessment of Holland, the son of a baker, is likely no coincidence, as another Footeism confirms. This one contains an explicit (and tasteless) reference to Holland's humble origins, although Foote now counts this actor as a "dear friend," and someone for whom he has "a serious regard"; when Holland dies of smallpox, the grieving Foote attends his funeral and afterward "smilingly" tells an acquaintance that, "*Yes, we have shoved the little baker into his last oven.*"[68] The Foote of anecdote is relentless in short-circuiting the veneration of other actors.[69]

Yet Footeisms were largely in the spirit of Foote's playwriting and performance practices, which wielded long-standing biases against the work of acting to insult specific Georgian actors. In *The Minor* (1760), he stereotypes actors as low people who keep coming up from the provinces or the London streets; playing himself in the play's metatheatrical "Introduction" (a prelude), Foote is the knowing manager to a bumpkin thespian: "Sir, this will never do," he chides this actor, "you must get rid of your high notes, and country cant. Oh, 'tis the true strolling—."[70] In act 1, the actor-mimic Tate Wilkinson, who spent part of his career in the provinces, is the individual target of Foote's biting satire.[71] The playwright gives him a scathing backstory as the actor-parvenu Shift, who relates that he started his prototheatrical life as "a link boy," not simply a "humble occupation" in the eighteenth century but one associated with crime and prostitution.[72] The skills that serve him onstage were drawn from this underworld, as he admits, "I learned dexterity from pick-pockets, connivance from constables, politics and fashions from footmen."[73] This putative Wilkinson, like Foote's real protégé, experiences a meteoric rise to stardom; his "art," Shift boasts, "is a *pass-par-tout*," translating into access to all levels of society.[74] Yet within the play's plot, he is simply a tool for aristocratic use, working to secure Sir William Wealthy's ends, as he later complains: "Zooks, I have toiled like a horse."[75] Sir William and his "ancient and honourable family"[76] are secure, the status quo firmly re-established, but Shift closes the play empty-handed, reduced from an earlier parvenu smugness to a begging epilogue addressed to the nobleman.

Footenote

After Foote's death in 1777, his career was memorialized in ways that gestured to the period's split conception of his artistry and more generally divergent attitudes toward the theatrical professions. "An

Elegy on the Death of Samuel Foote, Esq." by Boschereccio (a pseudonym) acknowledges the late comedian's appeal to devotees of both high and low art:

> Who arch Grimace and Pun admire,
> Friends of the Muse and Phœbus fire,
> Who set the Theatres on Roar,
> Your Samuel, your Foote deplore,
> For Foote, your Samuel, is no more![77]

The poet splits his subject into two personas, "Foote" and "Samuel," and uses "Esq." in his title to ratify Foote's place among the social elite, although as previously mentioned, by the late eighteenth century it was often used merely as a title of respect and a vague acknowledgment of gentility.

On every stage and at every stage in his life, Samuel Foote was an anecdotal personality: a character who adopted many characters in his artistic practice and a personage constituted for and by anecdote. Because of the way in which Foote the performer actively embraced the anecdotal mode, the putative Foote of the anecdote *is* Foote. Whether or not the anecdotes are historically true or authorized by Foote, they are largely on-brand, adhering to the image he crafted, and they gave him the recognition that enabled him to become a commercially successful artist. As I have uncovered in this chapter, classism, an overlooked element of his celebrity persona, is a staple within the myriad of comic anecdotes about Foote published in the eighteenth and nineteenth centuries, a time of social change and continued debate about the social worth of the actor.

Combining the low and high in novel ways, this English impresario left not only a deep legacy of theatrical anecdotes by his very presence in Georgian society but an anecdote-driven dramatic oeuvre as a playwright-performer. Foote, famous in the playhouse for his mimicry as well his own vendible peculiarity (his lost foot), depended on comic anecdotes—with caricature at their center—for the recognition, and hence profitability, of his impressions. Likewise, entertaining stories about him served to advertise, and, after his death, remember, his comic abilities; as Jacky Bratton argues, anecdotes are key to the making of myth and legend, especially in the performing arts.[78] Even as Foote's star as a playwright plummeted posthumously, comic anecdotes about this Georgian original were published well into the Victorian era. John Bee reflects that Foote's memory persists: "He has lived to these times, as these volumes give evidence: even his sayings and his bon-mots have been collected with the utmost care; they live, too, in the mouths of *all the wits*; and, by their many versions, prove how anxious their retailers are to give the good things 'as Foote said' them."[79] Perhaps influenced by James Boswell's belief in the anecdote's ability to preserve a subject's authentic character,[80] Foote's early biographers take Footeisms seriously, although ironically, the comedian himself was far more concerned with provocation and caricature than authenticity. Foote's plays, which reflect these attitudes, are themselves repositories of anecdotal material; and, as contemporary scholars of the eighteenth century increasingly turn their attention toward theatrical anecdotes as a significant literary genre and mechanism for establishing stage celebrity, Samuel Foote's anecdote-driven comedies seem ripe for rediscovery.

Notes

1. "Foote, Samuel," in *A Biographical Dictionary of Actors, Actresses, Musicians, Dancers, Managers & Other Stage Personnel in London, 1660–1800*, ed. Philip H. Highfill Jr., Kalman A. Burnim, Edward A. Langhans, vol. 5, *Eagan to Garrett* (Carbondale: Southern Illinois University Press, 1978), 354.

2. Jane Moody, "Stolen Identities: Character, Mimicry, and the Invention of Celebrity," *Theatre and Celebrity in Britain 1660–2000*, ed. Mary Luckhurst and Jane Moody (Basingstoke, UK: Palgrave Macmillan, 2005), 65.

3. Jane Wessel, "Mimicry, Property, and the Reproduction of Celebrity in Eighteenth-Century England," *The Eighteenth Century: Theory and Interpretation* 60, no. 1 (2019): 82.

4. Nigel Rees, *Brewer's Quotations* (London: Cassell, 1994), x.

5. Ruth Scobie, "Foote, Fox, and the Mysterious Mrs. Grieve," in *Intimacy and Celebrity in Eighteenth-Century Literary Culture: Public Interiors*, ed. Emrys D. Jones and Victoria Joule (Basingstoke, UK: Palgrave Macmillan, 2018), 252.

6. S[amuel] Foote, *Memoirs of the Life of Sir John Dineley Goodere, Baronet, who was Murdered by the Contrivance of His Own Brother, on Board the Ruby Man of War, in King's Road, Near Bristol, Jan. 19, 1740–1. Together Wtth* [*sic*] *the Life, History, Trial, and Last Dying Words of His Brother Captain Samuel Goodere* (Worcester: J. Butler, and James Grundy, 1785), 3.

7. A Gentleman, *Aristophanes: Being a Classic Collection of True Attic Wit, Containing the Jests, Gibes, Bon-mots, Witticisms, and Most Extraordinary Anecdotes of Samuel Foote, Esq. the Lords Chesterfield, Tyrawley, Messrs. Churchill, Thornton, Cox, Lloyd, and Their Cotemporaries* [*sic*]; *. . . Collected, During the Course of Twenty Years, by a Gentleman, . . . With an Engraved Head of Samuel Foote, Esq.* (London: Robert Baldwin, 1778), iv.

8. John Joseph Knight, "Foote, Samuel," in *Dictionary of National Biography, 1885–1900*, vol. 19, *Finch to Forman*, ed. Leslie Stephen and Sidney Lee (London: Smith, Elder, 1889), 370.

9. "Samuel Foote," *The Living Age*, vol. 43 (Boston: Littell, Son and Company, 1854), 401.

10. Ian Kelly, *Mr Foote's Other Leg* (London: Picador, 2012), 22.

11. Jon Bee, "Essay on the Life, Genius, and Writings, of Samuel Foote, Esq.," in *Samuel Foote: The Works*, 3 vols. (London: Sherwood, Gilbert, and Piper, 1830), 1:l.

12. Erin Mackie, "Boys Will Be Boys: Masculinity, Criminality, and the Restoration Rake," *The Eighteenth Century* 46, no. 2 (2005): 11.

13. James Boswell, *Life of Johnson*, ed. R. W. Chapman (Oxford: Oxford University Press, 1980), 686.

14. Boswell, *Life of Johnson*, 769.

15. Boswell, *Life of Johnson*, 769.

16. Henry Wilson, *Wonderful Characters: Comprising Memoirs and Anecdotes of the Most Remarkable Persons of Every Age and Nation* (London: J. Robins and Company Albion Press, 1826), 250.

17. William Cooke, *Memoirs of Samuel Foote, Esq: With a Collection of His Genuine Bon-mots, Anecdotes, Opinions, &c. Mostly Original. And Three of His Dramatic Pieces, Not Published in His Works* (London: Richard Phillips, 1805), 158.

18. Matthew Kinservik, *Sex, Scandal, and Celebrity in Late Eighteenth-Century England* (Basingstoke, UK: Palgrave Macmillan, 2007), 193.

19. Quoted in Highfill, Burnim, and Langhans, *A Biographical Dictionary*, 5:325.

20. Quoted in Highfill, Burnim, and Langhans, *A Biographical Dictionary*, 5:325.

21. A Gentleman, *Aristophanes*, 76.

22. A Gentleman, *Aristophanes*, 76.

23. James Boswell, *The Journal of a Tour to the Hebrides* (London: Henry Baldwin, 1785), 141.

24. For a fascinating account of Foote's surgery and its repercussions, see Ian Kelly's *Mr Foote's Other Leg* (both his biography of Foote and subsequent stage play).

25. William J. Burling, *Summer Theatre in London, 1661–1820, and the Rise of the Haymarket Theatre* (Madison, NJ: Fairleigh Dickinson University Press, 2000), 11.

26. Kazlitt Arvine, *The Cyclopedia of Anecdotes of Literature and the Fine Arts* (Boston: Gould and Lincoln, 1851), 179.

27. Cooke, *Memoirs of Samuel Foote, Esq*, 100.

28. Wilson, *Wonderful Characters*, 83.

29. *English Jests and Anecdotes (Nuggets for Travelers)* (Edinburgh: William Paterson, 1886), 107.

30. John Timbs, *Lives of Wits and Humourists*, 2 vols. (London: Richard Bentley, 1862), 1:249.

31. Timbs, *Lives of Wits and Humourists*, 1:249.

32. Timbs, *Lives of Wits and Humourists*, 1:250.

33. A Gentleman, *Aristophanes*, 28.

34. Alan Kendall, *David Garrick: A Biography* (London: Harrap, 1985), 7, 8.

35. Timbs, *Lives of Wits and Humourists*, 1:204.

36. Timbs, *Lives of Wits and Humourists*, 1:204.

37. Garrick supported numerous causes, arranged many a charitable benefit night, and aided the Drury Lane Theatrical Fund to support poor and aged actors. See Danielle Spratt's "Genius Thus Munificently Employed!!!": Philanthropy and Celebrity in the Theaters of Garrick and Siddons," *Eighteenth-Century Life* 37, no. 3 (2013): 55–84, and Leslie Ritchie's *David Garrick and the Mediation of Celebrity* (Cambridge: Cambridge University Press, 2019), 129–136.

38. Samuel Foote, *The Nabob*, in *The Works*, 3:187.

39. Foote, *The Nabob*, 204.

40. Quoted in Lionel Gossman, "Anecdote and History," *History and Theory* 42 (May 2003): 162.

41. William Davenport Adams, ed., *Modern Anecdotes: A Treasury of Wise and Witty Sayings of the Last Hundred Years* (London: Hamilton, Adams & Co., 1886), 156.

42. Adams, *Modern Anecdotes*, 156.

43. Adams, *Modern Anecdotes*, 159.

44. Adams, *Modern Anecdotes*, 159.

45. Richard Henry Stoddard, ed., *Personal Reminiscences: By O'Keefe, Kelly, and Taylor* (New York: Scribner, Armstrong, &. Company, 1887), 295.

46. Cooke, *Memoirs of Samuel Foote, Esq*, 70.

47. In turn, short descriptions of these plays, alongside Foote's other comedies, were compressed into anecdotes in later anecdotal biographies like John Timbs's *Lives of Wits and Humourists*.

48. Paula McDowell, *The Invention of the Oral: Print Commerce and Fugitive Voices in Eighteenth-Century Britain* (Chicago: University of Chicago Press, 2017), 184.

49. Samuel Foote, *The Orators*, in *The Works*, 2:151.

50. Cooke, *Memoirs of Samuel Foote, Esq*, 100.

51. Cooke, *Memoirs of Samuel Foote, Esq*, 100.

52. A Gentleman, *Aristophanes*, 81.

53. The *OED* defines "glyster" or "clyster" as "a medicine injected into the rectum, to empty or cleanse the bowels, to afford nutrition, etc.; an injection, enema; sometimes, a suppository." See "clyster, n.," *OED Online*, December 2020, Oxford University Press.

54. William Clark Russell, *Representative Actors* (London: Frederick Warne and Co., 1888), 52.

55. Russell, *Representative Actors*, 52.

56. Marc Martinez, "The Tricks of Lun: Mimesis and Mimicry in John Rich's Performance and Conception of Pantomimes," *Theatre History Studies* 29 (2009): 164.

57. Chris Rojek, *Celebrity* (London: Reaktion Books, 2001), 17. The antithesis of this earned celebrity status is "ascribed" celebrity, which is based on inborn qualities (i.e., born into the aristocracy).

58. *Bon-mots of Samuel Foote and Theodore Hook* (London: J. M. Dent and Company, 1894), 46.

59. Joel Fineman, "The History of the Anecdote," in *The Subjectivity Effect in Western Literary Tradition: Essays toward the Release of Shakespeare's Will*, ed. Joel Fineman (Cambridge, MA: MIT Press, 1991), 57.

60. A Gentleman, *Aristophanes*,13.

61. A Gentleman, *Aristophanes*,13.

62. Samuel Foote, *The Commissary*, in *The Works*, 2:336.

63. Foote, *The Commissary*, 336.

64. See Todd Gilman, *The Theatre Career of Thomas Arne* (Newark: University of Delaware Press, 2013), 204, 214–215, particularly his discussion of Charles Burney's views on Arne's philandering.

65. Joseph Cradock, *Literary & Miscellaneous Memoirs*, 4 vols. (London: J. Nichols, 1826), 1:33.

66. Bee, "Essay," lxxii.

67. A Gentleman, *Aristophanes*, 65.

68. Arthur Harold Engelbach, *Anecdotes of the Theatre* (London: Grant Richards, 1914), 296. A version of this line also appears in Cooke, *Memoirs of Samuel Foote, Esq*, 77.

69. In contrast, David Garrick penned an epitaph for Charles Holland that broadly served his own project of elevating the acting profession. Garrick highlights Holland's "Talents" as they "support the credit of the Stage" and his "Virtues which would honour any Rank and Profession." Quoted in Highfill, Burnim, and Langhans, *A Biographical Dictionary*, 7:370.

70. Samuel Foote, *The Minor*, in *The Works*, 2:10.

71. Foote, as Jane Wessel argues in her recent article on mimicry and intellectual property, felt the singularity of his celebrity threatened by the rival mimic Tate Wilkinson, who boldly imitated his mentor. See note 3.

72. Foote, *The Minor*, 21.

73. Foote, *The Minor*, 22.

74. Foote, *The Minor*, 24.

75. Foote, *The Minor*, 59.

76. Foote, *The Minor*, 25.

77. Boschereccio [pseud.], *An Elegy on the Death of Samuel Foote, Esq.* (London: G. Kearsley, 1778), 7.

78. See Jacky Bratton, "Anecdote and Mimicry as History," in *New Readings in Theatre History* (Cambridge: Cambridge University Press, 2003), 95–132.

79. Bee, "Essay," v.

80. For Boswell's explanation of this approach to biography, see his *Life of Johnson*, 22.

PART II
ANECDOTAL BODIES

4
PREGNANCY AND THE LATE STUART STAGE, 1661–1702

CHELSEA PHILLIPS

Despite excellent scholarship in the last thirty years furthering our understanding of professional actresses' experiences during the Restoration, questions remain. One such question concerns conflicting understandings of the relationship between pregnancy and the stage. While the author-editors of the *Biographical Dictionary* entry on Susanna Mountfort Verbruggen (1666–1703) confidently state, "Actresses of the Restoration and eighteenth century are known to have continued performing late in their pregnancies," Deborah C. Payne writes that "pregnancy lost [Restoration actresses] employment," and Felicity Nussbaum asserts that pregnant women could "face at least temporary dismissal."[1] Such divergent claims invite exploration and redress, as they have major implications for women's history within the theater. In attempting to reconcile these claims, however, we are often stymied by the nature of the evidence available from this time period, which is largely anecdotal. Here, I examine the case of Elizabeth Farley Weaver (fl. 1660–1678), the earliest-known woman to have performed on the Restoration stage while pregnant. I highlight the instability of evidence surrounding her story and subsequent, contradictory interpretations of this evidence by scholars. I then turn to later anecdotal evidence to map a broader picture of responses to the pregnant performing body. Ultimately, I argue that women were performing while pregnant during this time period, but that marital status and other elements of a performer's public reputation could have a powerful impact on audience response to their changing bodies.

The theatrical anecdotes surveyed here come from satires, play texts, state papers, and the diary of Samuel Pepys. They hold a variety of relationships to the literary genre of the anecdote, a word that entered the English language in 1676, only partway through the period of which I am speaking.[2] Most adhere to the word's original and most literal meaning: unpublished (i.e., secret or private) histories, often of public figures. Some, because of their inclusion in prominent archives, feel like something different: evidence, rather than the seemingly less formal and more gossipy anecdote. As Thomas Postlewait has reminded us, it is actually quite difficult to parse the differences between these two seeming opposites: "The distinction between facts and anecdotes (or records and legends) is impossible to maintain consistently in any examination of historical documents; many records are not factual; many anecdotes not only contain a kernel of factuality but also express representative truths."[3] Elizabeth Weaver's story is both anecdote and evidence, and has been used to suggest a variety of representative truths about actresses' experiences with pregnancy. When placed alongside the stories of other women, some known to us (Elizabeth Willis), some celebrated in their time (Jane Rogers), and some anonymous, however, it becomes clear that both the illegitimacy of Weaver's pregnancy and the novelty of the position in which she placed (or found) herself set hard limits on the extent to which her story can stand as reflective of a general attitude toward pregnant women on the late Stuart stage.

Elizabeth Farley Weaver was one of the first professional actresses in London, appearing under her maiden name in a King's Company personnel list from March 27, 1661. Although it is difficult to tell whether she was a celebrity in her own time, she is certainly a figure to whom we have often looked to understand the experiences of women on the early Restoration stage.[4] In part, this is because we have interesting and useful—although far from complete—evidence about her career. According to actress and singer Mrs. Knepp, who reported it to Samuel Pepys, Mrs. Weaver was "first spoiled" by the king, implying he was her first sexual partner.[5] If true, this may have been before she began living with James Weaver as his wife. The Weavers had a daughter, Elizabeth, baptized on May 20, 1661, just shy of two months after Elizabeth Farley signed on to the company. Early the following year, however, James Weaver asked permission to sue Farley for debts incurred in his name, making it clear they were not actually married.[6] By the fall of 1662, a petition against her by Henry Dobson implies that knowledge that she was "none of [Weaver's] wife" was becoming widely known, and there are six recorded legal actions against her between 1662 and 1665.[7] Despite this change in public understandings of her marital status, Elizabeth Farley remained on the stage as Mrs. Weaver until 1666, and may have returned between 1671 and 1678 under her maiden name.[8]

Early in her career, in either 1662 or 1664, Weaver left the company unexpectedly while pregnant with an illegitimate child.[9] Her departure was brought to the attention of the company's royal patron, prompting shareholder Sir Robert Howard (1626–1698) to write to Secretary of State Henry Bennet (1618–1685) to explain the situation. This letter is often excerpted, sometimes in ways that create causal connections that are not necessarily present in the original, so I offer it in full here:

> In the absence of Mr Killegrew I have receiv'd his Maties Command by you. I wish Mr Killegrew had been in the way, or that I had been thought worthy to have been heard before his matie and your selfe had been soe ill informd. your letter I receivd just now beinge too late in all particulars to have obeyd it, but the information beinge so exactly false, I hope you'll be pleasd not to looke upon us as person's concernd in it, for Mrs. Weaver's three weeks agoe and above of her owne accord brought in all her part's and warn'd the Company that after such A day which is expird shee woud act noe more, I my selfe spoke with her twice about it and shee continu'd her resolution to goe and then all her part's were given out; since indeed shee has appeard big with Child and now knowne to be shamefully soe for wch many women of quality have protested they will never come to thee house to see A woman actinge all parts of vertue in such A shamefull Condition. This Sr has been the cause that wee are not troubled for the losse of her, but the first cause of her leaving the house came from her selfe and truly Sr wee are willing to bringe the stage to be a place of some Creditt and not an infamous place for all persons of honour to avoide if we may be

> permitted; and when his Matie receives A true information his commands shall be joyfully obeyd; but this sir as A person wth out any power here I relate only as an information as [becomes]
>
> yr most humble servant
> Ro: Howard[10]

Howard's letter appears to answer two implicit charges: that Weaver may have been wrongfully terminated, and that the company was not sufficiently "troubled for the losse of her," presumably because they either refused to readmit her or had not pursued her to return to the company. Howard's anecdotal evidence is in the form of a personal testimonial, which he is uniquely placed to offer to the Secretary of State, having "spoke with her twice" before she left. Importantly, Howard claims it was only since her departure that her condition became known, denying any idea that the pregnancy caused a termination of her theatrical contract. While Howard had attempted to convince her to stay, ultimately the company did not regret her departure as her "shamefull" pregnancy might have caused problems with "many women of quality" had she remained.

Even this fairly detailed account leaves us with questions. The repetition of "shameful" suggests the illegitimacy of the pregnancy was a considerable problem. Was it only this, or was pregnancy itself also objectionable? Were the "women of quality" specifically responding to Weaver, or was this an opinion expressed independently of the situation at hand? Did women of quality actually object, or is Howard finding a way to make the theater the disadvantaged party? Howard is not an unbiased source, writing as he is on behalf of the company in which he was a shareholder. We have little to corroborate anything he says or the timeline of events he implies. We are not even sure when he wrote the letter. The anecdotal evidence he supplies is important, but frustratingly incomplete. Unsurprisingly, this has led to an array of scholarly interpretations. In turn, these interpretations have led to divergent narratives about early actresses, pregnancy, and the stage.

One detail inconsistently construed is the exact relationship between Weaver's pregnancy and the timing of her exodus from the company. John Harold Wilson, whose work on early actresses is still a staple of Restoration scholarship, believes Weaver concealed the pregnancy, and gave up her parts once it could no longer be hidden. He writes: "She was pregnant, and although the loose-bodied gowns and full petticoats then in vogue allowed her to continue acting much longer than was safe or proper, eventually, in the autumn of 1662, she had to turn in her parts and leave the King's Company."[11] Wilson's notion of "safe or proper" may be ahistorical, as may his assumption that the performing pregnant body was always already taboo.[12] Reading between the lines of Howard's account, however, this is a perfectly possible justification for why her pregnancy only became known after she left the stage: Weaver had hidden it, and departed before she was found out. In Wilson's mind, Weaver offers the representative truths that pregnancy was bad for business and had to be concealed. As we will see in the latter half of the chapter, however, by 1675 such attitudes (if they indeed existed) seem to have changed.

Other interpretations suggest Weaver's attempts at concealment failed, and this is what prompted the crisis. Rhetorician Lindal Buchanan, for example, claims that Howard, "Fearful of offending sensitive members of the audience," fired Weaver because of audience objections.[13] Again reading between the lines of Howard's letter, this may well be the charge against which Howard is attempting to defend the company; but it is not, importantly, what he says happened. Howard takes great pains, in fact, to stress that Weaver's "first cause of her leaving the house came from her selfe." Deborah Payne Fisk's entry for Weaver in the *Oxford Dictionary of National Biography* (2004) also assumes that her pregnancy was visible and a source of conflict before she left rather than being revealed after the fact: "In 1664 the dramatist Sir Robert Howard wrote to Henry Bennet, Lord Arlington, explaining why Mrs Weaver 'of her own accord brought in all her parts and . . . wou'd act noe more'. 'Big with child' and clearly unmarried, her appearance offended 'women of quality'; and the actress, indignant her parts had been reassigned, 'continued her resolution to goe.'"[14] The order of events is slightly reversed in both cases, pregnancy now driving the management's actions rather than being revealed after the fact. In Buchanan's account, Howard feared audience objections and fired Weaver. In Fisk's, Weaver was not technically fired; instead, she was provoked into leaving by managerial machinations—out of deference to women of quality—that sidelined her career during pregnancy. When Weaver returned (presuming this was ca. 1664), Fisk argues that she appeared in smaller roles than previously; hence, a direct consequence of Weaver's "notorious pregnancy" was a permanent loss of prestige in the company.[15] We have here two other representative truths being read from Weaver's story: that pregnancy got women fired and/or did permanent damage to their careers.

Historian Geoffrey Smith's interpretation follows John Harold Wilson's assumption that Howard's letter was prompted by Weaver's request to be reinstated in the company:

> Elizabeth Weaver, one of the original actresses in the King's Company, with support from Charles II discreetly in the background, [petitioned] for reinstatement in the company from which she had suddenly withdrawn. Weaver's career, replete with short-term liaisons, possibly including one with Charles, had, not surprisingly, left her "big with Child," but Howard opposed her readmission to the company when she regretted her rash decision to leave it. As "many women of quality have protested that they will never come to thee House to see a woman actynge [*sic*] all parts of virtue in such a shameful condition."[16]

Here, we have an interpretation that makes space for the possibility that pregnancy did not initially drive Weaver from the stage. In fact, the implied timeline suggests Weaver was petitioning for a return to the company while she was still pregnant and still at risk of offending the women of quality. If the pregnancy or her now widely known marital status made her return more difficult because of audience protests, it does not appear to have made it impossible: Bennet and the king were aware of both and apparently still supported her return. Smith mentions Weaver in the context of an argument about Howard's powerful position in the company; one representative truth here is that Howard had sufficient authority in the company to make a decision about Weaver's readmittance.[17] Another representative truth, particularly in light of Smith's conflation of Weaver's career with her sexual history, is that Weaver (and by implication, other women) leveraged her offstage "career" to force the continuance of her onstage career over the objections of audiences and management.[18]

These interpretations draw different conclusions from a single, less than clear source. While it may seem obvious to connect the idea that Weaver was pregnant with her "resolution to goe," we actually do not know if there is a causal relationship between the two events. Howard says that learning Weaver was pregnant lessened the inconvenience of her departure, sparing them the potential loss of female audience members who objected to her "shamefully" pregnant body. In fact, that it would have been an issue at all implies she would have continued to perform were it not for her own insistence on leaving. The various representative truths read from Weaver's story align with the spectrum of general narratives about pregnancy on the stage, which were presented at the opening of this chapter: Buchanan claims Weaver was fired and Fisk that she was forced out. These interpretations align with Payne's claim (in "Reified Object") that pregnancy meant the loss of a position. Wilson's reading, meanwhile, supplies evidence for Nussbaum's claim that women might be forced to retire temporarily. Finally, Smith's version leaves room for the possibility that Weaver might have returned (still pregnant) to the stage if Charles had commanded it, supporting the *Biographical Dictionary*'s claim that women could perform throughout pregnancy. Despite these congruencies, we do not know to what extent Weaver's story lies behind these generalized claims about pregnancy on stage. While the *Biographical Dictionary* implies that Susanna Mountfort Verbruggen is one of the "actresses of the Restoration and eighteenth century . . . known to have continued performing" during pregnancy, it offers no further examples, and neither Nussbaum nor Payne cite specific instances to support their claims. Unfortunately, since we do not know the result of this conflict, Weaver's story ends with the tensions between these narratives unresolved. To ensure a broader sample, then, other evidence is needed. Turning to later anecdotes does not give us additional information about Weaver herself or what happened to her, but it does offer us an opportunity to compare later incidents against Howard's claims about actual or presumed audience response.

In his letter, Howard claims the foundation of the women of quality's objections to seeing pregnancy onstage is that the performer's body conflicts with the "parts of virtue" being performed. He presents the dilemma as one that will determine the fundamental identity of the stage, anticipating debates about the theater's morality at the end of the century: Will the theater be "a place of some Creditt" or not?[19] The decision does not ultimately seem to rest with the company's management, but with its patron. If, as Jacky Bratton has argued, theatrical anecdotes help theater create and preserve its identity and write its own history, Howard's play-by-play of the conflict does something similar.[20] It is Weaver who severs her connection to the company, despite entreaties to stay, and the redistribution of her parts is simply the way the company must function in order to survive. Howard is drawing lines around the theater and what it is striving to be: "A place of some Creditt" where "persons of honour" can appear without being offended by "shamefull" displays onstage. For the theater to be all these things, he suggests, it was ultimately better for all that Weaver left, but she was not driven from the stage. The implicit question begging to be asked is whether a legitimate and therefore shame*less* pregnancy would evoke the same response? If people had still thought Elizabeth Farley was married to Mr. Weaver, would we even have this letter? Later anecdotal evidence suggests the answer might be no.

Between 1675 and 1702, anecdotes about pregnant women on the late Stuart stage focus heavily on unmarried women, and specifically on the idea that some were attempting to maintain virgin reputations in the face of clear evidence of sexual activity. These anecdotes rarely identify individual women directly. Instead, satirical sources and play texts focus on actresses as a class, suggesting representative truths about this new category of publicly and economically active women. In satirical sources, pregnancy is used as evidence for complaints familiar from antitheatrical texts; namely, the hypocrisy and immorality of stage performance in general and actresses in particular. In 1702, for example, Thomas Brown added to a long list of hypocrisies currently in vogue: "Hypocrisie has infected the Stage too, where *Whores with great Bellies* wou'd thrust themselves off for *Virgins*, and *Bully* the Audience out of their sight and understanding."[21] A major problem with pregnant actresses, this suggests, was the disconnect between their bodies and the persons and personas they projected on stage. The slippages in Brown's account between passing oneself off as a virgin within the fiction of a play, or asserting a virginal identity in real life are significant, for "audience" describes not only a temporally bounded relationship that dissolves when stage time expires but an ongoing configuration that extends into the green room and beyond. For the professional actress, always on display, audience is everywhere.

In the anonymously authored *Comparison Between the Two Stages* (1702), the Critic suggests the bullying of the audience's senses extends beyond the stage, describing the strategies actresses use to maintain their public reputations while pregnant:

> *Rambler.* There are some that wou'd be thought honest.
> *Critic.* Yes, tho' they are Mothers and never were marry'd . . . They Trade like our *East-India* Ships, they take in their Lading the beginning of Winter, and having calculated the Voyage just for Nine Months, it falls out very opportunely for 'em to unlade again in the long Vacation.
> *Sullen.* . . . a ramble into the Country for six Weeks brings it all about: The Lady lies in, the Child goes to Nurse, every thing is husht up, and she returns to Town again, and fancies no body knows anything of the Matter.[22]

This discussion begins by painting unmarried actresses with a broad brush: they cannily use the length of the theatrical seasons and summer breaks to avoid detection when having illicit children. This is a deception available to all, and evidence of the fundamental mistrust to which women, actresses (particularly if unmarried), and the theater could be subject. The problem is not pregnancy specifically; it is the way the stage can enable women to appear to be one thing while actually being something else. Instead of fears of a failed performance (Weaver), we have fears of a successful one. The Critic then elaborates, purporting to offer an anecdote about a specific (albeit unnamed) woman to shore up and embellish what he has touted as a widespread tactic:

> *Critic.* I have seen one of 'em cramp her Belly so confoundedly with her Stays, to hide it from the Audience, that when the Child has been born, the Jade had mawl'd it into such a deform'd condition, that the good Women have been frighted out of their Wits, and the Midwife . . . has mistaken it for a false Conception . . . to this Day, after such an exploit as I have been telling you, one of

'em wou'd perswade the Town that she's an immaculate Virgin.[23]

Sullen. Ridiculous and foolish!

Critic. So that upon the whole I tell you, what for the Players, the Dancers, the Poets and the Masters, it's easier matter for an honest young Fellow of the Town, to lose his own good Name, than to fix a scandal on one of theirs.[24]

In turning to the specific, the Critic's anecdote takes on the qualities of other, related genres, including amorous fiction, which titillates with revealed secrets, and the scientific report.[25] As James Robert Wood has argued, both scientific reports and anecdotes attempt to create the sensation of "virtual witnessing" while offering the evidence that led the investigator or observer toward the broader law or conclusion for which they advocate.[26] Moving from a general assertion (that unmarried actresses hide pregnancies) to a specific one ("one of 'em"), the Critic's example allays any questions the broader story might provoke. The "touches of the real" that make a convincing anecdote are marked: the tactics the woman used to conceal her body, the presence of a significant number of witnesses (including the speaker), and implied visual evidence in the form of the "mawl'd" child.[27] We know, moreover, that unlike Weaver, this "one" has a clear status and the ability to wield celebrity to shape reality. If strait-lacing is one tactic for concealing pregnancy, the Critic suggests that celebrity may be another.[28] The *Comparison*'s representative truth is thus: in deference to their theatrical work, unmarried, sexually active actresses become monstrous mothers who damage their unborn children while using their celebrity allure to avoid detection.

Beyond the unnatural bodily control of strait-lacing, these deceptions require control of nature itself: to "unlade in the long vacation," the women must precisely time their conceptions. Such emphasis on timing tacitly adds to the validity of the story: This is why, it seems to say, one may not have noticed a large number of pregnant women on the public stages, or seen a woman go into labor, or noted a particularly long mid-season absence. Women go to great lengths to deceive.[29] Although their wiles are judged "ridiculous and foolish" in theory, the opacity of the pregnant body and the power of the theater as a public platform mean that in practice some women get away with it; they do what Brown suggests, causing audiences to doubt or ignore their "sight and understanding" in preference of a hollow virtue projected from the stage. The wider implication is clear: If one can make people disbelieve their eyes and ears regarding a pregnancy—something which should be so obvious and undeniable—what other dangerous powers might these new, unmarried, celebrity women possess? Rather than women of quality driving or keeping Elizabeth Weaver from the stage, brazen and emboldened celebrity actresses are now concealing pregnancies badly and fomenting ire against those who attempt to expose them. In doing so, they blur the line between real and represented and avoid the consequences of their actions.

The commentaries on pregnant performance from the *Comparison* and Brown's *Letters* have several features in common. First, the visibly pregnant body in each instance marks the woman as either a whore or shameless, or both. Second, the women under discussion are unmarried, which may indicate a wide gap between married and unmarried women's experiences with pregnancy and performance. If so, perhaps Elizabeth Weaver's abrupt departure was more closely tied to such a revelation than we have appreciated; perhaps the most important thing Howard's letter tells us—has been telling us—is that her body signaled shame, not just pregnancy. In later cases, marital status appears to be partially behind the drive to conceal the body; what would signal normative femininity within marriage is damaging outside it, particularly for actresses attempting to trade on an appearance of virginity for celebrity status.[30] Finally, as none of these sources identifies specific figures, the sense is that these deceptions could be happening at any time. By not naming a subject, the Critic renders all suspicious; Brown calls any and all actresses claiming to be virgins, whores. Criticisms of pregnant actresses reveal underlying anxieties about women and/on the stage, and perhaps especially about single women whose sexuality, commercial potential, and identity were not circumscribed by male control in the same ways as their married counterparts.[31] There are certainly representative truths here, but they may center much more on these wider cultural anxieties than they do on the specific phenomenon of pregnancy on the stage. Nevertheless, such comments would not exist if there were no pregnant bodies on the stage. The "Inchanted Island" of the playhouse had many delights and dangers to offer; pregnancy was one feature that could become a locus for anxiety around what was real and what was not.[32]

Despite the vehemence of the complaints in Brown's *Letters* and the *Comparison*, other evidence suggests that pregnancy was not an equal problem for all actresses. A decade or so after Weaver's experience, pregnancy was a common enough sight to make a good joke. Dorilant in Wycherley's *The Country Wife* (1675) compliments Horner (who is being publicly proclaimed a eunuch to better enable his libertine habits) for having "most theatrical impudence; nay, more than the orange wenches show there, or a drunken vizard mask, or a great bellied actress."[33] Dorilant places the "great bellied actress" in a group with other common sights in the theatrical space: sex workers in the pit (orange wenches) and galleries (vizard masks). Like them, the pregnant actress displays her sexualized body in public as part of an economic exchange, failing to feel the shame of her condition properly. Dorilant casts the playhouse as a permissive space that facilitates and encourages such shamelessness. The "great bellied actress" is presented as a proverbial figure: a "great bellied actress" walks onto a stage . . . wakka wakka. To have become such, in theory, she must have been visible during women's first fourteen years on the professional English stage.

A generation later, in a mock visit to the playhouse in the third volume of his *Works*, Thomas Brown hints at William Congreve's fawning love for Anne Bracegirdle, who originated the role of Millamant in his *The Way of the World* (1700). Brown laments that Bracegirdle cannot have a "Humble Servant" (lover) when other women, namely a "Mrs. Abigail . . . can be brought to bed of a Living Child without any Manner of notice taken of her."[34] Brown's comment asks us to consider why Bracegirdle and "Mrs. Abigail" are permitted such different behavior. That Mrs. Abigail has given birth to "a Living Child" suggests she has not damaged the child by tightening her stays to conceal her condition, and so has performed while visibly pregnant without incurring audience disfavor, or even interest. Fortunately, we have a reasonable idea who he means. There is no attendant or actress named Abigail in Congreve's play, but there are two ladies' maids (abigails), originally played by Mrs. Prince and

Mrs. Willis. Elizabeth Willis acted Foible, the larger of the two parts, and was married to a fellow player. She was also the mother of two daughters, one born the year before *The Way of the World* premiered, and the play appears to contain a metatheatrical joke about this recent pregnancy.[35] Having been deceived by her maid Foible, Lady Wishfort rages, "Oh, thou frontless impudence, more than a big-bellied actress."[36] The joke is partially predicated on the idea that at least some members of the audience had seen Willis's pregnant body, would remember it in this moment, and would find a reference to it humorous. Rather than a reason to drive her from the stage or a threat to public morals, Willis's body (and the audience's memory of it) heightens the comedy and diffuses any implied danger from a concealed pregnancy. The line parallels Wycherley's reference in *The Country Wife*, but now points to a specific body present on stage at the moment of the line's delivery. That it is Lady Wishfort, the dupe of the play, who delivers the insult to one of the heroes, moreover, blunts its edge. Perhaps Willis's marriage, combined with her less prominent place in the company, allowed her to perform without censure in ways that Anne Bracegirdle, nearly as famous for her off-stage virginity as for her onstage performances, would never have been able to do.

Willis was not the only married woman who performed during pregnancy. Anne Shadwell (fl. 1661–1705) and Elinor Leigh (fl. 1670–1707) appear to have done so occasionally in the 1670s and 1680s, and in the 1690s Susanna Mountfort (later Verbruggen) (1666–1703), Katherine Shore Cibber (1669–1734), and Elizabeth Bowman (ca. 1677–1707) did the same. In the early 1660s, Elizabeth Weaver introduced to the London stage what is still a persistent issue for childbearers today: the balance of reproductive and professional labor. Public knowledge of her marital status appears to have made her situation particularly fraught. When Weaver lost her stable identity as a married woman, understandings of her as a person and a pregnant woman shifted and may have led to a temporary disruption of her career. Just a generation later, however, anecdotal evidence points to unmarried women who found ways to continue their stage careers during pregnancy, even in the face of negative commentary. Anecdotal evidence, particularly from a time period in which our archives of bibliographic and repertory material are so scant, testifies to the presence of the pregnant body on the late Stuart stage. When examined together, these disparate stories also help to nuance our hypotheses about what impact pregnancy had on women's careers. Collectively, these anecdotes suggest that public reputation, including stage repertoire and marital status, helped to establish the bounds of behavior in which a woman might engage. Pregnancy, if it challenged that identity, had to be approached carefully, but was not the end of a career.

Notes

1. "Verbruggen, Mrs. John Baptista, Susanna, née Percival, formerly Mrs. William Mountfort," in *A Biographical Dictionary of Actors, Actresses, Musicians, Dancers, Managers & Other Stage Personnel in London 1660–1800*, ed. Philip H. Highfill Jr., Kalman A. Burnim, and Edward A. Langhans, 16 vols. (Carbondale: Southern Illinois University Press, 1993), 15:137; Deborah C. Payne, "Reified Object or Emergent Professional? Retheorizing the Restoration Actress," in *Cultural Readings of Restoration and Eighteenth-Century English Theatre*, ed. J. Douglas Canfield and Deborah C. Payne (Athens: University of Georgia Press, 2005), 17; Felicity Nussbaum, *Rival Queens: Actresses, Performance, and the Eighteenth-Century British Theater* (Philadelphia: University of Pennsylvania Press, 2010), 49.

2. "Anecdote, n.," *OED Online*, June 2019, Oxford University Press.

3. Thomas Postlewait, "The Criteria for Evidence: Anecdotes in Shakespearean Biography, 1709–2000," in *Theorizing Practice: Redefining Theatre History*, ed. W. B. Worthen and Peter Holland (New York: Palgrave Macmillan, 2003), 65.

4. Joseph Roach's definition of celebrity, for example, emphasizes an element of visual culture ("images circulat[ing] widely in the absence of their person") that cannot be tied to Weaver, nor does her known repertoire suggest renown; Joseph Roach, *It* (Ann Arbor: University of Michigan Press, 2007), 17. Lack of evidence from this period, however, is profound.

5. Samuel Pepys, *The Diary of Samuel Pepys, M.A., F.R.S.*, ed. Henry B. Wheatley, 10 vols. (London: George Bell & Sons, 1893), 7:277 (January 11, 1667–1668).

6. If they had been married, James Weaver would have been responsible for her debts. He had to seek permission to sue Elizabeth because she was one of the king's servants, which made her immune to prosecution without permission.

7. "Weaver, Mrs. James, Elizabeth, née Farley," in *A Biographical Dictionary of Actors*, 15:306.

8. As "Mrs. Farlowe," see *A Biographical Dictionary of Actors*, 15:305–306.

9. The dating of this event is uncertain. A letter about the event is collected in the State Papers for 1664–1665, but the revelation that Elizabeth Farley was unmarried appears to have come to light in 1662. The *Biographical Dictionary* and John Harold Wilson both date her departure to 1662; see John Harold Wilson, *All the King's Ladies: Actresses of the Restoration* (Chicago: University of Chicago Press, 1958). Deborah Payne Fisk and Geoffrey Smith give 1664; see Fisk, "Weaver [née Farley], Elizabeth (fl. 1661–1678), actress," *Oxford Dictionary of National Biography* (Oxford: Oxford University Press, 2008), and Smith, "'A Gentleman

of Great Esteem with the King': The Restoration Roles and Reputations of Thomas Killigrew," in *Thomas Killigrew and the Seventeenth-Century English Stage*, ed. Philip Major (Burlington, VT: Ashgate, 2013).

10. Sir Robert Howard to Secretary [Henry] Bennet (SP 29/109 f.19), ca. 1664–1665, *State Papers Online, 1509–1714: Early British State Papers*. Gale, Cenage Learning, 2021. https://lst.gale.com/mss/i.do?id=GALE|MC4327681233&v=2.1&u=wash46354&it=r&p=SPOL&sw=w&viewtype=Manuscript.

11. Wilson, *All the King's Ladies*, 18.

12. Charles II's grandmother, Anne of Denmark, performed in Ben Jonson's *Masque of Blackness* (1605) while six months pregnant, for example, and Weaver herself joined the company during or shortly after her 1661 pregnancy.

13. Lindal Buchanan, "Angels in the (Theatrical) House: Pregnancy, Rhetorical Access, and the London Stage," *Rhetorica: A Journal of the History of Rhetoric* 30, no. 3 (Summer 2012): 277–305, see 284.

14. Payne Fisk, "Weaver [née Farley]."

15. But in 1666–1667, we have Pepys noting that Mrs. Knepp is going to act in Weaver's "great part" in *The Indian Emperor*, so she seems to have still had at least one major role even if the event dates to 1664 (Pepys, *Diary*, 6:131 [January 15, 1666–1667]).

16. Smith, "'A Gentleman of Great Esteem with the King,'" 162.

17. This seems counter to Howard's assertion that he is "without any power heer," but such a claim might also be a rhetorical move to lend credence to his account.

18. For this typical conflation, see Elizabeth Howe, *The First English Actresses: Women and Drama 1660–1700* (Cambridge: Cambridge University Press, 1992); Payne, "Reified Object"; and Gilli Bush-Bailey, *Treading the Bawds: Actresses and Playwrights on the Late-Stuart Stage* (New York: Palgrave, 2006), among others.

19. See, for example, Jeremy Collier, *A Short View of the Immorality and Profaneness of the English Stage*, 4th ed. (London: S. Keble, R. Sare, and H. Hindmarch, 1699), *Early English Books Online*, and subsequent replies to Collier.

20. Jacky Bratton, *New Readings in Theatre History* (Cambridge: Cambridge University Press, 2003), 95–132.

21. Thomas Brown, *The Second Volume of the Works of Mr. Tho. Brown, containing Letters from the Dead to the Living, Both Serious and Comical* (London: B. Bragg, 1707), 73–74. The *Letters* first appeared in 1702.

22. *A Comparison Between the Two Stages, with an Examen of "The Generous Conqueror"; and Some Critical Remarks on "The Funeral, or Grief Alamode," "The False Friend," "Tamerlane" and Others. In Dialogue* (London: n.p., 1702), 19–20.

23. Jane Rogers might be the woman behind both Brown's *Letters* and the *Comparison*. Rogers initially positioned herself as following in Anne Bracegirdle's footsteps and maintaining a virgin reputation despite her career on the stage. Sometime in the 1690s, however, she had a daughter by Robert Wilks (see "Rogers, Jane, later Mrs. Thomas Brome Whorwood," in *A Biographical Dictionary*, 68–71). As late as 1709, Delarivier Manley's *The Female Tatler; by Mrs. Crackenthorpe, a Lady that knows every thing* referred to this earlier reputation, sarcastically calling Rogers the

"virtuous Imoinda" who was then lying in of a fourth illegitimate child; in no. 29 (London: B. Baggs: September 9–12, 1709).

24. *A Comparison*, 20–21.

25. The Critic's account is a shadowy forerunner of the concealed pregnancy in Eliza Haywood's *Fantomina* (1725).

26. James Robert Wood, "Mr. Spectator's Anecdotes and the Science of Human Nature," *Eighteenth-Century Life* 38, no. 1 (Winter 2014): 64.

27. Catherine Gallagher and Stephen Greenblatt, "The Touch of the Real," in *Practicing New Historicism* (Chicago: University of Chicago Press, 2000), 20–48.

28. For work on women's creation and manipulation of celebrity personas, see Nussbaum, *Rival Queens*, and Helen E. M. Brooks, *Actresses, Gender, and the Eighteenth-Century Stage: Playing Women* (London: Palgrave Macmillan, 2015), among others.

29. Lack of pregnancy could also be construed as suspicious and cause for censure if the woman was assumed to be sexually active. *A Satyr on the Players* (1682–1684) rails, "Impudent *Sarah* [Cooke] thinks she's praised by all / Mistaken Drab, back to thy Mother's stall, / And let true Savin whom thou hast prov'd so well / 'Tis a rare thing that belly will not Swell / Tho' fuck't & fuck't and as debauch'd as Hell" (quoted in Bush-Bailey, *Treading the Bawds*, 59). Savin, a juniper derivative, was a common abortifacient.

30. Joanne Bailey demonstrates that cultural expectations of men and women required both spouses to make financial contributions to marriage, as well as to the production of children. Though she does not discuss the position of professional actresses specifically, this suggests that married actresses' appearances during pregnancy helped make visible their participation in expected spousal behavior. See Joanne Bailey, *Unquiet Lives: Marriage and Marriage Breakdown in England 1660–1800* (Cambridge: Cambridge University Press, 2009).

31. Among these controls, some single women could enter into contracts for themselves, while married women could not. In her unpublished dissertation, Susan M. Martin calculates that 42 percent of known women on the stage between 1670 and 1675 were married, and 48 percent of known women between 1710 and 1715. This rose to 67 percent between 1750 and 1755. Susan M. Martin, "Actresses on the London Stage, 1670–1755: A Prosopographical Study" (PhD diss., Pennsylvania State University, 2008), 262.

32. Thomas Brown, *Amusements both Serious and Comical Calculated for the Meridian of London*, (London: John Nutt, 1700), 48.

33. William Wycherley, *The Country Wife* (1675), in *The Broadview Anthology of Restoration and Eighteenth-Century Drama*, ed. J. Douglas Canfield (Toronto: Broadview Press, 2005), 1042.

34. Thomas Brown, *The Third Volume of the Works of Mr. Thomas Brown* (London: B. Bragg, 1708), 39. Brown died in 1704, so the reference dates from at least several years prior to publication.

35. "Willis, Mrs. Richard, Elizabeth, *c. 1669–1739*," in *A Biographical Dictionary*, 16:155–158.

36. William Congreve, *The Way of the World*, in *The Broadview Anthology of Restoration and Eighteenth-Century Drama*, 800.

5

"A HIGH TREAT TO THE ANECDOTE HUNTERS!"

The Body of Mrs. Sophia Baddeley

NEVENA MARTINOVIĆ

When the notorious actress and courtesan Sophia Baddeley died, her July 14, 1786, obituaries were printed in newspapers under the heading "Anecdotes of Mrs. Baddeley."[1] These anecdotes, like those that proliferated throughout her life, focused on the transformation of her youthful, pure body into one that was beaten, ill, withered, and corpse-like, even though Baddeley was at most forty-two when she died.[2] Descriptions of this second disfigured body appear in anecdotes whenever Baddeley's inappropriate romantic and sexual liaisons are discussed. Her perceived moral failings are projected onto her physical body, and it is depicted as less and less desirable. The ongoing publication of these anecdotes in newspapers and standalone texts suggests the English public's desire for this kind of devastating transformation narrative.

I contend that anecdotes depicting Baddeley's notoriety function as a form of social policing against immoral behavior by showing punishments enacted on the physical female body. This representation is particularly effective because of Baddeley's theatrical career: her audience was used to reading cues from her physicality. Her most celebrated characters were those of women of virtue in distress, notably Fanny in George Colman the Elder and David Garrick's *The Clandestine Marriage* (1766). Anecdotes provided plots similar to those in the dramas through which audiences had already been conditioned to read Baddeley's body. However, these anecdotes do not have a comedic resolution. Her corpse-like body—and later, her corpse—are presented as both a fitting punishment and a warning to other women tempted into similar pursuits.

Descriptions of Sophia Baddeley's body as ailing were not entirely unfounded. She had a severe laudanum addiction, suffered miscarriages, and never fully recovered from her 1769 suicide attempt.[3] However, the representations of her illnesses and deteriorating physical body are exaggerated and narrated as the physical consequences of female moral failings. I take my cue here from Diana Solomon's "Anecdotes and Restoration Actresses: The Cases of Elizabeth Barry and Anne Bracegirdle." Solomon urges scholars who use anecdotes in their research to interrogate the motives of the sources supposedly recording these recollections and ask, "What myths do they perpetuate about women that are antifeminist, when other ways of narrating such stories are available?"[4] The narrative function (and by extension the authorial motive) of these Baddeley anecdotes is the social policing of women's bodies.

Characters of the Present Most Celebrated Courtezans (1780) is explicit in its description of the transformation of Baddeley's physical body. The anonymous publication contains a sixteen-page section on Baddeley, which opens with a description of her youthful self under her maiden name of Snow. The narrative quickly constructs a contrast between the youthful Miss Snow and the cadaverous Mrs. Baddeley:

> The utmost stretch of human imagination is inadequate to conceive anything more delicately lovely than the *tout ensemble* of this adorable girl; her figure—her feature—her complexion—the unsullied purity and whiteness of her skin—the inexpressible softness and feminality [*sic*] of her air—her voice and manner—formed all together an object which the delighted eye was never satisfied with gazing. Such were the heavenly beauties of the charming Miss Snow; the wretched vestiges of which are scarcely to be traced in the present emaciated remains of Mrs. Baddeley.[5]

Miss Snow's beauty is rhetorically constructed for the "delighted eye" and the pleasure it bestows on the viewer. This quality is connected to her "feminality" (i.e., femininity), suggesting that beauty, youth, and purity are feminine qualities and, therefore, that their loss detracts from Baddeley's "feminality." Furthermore, the description of "the unsullied purity and whiteness of her skin" equates her unblemished complexion with her unblemished soul. The language suggests that the illnesses and wounds that impact the aesthetic quality of her body similarly impact her character. This aesthetic and moral degradation is directly tied to her romantic and sexual affairs offstage.

In the excerpt from the *Courtezans*, Baddeley's transformation is described as so extreme that she is narrated as if she were two separate women: the heavenly Miss Snow and the wretched Mrs. Baddeley. Her new married name signals that the boundary between the two female bodies is distinguished by interactions with men, beginning with her husband. The text describes the physical abuse that she experienced at the hands of her husband and it narrates this violence through its effects on her aesthetic form: her "tenderness and beauty were no preservative; scarcely did a day elapse without her lovely face or tender frame receiving some wound, mark or contusion from the hand of the tyrant on whom she had bestowed herself."[6] The text puts the onus on Baddeley for instigating this violence; her husband is described as the tyrant on "whom she had bestowed herself" in a marriage in which she had "prostitute[d] her mind and person."[7] The then fifteen-year-old Miss Snow is not given any allowances for her youth and naïveté. Instead, her legal marriage is described as a prostitution of the self. She is depicted as misappropriating her own beautiful face, as well as her mind. The text makes explicit the connection it previously drew between her aesthetic form and moral character. Not only is Baddeley described as initiating this "prostitution," but her body is also blamed for its inability to stop the violence it receives as a result of her actions. The narrator mournfully declares that her "tenderness and beauty were no preservative" to the harm she received, and the blame is again placed on her for not being able to defend herself against her abuser. Considering the mind–body connection that the text has created, the language of "beauty and tenderness" suggests that it is not just her physical beauty but also her virtue that was unable to protect her from her abuser. This rhetoric of virtue serving as a preservative against immorality echoes many sentimental narratives of the period. Baddeley is divided into two irreconcilable selves: abuser and victim, both of which are to blame for the consequences her physical form endures.

Her relationship with Charles Holland is described in *Characters of the Present Most Celebrated Courtezans* as a "violent" "attachment" that ended abruptly when Holland died of smallpox on December 7, 1769. Her resulting "grief and solitude began to impair her beauties and 'steal the rose from her cheek.'"[8] Baddeley is again described as not taking preventative measures to preserve her beauty, for her complexion is compromised by her own excessive reveling in grief and solitude. The text goes on to narrate a list of Baddeley's subsequent relationships and labels them as the "short-lived paramours of her insatiate concupiscence."[9] The tension between victim and abuser in her characterization disappears, along with any sympathy the text offered her. She is no longer a victim of her own bad behavior but a lustful, destructive force, whose "insatiate" sexual body reaps the consequences of her actions. The ending of the Baddeley section presents a more complete image of the "wretched Baddeley" that opened the text: "She has arisen to great theatrical eminence; which, wonderful to say, she still preserves, though she is scarcely half a degree removed from an idiot. Her eyesight is decayed, her memory extinct, and her whole frame relaxed to a degree of almost infantine imbecility, by a dreadful and excessive indulgence in love, liquor, lust and laudanum."[10] Her theatrical career is secondary to the main narrative of her physical degradation, and her public acclaim is described as remarkable considering her decaying body. That body, the result of her excessive indulgences in the alliterative list of "love, liquor, lust and laudanum," is beyond use to theatergoers, but serves as material for authors of anecdotes. Her immoral behavior has been excessive—after all, she is included in a book about courtesans—and as a result her body has almost entirely deteriorated. Unlike other actresses who left the stage when their bodies became ravaged by age and illness, Baddeley had not retired, and similar commentary on her morals and her deteriorating body was presented in newspaper reviews, theatrical anecdotes, memoirs, and her obituaries.

Baddeley's narrative of physical decline transforms from its representation in obituaries, to "Anecdotes of Mrs. Baddeley," and ultimately, to advertisements for her forthcoming memoirs. This transition suggests that printers contributed to the public's interest in

Baddeley's life story to sell periodicals and books. The blame placed on Baddeley for the mismanagement of her body in *Courtezans* is reiterated in the opening lines of her *London Chronicle* obituary: "Mrs. Baddeley, the comedian (formerly belonging to Drury Lane Theatre, whose beauty and talents, prudently managed, might have ensured her both fame and fortune), died [in Edinburgh] on Sunday last."[11] The obituary rhetorically attaches her poverty to her demise, intimating that the loss of her "beauty and talents" directly contributed to her untimely death; the wording "prudently managed" suggests that Baddeley's theatrical managers were complicit in her deterioration. Moreover, the phrasing of her "beauty and talents" speaks to Judith W. Fisher's observation that "appearance and ability were often juxtaposed by the critics in their reviews of actresses' performances."[12] These are not two separate qualities that the obituary is discussing; Baddeley's "beauty and talents" have an interdependent relationship that her actions negatively affected.

Later that week, the obituaries were replaced with articles titled the "Anecdotes of Mrs. Baddeley." The *London Chronicle*[13] dedicated a column and a half to these anecdotes, with other periodicals, such as the *Morning Post and Daily Advertiser*[14] and the *Public Advertiser*,[15] publishing nearly identical reports. The *London Chronicle*'s collection of anecdotes opens with Baddeley's theatrical merit, specifically describing her role as Fanny in the October 12, 1769 command performance of *The Clandestine Marriage*, and the subsequent oil painting by Johan Zoffany depicting Thomas King, Baddeley, and her husband, Robert Baddeley, in character (see this volume's cover image). Baddeley is prized for "the beauty of her person, and the elegant simplicity of her performance," which were "extremely conspicuous and so much attracted his Majesty's notice, that he [King George III] commanded a picture to be taken of Fanny's principal scene with Lord Ogleby in the fourth act." This extended depiction of the theatrical Baddeley is focused on a youthful aesthetic beauty that is so pleasing to an elite audience that it has been captured in portraiture. As a result of this portrait, subsequent references to Baddeley in the role of Fanny call to mind both general audience memories of her Fanny performances and this specific visual representation of her in her mid-twenties. This reflects the "tension between the temporal and permanent" that Shearer West describes in her discussion in *Portraiture* (2004) of the paradoxical function of the portrait.[16] A portrait depicts "the appearance of an individual in the fugitive moment in which it was produced," as it simultaneously "serves magically to freeze time and to extend artificially the life of the represented individual."[17]

The Zoffany portrait is especially significant to Baddeley's public image because of the similarities it emphasizes between the actress and her character. This speaks to a phenomenon that Elaine McGirr describes whereby "the staging of interiority, the fascination with what Felicity Nussbaum has dubbed the 'interiority effect' and Joseph Roach calls 'public intimacy' is about more than interiority; it is about the slippage between the actor and her/his role."[18] Fanny was a prized role that Baddeley successfully repeated for years. A 1776 review from the *Morning Chronicle and London Advertiser*[19] is as flattering to Baddeley's presentation of Fanny as her early reviews, stating that her performance "gave us infinite pleasure. Her tone of enunciation, and her remarkable delicacy of deportment, rendered Fanny as fully a favourite with every friend of distressed virtue as the authors of the comedy would possibly desire." The focus on the character's connection to "distressed virtue" again signals what the actress had in common with her character, and what was so entertaining for the play's public.

The main plot of *The Clandestine Marriage* is concerned with Fanny Sterling's various romantic entanglements. She is a beautiful young woman who has secretly eloped with Lovewell and is now pregnant with his child. These developments are hidden from the rest of the characters in the play, and unfortunately, her sister's suitor, as well as her suitor's uncle, try to gain Fanny's hand in marriage. As a result of various comic miscommunications, she appears to be leading on several of the male characters, which initially harms her reputation. All the while, her pregnancy means that her body is physically manifesting the consequences of her clandestine courtship. Fanny's reputation is ultimately saved by her virtue, the legality of her marriage, and the conventions of comic structure. At the time of the 1769 performance, Baddeley and her husband were separated, and Baddeley had already begun her affair with Holland, who often portrayed the role of Fanny's love interest, Lovewell. *Courtezans* even attributes this affair to Baddeley's success in the production:

> By this intimacy, she considerably improved her theatrical talents, and acted a variety of characters with the greatest applause, but the part in which she seemed to shine with more than common brilliancy, was Fanny in the Clandestine Marriage; for the interesting tenderness, and pathetic softness that were so inimitably blended in her performance of it, received a glow, an animated effect, and a thousand natural beauties, from the reality of that tenderness which she felt for Mr. Holland, who acted the part of Lovell [*sic*], and with whom she availed herself of every opportunity of rehearsing in the dressing rooms.[20]

Baddeley and Fanny are "blended" in these performances from which she receives the "greatest applause," and her reception is influenced by her offstage relationships with her onstage peers.

The association *Courtezans* draws between the onstage love plot and the players' amorous interactions in the dressing rooms interested audiences of both the play and the painting. The scene that Zoffany depicts is equally charged with Baddeley's offstage sexual liaisons. Although Holland is not pictured,[21] her estranged husband Robert Baddeley is. Moreover, he is depicted in the background, having just encouraged Thomas King's Lord Ogleby to make love to Baddeley as Fanny. John Galt's *The Lives of Players* (1831) supports this explanation for the scene's popularity: "In the scene where the Swiss [Robert Baddeley's servant character Canton] exhausts all his adulation to recommend [Fanny] to Lord Ogleby, their relative situation caused a universal laugh, in which the King and Queen heartily joined. And she was the next day honoured with a message from King George the Third, desiring her to go to Zoffany."[22] The anecdote makes it clear that the audience's enjoyment of the scene was a result of its similarity to Baddeley's offstage life. This story becomes part of the standard repertoire in the Baddeley biographies that followed the publication of this text.[23]

The portrait and accompanying anecdote serve to represent the youthful and beautiful Baddeley at the height of her theatrical and sexual appeal. She is depicted as being in a loving and beneficial relationship with Holland and separated from her abusive husband, who condones her affair. The anecdote's placement at the beginning of her obituary and biographical notices sets up this representation as her earlier and *former* public image. In the same way that she is no longer the virtuous and beautiful Miss Snow, Baddeley is no longer the virtuous and beautiful Fanny Sterling. Instead, the portrait comes to represent the youthful and beautiful Baddeley before the accumulation of her various misdeeds, and before the consequences of those misdeeds ravaged her body. Instead of merely a memory of the younger Baddeley, the portrait represents Baddeley before her transformation and contrasts with her debilitated body and downfall at the end of her obituary. Shearer West's "Siddons, Celebrity and Regality: Portraiture and the Body of the Ageing Actress" provides a framework for understanding how Zoffany's painting influenced these contrasting images of Sophia Baddeley. West suggests that Sarah Siddons's use of portraiture early in her career was risky, as it could consolidate "an iconic view of herself that would not last the vagaries of changing theatrical fashion or withstand public awareness of inevitable alterations in her physical appearance."[24] While the production of Zoffany's painting was not Baddeley's decision, it still iconicized an image of Baddeley that her physical body could not maintain. This image could then be contrasted with her later debilitated body, which was iconicized in its own way in the printed descriptions of her body.

The other role that the obituaries praise Baddeley for portraying is her tragic role as Mrs. Beverly in Edward Moore's *The Gamester* (1753). The contrast between the roles of Fanny and Mrs. Beverley echoes the transition that Baddeley experienced as a result of her romantic and sexual relationships. Mrs. Beverly is married to the eponymous gamester of Moore's domestic tragedy. The family falls into ruin because of his gambling and must rely on the charity of their friends. Baddeley's similar experience appears in her *London Chronicle* obituary: "Owing to some private motives, she unexpectedly quitted London for an engagement in Dublin, from which period her theatrical career seems to have been checked by misfortune. For some years past she labored under a nervous disorder, which during the last winter prevented her from making any theatrical engagement; from which time, until her death, she was supported by a subscription raised among the ladies and gentlemen of the theatre here." The "private motives" that the *Chronicle* here describes have elsewhere been depicted as an attempt to evade her creditors. Baddeley's reckless spending of the money that she received from her various lovers inspired her move to Dublin, from which point on, her "theatrical career," and ultimately, her life, was ill-fated. This misfortune is epitomized by her bodily ailments: her "nervous disorder" that restricts her from her profession. Like her character, Mrs. Beverly, she relied financially on the charity of others.

In the following days, her obituaries and anecdotes are replaced with advertisements for Baddeley's Elizabeth Steele–authored memoirs. This transition reflects the public's desire for narratives of Baddeley, while also reflecting the progression of the form of newspaper obituaries. As the August 9 issue of the *Morning Chronicle and London Advertiser*[25] states, the incompleteness of the anecdotes had heightened the public's desire for the expanded memoirs: "The editor of the life and memoirs of Mrs. Baddeley finds himself indispensably bound to inform the publick that he only, is possessed of the original letters and documents that comprise that Lady's life, which is now printing and will be delivered as soon as a proper actuary (which a work of that nature requires) will permit. All newspaper accounts must therefore be totally erroneous, and can afford no real satisfaction or entertainment."[26] The newspaper report decries all previous accounts of Baddeley's life and suggests that "real satisfaction or entertainment" can only be attained from the forthcoming publication. The *Public Advertiser* blames Samuel Johnson for the public's "rage for life-writing" that inspired such publications.[27] This statement reflects a trend that N. D. Norman tracks in his work on biographical obituaries within *The Gentleman's Magazine*, which he credits as originating the genre in response to the popularity of the theatrical biography. Under John Nichols's editorial purview, death notices (which had been an average of 2.24 lines per entry) transformed into biographical obituaries (an average of 42.79 lines per entry) during the 1780s.[28] The form of these entries followed the conventions of the biographical portraits that Samuel Johnson popularized and published in the magazine.[29] Anecdotes were included in these portraits, as they were one of the formal features of theatrical biography through which biographers illustrated the character of a player.[30] By 1785, the obituaries in the *Gentleman's Magazine* were titled "Obituary of considerable Persons; with Biographical Anecdotes."[31] Norman suggests that the nine-volume collection of anecdotes that Nichols published from 1812 to 1816 is even modeled after these early biographical obituaries.[32] The transformation of Baddeley's brief death notices to long-form obituaries with anecdotes, and ultimately to advertisements for her memoirs, echoes the transformation of this periodical form. Both transformations were responses to the public's growing interest in biographies, and the lives of sexually scandalous women such as Baddeley in particular.

However, the issue of the *Public Advertiser* which evokes the Johnsonian connection has a bleak perspective on the publication of Baddeley's life story, stating, "We are now threatened with the lives of Mrs. Robinson and Mrs. Baddeley, which were so truly exemplary, that they must undoubtedly add much to the morality of the age; the literary abilities of Mrs. Baddeley will prove a high treat to the anecdote hunters!" The specific, named market of "anecdote hunters" addresses the popularity of the form and the insatiable desire of the "hunters." The newspaper's satirical tone is obvious from its pairing of Baddeley and Robinson, and its mock suggestion that the women's stories will add to the "morality of the age." These women are obviously connected by their common theatrical profession, but even more so by their high-profile sexual affairs. Robinson also married young and had public relationships while she was estranged from her husband, most notably with the Prince of Wales—the future King George IV—and Banastre Tarleton. By the date of this publication, she had been abandoned by both men and was afflicted with a mysterious illness that left her partially paralyzed. These were both women with scandalous lives and deteriorating bodies, but while Baddeley's memoirs were released shortly following these advertisements, Robinson's were neither completed nor published until after her death in 1801, fifteen years following this report.

Robinson's memoirs were not the only thing advertised prematurely: her obituary was also published directly below Baddeley's in the July 14, 1786, edition of the *Public Advertiser*, fourteen years before her death. In Robinson's premature obituary, Baddeley appears as a recipient of Robinson's touching generosity. This portrayal reflects Baddeley's impoverishment and dependence on others for financial survival, as it reiterates Baddeley's representation as a public "example": "[Robinson's] heart was open to the feelings of humanity, of which the late Mrs. Baddeley was a striking example. Mrs. R. relieved her when in Chelsea, in the most deplorable and wretched situation that helpless woman could be in—having the cravings of nature, without the means of supplying them, added to the pangs of labour, and all the horrors of an out-cast and forlorn wretch to combat." Robinson is portrayed positively in relation to Baddeley, and the obituary narrates the time when she gave the impoverished Baddeley money. However, Baddeley's memoirs state that this event happened when Robinson was with the Prince of Wales, which was from 1779 to 1781, when she was between the ages of twenty-two and twenty-four.[33] This is Robinson at her aesthetic and social prime. This anecdote, especially as it concludes Robinson's fake obituary, serves as a warning to Robinson and other women, suggesting that immoral sexual behavior is debilitating to the physical female body. Additionally, it suggests the diminishing independence of these bodies, as they can only survive on the generosity of others. Robinson's connection to Baddeley through their shared sexual proclivities has doomed Robinson to an early death in the public eye.

The fact that these anecdotes appear in obituaries further emphasizes that these women's deaths (whether having actually occurred or not) were related to their immoral actions. Death notices were brief and provided a digestible overview of deaths that "enabled creditors and financiers to make claims against outstanding debts."[34] Obituaries—with their greater length and narrative flexibility—had a variety of functions, and one of these functions was to edify and produce "cultural value judgements."[35] In some cases, these value judgments even prescribe gender norms and punish transgressive women, which is demonstrated in one subgroup of female obituaries that Norman analyzes: women who have burned to death as a result of reading in bed by candlelight. The obituary of one unfortunate victim distinguishes her as a "young lady." Norman suggests that "stressing initially that Miss Tredaway was a young lady seems to stress some impropriety in her reading, the consequence of which is how shockingly she was burned. It is seemingly shocking that reading can bring about such a fatal catastrophe. The implication, then, is that a young lady has no business reading."[36] The obituaries of Robinson and Baddeley similarly offer a punishing lesson, though the actresses' social crimes are not reading but other activities in bed.

Anecdotes and anecdotal obituaries are not alone in their representation of Baddeley as a public example against socially inappropriate behavior. Her entry in *A Biographical Dictionary* explicitly states that contemporary "accounts of Mrs Baddeley would stress the 'public example' she offered of the dangers of seduction," [37] and this was especially true of Anthony Pasquin's *The Children of Thespis* (1787), a satirical collection of verses on players.[38] As with her obituaries, Baddeley's decimated corpse is presented as the necessary consequence of her improper actions:

> There view lovely Baddeley stretch'd on her bier,
> Whose pallid remains claim the kindred tear:
> Emaciate and squalid her body is laid,
> Her limbs lacking shelter, her muscles decay'd.
> An eminent instance of feminine terror,
> A public example to keep us from error.[39]

Pasquin's verse keeps Baddeley's "emaciate[d]" and "decay'd" body in the public eye for the purpose of social instruction, and the "public example" he presents is gendered: the body presented is the result of "feminine terror." Baddeley's "error[s]" and the consequences they have wrought on her physical body are those of a transgressive woman.

While Pasquin's verse, the obituaries, and *Courtezans* all blame Baddeley for her bodily decay, none of these texts offer the actress agency in her representation or reception. These narratives are all the production of anonymous or anonymized outside sources intent on publicizing her private actions and exploiting the image of her ailing form for entertainment and social edification. Elizabeth Steele complicates the correlation between Baddeley's immoral sexual behavior and her deteriorating body in *The Memoirs of Mrs. Sophia Baddeley*, as the memoirs represent Baddeley as maintaining some agency in the representation of her body. While her physical body is figuratively punished in the social sphere for her immoral behavior, she is depicted by Steele as simultaneously manipulating the public's knowledge of her ailing body in her romantic engagements. In *The Memoirs*, Baddeley is shown to fake headaches in order to manipulate interactions with her suitors. She is described as using her perceived weaknesses to her benefit in the relationships for which she is criticized. In one instance, her "old complaint"—a headache—reappears when she is in the company of a suitor; as a result of her apparent affliction, she is given use of the gentleman's larger, covered carriage, and he rides in her smaller, open-air phaeton.[40] Steele is not let into Baddeley's machinations, and so her narration often leaves the credibility of Baddeley's headaches in doubt. However, these suspicious illnesses are represented as conveniently timed or beneficial to Baddeley. There are a few select times when Steele is aware of the performativity of Baddeley's illnesses, and these take place as Steele describes Baddeley's relationship with Lord Melbourne. This is revealed when Steele goes to Baddeley's bedroom to check on her indisposed friend: "I went up to her, and found her head-ach [*sic*] was a pretence to quiet Lord Melbourne, who, from being in high spirits, was as noisy as he could be."[41] Later in the same volume, Baddeley again pleads illness, although this time to avoid a visit from Lord Melbourne entirely, as she has grown tired of him.[42] These sickly performances complicate the reading of Baddeley's body in relation to her love affairs, as Steele depicts Baddeley as more than merely an object on display for public example; she is an active participant in her representation.

The body narratives of Baddeley's anecdotes perform a larger social function. They are not depicting an extraordinary situation with unexpected physical consequences but a direct cause and effect of transgressive female sexual behavior and bodily deterioration that is not unique to Baddeley. Nor are these narratives unique to Baddeley's obituaries and *Characters of the Present Most Celebrated Courtezans*. As a female player aging and misbehaving in the public sphere, a narrative of self-inflicted decline is attached to descriptions of Baddeley's body, which rhetorically punishes the actress for her socially unacceptable actions, while warning other women that should they follow in Baddeley's pursuits, they too will face ultimate deterioration. In eighteenth-century anecdotes, women's bodies were presented as potent symbols of decline and served more broadly as stages for narratives about the "bad" actress, and by extension, the "bad" woman.

Notes

1. *Morning Post and Daily Advertiser* (London, England), July 14, 1786, *Seventeenth and Eighteenth Century Burney Newspapers Collection*. All newspaper references are to this database.

2. The obituaries vary and place her age between thirty-eight and forty-two at her death.

3. Elizabeth Steele, *The Memoirs of Mrs. Sophia Baddeley*, in *Women's Theatrical Memoirs*, ed. Sue McPherson and Julia Swindells, vols. 6–8 (London: Pickering & Chatto, 2008), 1–2, 34.

4. Diana Solomon, "Anecdotes and Restoration Actresses: The Cases of Elizabeth Barry and Anne Bracegirdle," *Restoration and Eighteenth-Century Theatre Research* 31, no. 2 (2016): 34.

5. Anonymous, *Characters of the Present Most Celebrated Courtezans* (London: M. James, 1780), 30–31.

6. Anonymous, *Courtezans*, 31–32.

7. Anonymous, *Courtezans*, 32.

8. Anonymous, *Courtezans*, 36–37.

9. Anonymous, *Courtezans*, 41.

10. Anonymous, *Courtezans*, 42.

11. *London Chronicle* (London, England), July 8–11, 1786.

12. Judith W. Fisher, "Creating Another Identity: Aging Actresses in the Eighteenth Century," *Journal of Aging and Identity* 4, no. 2 (1999): 57.

13. *London Chronicle* (London, England), July 11–13, 1786.

14. *Morning Post and Daily Advertiser* (London, England), July 14, 1786.

15. *Public Advertiser* (London, England), July 14, 1786.

16. Shearer West, *Portraiture* (Oxford: Oxford University Press, 2004), 44.

17. West, *Portraiture*, 43–44.

18. Elaine McGirr, "'Nell Gwyn's Breasts and Colley Cibber's Shirts': Celebrity Actors and Their Famous 'Parts,'" in *Intimacy and Celebrity in Eighteenth-Century Literary Culture: Public Interiors*, ed. Emrys D. Jones and Victoria Joule (Basingstoke, UK: Palgrave Macmillan, 2018), 14.

19. *Morning Chronicle and London Advertiser* (London, England), October 7, 1776.

20. Anonymous, *Courtezans*, 34–35.

21. The part of Lovewell was played by Cautherley in this performance. George Winchester Stone, ed., *The London Stage, 1660–1800: A Calendar of Plays, Entertainments & Afterpieces Together with Casts, Box-Receipts and Contemporary Comment*, part 4, 3 vols. (Carbondale: Southern Illinois University Press, 1968), 3:1423, 1429.

22. John Galt, *The Lives of the Players* (London: Henry Colburn and Richard Bentley, 1831), 222.

23. This anecdote is repeated in both Leslie Stephen, ed., *Dictionary of National Biography*, vol. 2, *Annesley-Baird* (London: Smith, Elder & Co., 1885), 384, and "Baddeley, Mrs Robert, Sophia, née Snow," in *A Biographical Dictionary of Actors, Actresses, Musicians, Dancers, Managers & Other Stage Personnel in London, 1660–1800*, ed. Phillip H. Highfill Jr., Kalman A. Burnim, and Edward A. Langhans, vol. 1, *Abaco to Belfille* (Carbondale: Southern Illinois University Press, 1973), 204.

24. Shearer West, "Siddons, Celebrity and Regality: Portraiture and the Body of the Ageing Actress," in *Theatre and Celebrity in Britain: 1660–2000*, ed. Mary Luckhurst and Jane Moody, (Basingstoke, UK: Palgrave Macmillan, 2005), 194.

25. *Morning Chronicle and London Advertiser* (London, England), August 9, 1786.

26. *Morning Chronicle and London Advertiser* (London, England), August 9, 1786.

27. *Public Advertiser* (London, England), August 10, 1786.

28. N. D. Norman, "From a Record of Death to a Memory of Life: The Rise of the Biographical Obituary in the *Gentleman's Magazine*" (Master's thesis, Virginia Tech, 2008), 9.

29. Norman, "From a Record of Death to a Memory of Life," 17.

30. Amanda Weldy Boyd, *Staging Memory and Materiality in Eighteenth-Century Theatrical Biography* (London: Anthem Press, 2017), 8.

31. Norman, "From a Record of Death to a Memory of Life," 29.

32. Norman, "From a Record of Death to a Memory of Life," 29.

33. Steele, *The Memoirs of Mrs. Sophia Baddeley*, 3:398.

34. Norman, "From a Record of Death to a Memory of Life," 2.

35. Norman, "From a Record of Death to a Memory of Life," 33.

36. Norman, "From a Record of Death to a Memory of Life," 14.

37. Highfill, Burnim, and Langhans, *A Biographical Dictionary*, 1:207.

38. Pasquin was the pseudonym of John Williams (1754–1818).

39. Pasquin, Anthony, *The Children of Thespis* (London: Denew and Grant, 1786) 2:26, quoted in Highfill, Burnim, and Langhans, *A Biographical Dictionary*, 1:207.

40. Steele, *The Memoirs of Mrs. Sophia Baddeley*, 3:217.

41. Steele, *The Memoirs of Mrs. Sophia Baddeley*, 4:415.

42. Steele, *The Memoirs of Mrs. Sophia Baddeley*, 4:428.

6

A BELLYFUL OF NIGHTINGALES

Seven Stories of Seven Singers

MICHAEL BURDEN

> When a celebrated vocal performer was taken ill, on the night of his promised performance, an inferior singer was introduced to supply his place. The man was hissed by several of the audience, and came forward very humbly, saying, "Gentlemen, you expected a voice of fifty guineas a week; but consider, I have only ten."
>
> —Gridiron Gabble (Joseph Haslewood)

The above tale usefully illustrates both aspects of a singer's profession in the eighteenth century and how those professional details could be useful in constructing anecdotes, defined here as "the narrative of a detached incident or of a single event, told as being in itself interesting or striking" and often starting as "an item of gossip."[1] Firstly, we have the mechanism used by the theaters to replace a performer absent through illness. The theater or opera house would normally employ a singer at a lesser cost and make an announcement that a substitute had been hired. This was a signal for the crowd to respond by hissing and catcalling; many singers suffered through such treatment. Secondly, in the singing profession, there was endless discussion of cash—who was paid what, when, and how—and there were many quarrels arising from such matters.[2] Lastly, the production of such repartee between performers and members of the audience was expected. Numerous reports of responses to hecklers were noted, and a singer able to produce an effective put-down showed both spirit and style, and could expect their response, as here, to be "anecdotable." And, as these three aspects suggest, it could be to a performer's advantage to be the subject of an anecdote, for it kept their names before the public, perhaps advancing their reputations and giving them something they could play up to.

Theatrical gossip and anecdotes appear both on their own and in collections, each with its own purpose and style, or in similar volumes purporting to be quite something else, from the 1760 *Memoirs of the celebrated Mrs Woffington Interspersed with several Theatrical Anecdotes*, to David Erskine Baker's 1764 *Companion to the Playhouse*, to the anonymous 1789 *The Hive*. These are all eighteenth-century collections, and it has been argued that they represent the period's predilection for the exchange of curios in all forms.[3] Indeed, it has been suggested that these collections resemble "the cabinets of curiosities of the period."[4] The rest of this article concentrates on the anecdotes concerning singers of one of these small "cabinets of curiosities," a volume titled *Green Room Gossip; or, Gravity Galliniput: a gallimaufry, consisting of theatrical [anecdotes—bon mots—chit-chat—drollery—entertainment—fun—gibes—humour—jokes—kickshaws—lampoons—mirth—nonsense—oratory—puns—quizzing—repartee—stories—tattle—vocality—wit—yawning—zest.] Got up to guide Gymnastical and Gynecocratic Governments. With an appendix of grave subjects.* In approaching this collection, one might be tempted to pursue a definition of each of these terms to see what refinements could be teased out. This would, however, be a mistake. A reading of the list shows that it includes a word beginning with every letter of the alphabet—with the usual eighteenth-century omission of the *i*—and in alphabetical order. It is a joke of a different kind, then, one that suggests the anecdotes are all-encompassing, includes the form of delivery as well as content, and has a broader function in the world of jests and jestbooks. How much truth can be found in an anecdote is, of course, anybody's guess. The title page of *Green Room Gossip* notes that its contents have been "gathered and garnished," advertising not just that truth or accuracy are both irrelevant but also that the compiler went out of his way to embellish the included anecdotes.

Figure 1. George Moutard Woodward, *Preperations* [*sic*] *for a New Comedy;—A Green Room in Town*, 1790. Watercolor, 32×47.9 cm. London, Victoria and Albert Museum, P.14-1931.

The title *Green Room Gossip* obviously draws on the public's obsession with what went on in the green room backstage. Circulating stories included duels, fights, and flirtations, and a visit to the green room to meet the great performers who lounged there also offered the possibility of some offstage drama. The purpose of the green room was to provide an administrative meeting point for the performers and the managers to conduct business that included negotiating contracts, hosting cast meetings, and holding rehearsals. A watercolor by George Woodward shows a cast apparently working with their parts, a process that always began with a read-through in the green room (Figure 1). Thomas Rowlandson's image of Sarah Siddons (one of the best-known images of a performer from the eighteenth century) shows her rehearsing in the green room.[5] Both images play on the public's interest in this strange no man's land, where performers were caught between the world outside the theater and the stage on which they performed. And their interaction with visitors to the green room supposedly gave rise to the gossip contained in the *Green Room Gossip* volume, the venue thereby framing the context in which the tales of appropriately inappropriate activities were told and retold. These visits were encouraged by the management—the King's Theatre built a room for the dancers for that very purpose[6]—who treated the green room as an asset in the entertainment of subscribers and the public.

"Gravity Galliniput" embodies the character of Giovanni Gallini (1728–1805), a dancer at and then manager of the King's Theatre.[7] Strangely, he plays no role in the narrative, and none of the stories concerning him in circulation—such as those Henry Angelo recounted in his *Reminiscences*—make it into the collection. And what bizarre stories they are. On one occasion, Angelo visited Gallini with the dancer Petrot and others, and the manager, reputedly mean to a fault, showed them his concert room by the light of the stub of a candle. On his leaving the room, the party lit all the candles prepared for a future concert, causing the old miser to come back and run about the room like a madman trying to puff them out. On another occasion, it was reported that, finding no food in the house, Gallini fried and ate a domestic cat's dinner.[8] The essence of these tales is not just his eccentricity—who else would eat a cat's dinner?—but his apparent parsimoniousness, which is in stark contrast to his reputed wealth and his 1763 aristocratic marriage to Lady Elizabeth Peregrine Bertie, the daughter of the third Earl of Abingdon. But it also references incidents in his career as manager, particularly in the turbulent years surrounding the destruction of the King's Theatre by fire in 1789, behavior that allowed the performers to claim he was both a mean and unjust impresario. These circumstances resulted in one of the greatest late eighteenth-century theatrical prints, *The Prospect Before Us*, one that was a counterblast to an engraving of the same name that marked the opening of the new Pantheon Opera. Published on January 13, 1791 in advance of the first season, the Pantheon version shows the ballet d'action *Amphion et Thalie*, performed by Charles-Louis Didelot and Madamoiselle Théodore, in the rich surroundings of the new theater.[9] But also published on that same day was the second print that shows the performers of Gallini's King's Theatre, deprived by the Pantheon of a license to operate, faced with beggary and penury as *The Prospect Before Us*.[10]

Green Room Gossip's compiler went by the name of "Gridiron Gabble," a pseudonym of the writer Joseph Haslewood, who had a successful practice as a solicitor. Haslewood was to become a bibliographer, an antiquary, and a book collector; in 1812, he founded the Roxburghe Club, the world's oldest society of bibliophiles, with his friends Philip Bliss and Thomas Frognall Dibdin, and went on to publish new editions of sixteenth- and seventeenth-century texts.[11] The pseudonym "Gridiron Gabble" was one he used only for this publication. A "gridiron" is the theatrical term for the arrangement of beams over a theater stage supporting the flying scenery and drop scenes.[12] "Gabble" can be assumed to refer to the manner in which the fast-flowing gossip contained in the volume's pages was conveyed in conversation. Why Haslewood chose to use a pseudonym on the volume is unclear. It may be significant that the only other time he appears to have used one is also in a theatrical context; he signed himself "Eu. Hood" for his series of articles titled "Of the London Theatres." These appeared in the *Gentleman's Magazine* in 1813 and 1814 and included pieces on the theaters at Whitefriars and Dorset-Gardens, the Vere Street Theatre, and Sadler's Wells.[13]

Haslewood is also credited with the anonymous *Secret History of the Green Room*, a two-volume set of biographies of performers at all the theaters; published in the 1790s, it ran into three editions. While they are indeed biographical sketches, they do, of course, contain numerous anecdotes of the figures described. There are nine volumes of cuttings, playbills, and dramatic prints in the British Library, a collection that is clearly preparatory material for the *Gentleman's Magazine* articles, and also doubtless a source for material in both *The Secret History* and *Green Room Gossip*. In his introduction to *Green Room Gossip*, Haslewood claims that the anecdotes were collected far and wide "from those who rant in royal robes, to the mute moppets of a procession," an assertion that he buttresses with a dedication referring to the players of both the metropolis and the provinces.[14] He also makes a claim to have been the first on the block: "Incredible it is that two centuries should elapse, and with the drama forming the moral principle and rational entertainment in this country, without some attempt to collect those sparks of wit and humour that are produced by the collision of the abstract work of the author, and natural of the actor."[15] He goes on: "Especially at a

period when your conversations, sallies of pleasantry, and whimsical anecdotes continually give to the social board of friendship and harmony, the highest zest."[16] Haslewood's suggestion is of a particular bond between members of this generation of singers and actors, and while he is not specific, a clue lies in his sign-off: he "deeply regrets the late calamity, and general misfortune in the destruction of the two principal theatres," a reference to the recent fires at Covent Garden and Drury Lane, indicating that the generation of players contemporary with him saw themselves thrown together in a year of "calamity."[17] Haslewood's references to "the two principal theatres" narrow the window of publication; Drury Lane burned on September 20, 1808, while Covent Garden was destroyed on February 24, 1809, the latter event possibly placing publication toward the middle of 1809.

The contents of the volume range widely, and the result is a mixed bag of stories about personnel from all levels of the business, including anecdotes of well-known incidents. They are randomly organized (but indexed); the only principle that can be seen to operate is that anecdotes about the same figures are scattered throughout the volume and do not appear together. There are fewer anecdotes of singers than one might expect; in fact, the anecdotes discussed below are all that are included in the collection. This is inexplicable, given that some singers' behavior made for interesting retelling and, à la Haslewood, embellishment. Another peculiarity is that Francesca Cuzzoni is almost the only singer—and almost the only performer—who is a foreigner, and it might be argued that she was only included because the anecdote involves Handel, who, after the 1784 Commemoration, had more currency than any other musical figure in England. In fact, both the *Secret History* and *Green Room Gossip* feel very English indeed. Further, all singers of whom anecdotes are included are women; the tales of the rest of the personalities, include those of many women but ultimately favor male performers as subjects. There is nothing about the anecdotes included, though, that is particularly misogynist; they present the singer in a number of different ways including as virtuous, adventurous, and humorous; and as discussed below, some anecdotes did several things at the same time.

Mary Porter: A Brave and Virtuous Woman

Mary Porter is not well known today, even in writings about eighteenth-century theater, where most of her career was spent. Having been discovered performing at Bartholomew Fair by Elizabeth Barry and Anne Bracegirdle, she was taken up by Thomas Betterton and boarded with a Mrs. Smith, sister to the treasurer of the playhouse.[18] Some years ago, it came to light that she was the most likely candidate for the girl who, at the age of twelve, played the role of Titania in Henry Purcell's opera *The Fairy-Queen*.[19] Her theatrical career was dynamic, and she succeeded to most of Barry's great roles.[20] *Green Room Gossip* contains a rather long anecdote concerning an incident in her life outside the theater, although the two worlds ultimately intersected: "Mary Porter lived at Heywood-Hill near Hendon—After the play, she usually went home in a one-horse chaise; her constant companions were a book and a brace of horse-pistols."[21] The horse pistols were to protect her from the footpads that haunted her way home. The anecdote goes on to tell us that she was indeed attacked in the summer of 1731, when a highwayman demanded her money: "She had the courage to present one of the pistols to him; the man, who had perhaps only had with him the appearance of firearms, assured her that he was no common thief." On being persuaded by him that he wanted to feed and clothe his family, Porter gave him all the money in her purse, and then having investigated his case, raised £60 among her friends to aid the robber. Porter, then, was not only shown as brave and generous but as not content with merely sitting on the sidelines; she was prepared to take action.

The anecdote is lent credence by the real-life details of Porter's independence; for example, when she needed money in 1758, she realized a substantial sum by publishing Henry Hyde's play *The Mistakes*. When she died in 1765, she was described at her burial in St. Paul's, Covent Garden, as "a spinster of the Parish of St George, Hanover Square," her unmarried state prompting an even more impressive assessment of her possession of a brace of pistols.

Susannah Cibber: A Redemption through Performance

Susannah Cibber, the singer and estranged wife of the playwright, the dreadful Theophilus Cibber, is the subject of one of the most famous musical anecdotes of the eighteenth century (although given the factual details about their life together, it has to be said that the marriage between them was a wilder ride than any invention). Sometime before 1738, the Cibbers had established a ménage à trois in a house in Kensington with a country squire called John Sloper. Theophilus, in attempting to gain the upper hand as things deteriorated, mounted an absurd (but successful) attempt to abduct Susannah Maria from Sloper's country house, an event that ended with all three of them staying, à la Fielding, at the same inn.

Theophilus then confined his wife to a house in Wild Court, Great Wild Street, from where she was rescued by her brother, the composer Thomas Arne, who broke in and knocked out the guard. The whole affair gained notoriety when Cibber sued Sloper twice: once for damages for criminal conversation, and again for £10,000. As the scandal died down, Susannah went to Dublin to sing with Handel, an engagement that led to this anecdote: "When the celebrated actress, Mrs Cibber, was in Dublin, she sang in the Oratorio of the Messiah. A Bishop that was present, struck with the extreme sensibility of her manner, could not refrain from saying loud enough for the numbers round him, *Woman! Thy sins be forgiven thee!*"[22] Versions of this anecdote have done the rounds ever since, being used even in Simon Callow's Channel 4 program about the life of Handel, in which, at the end of "He was despised," a clergyman stood up in the audience and cried out "For this, all thy sins will be forgiven."[23] The program did, of course, choose to tie the story to an appropriate aria, thus producing a twentieth-century trope of the anecdote. In all accounts of this event, the key part was that it was Cibber's *interpretation* of the aria, her "sensibility," that was the means of rescuing her from hell, *not* Handel's music.

Charlotte Brent, Arne's Mistress?

Another scandal involving infidelity was the case of Susannah Cibber's brother—the one who rescued her from Wild Court. Thomas

Arne is reputed to have left his wife for his pupil, Charlotte Brent, a brilliant soprano, for whom he wrote the role of Mandane in his opera *Artaxerxes*:

> When Dr Arne first brought the Opera of Artaxerxes to a rehearsal, Tenducci sung the Air "Water parted from the Sea" with such effect that Miss Brent (afterwards Mrs. Pinto) for whom the part of Mandane was composed, flew to Dr Arne with some violence, and told him "he might get whom he pleas'd to take Mandane; because he had given the best air in the piece to Tenducci." In vain the poor Doctor strove to sooth her—she was ungovernable. He retired from the theatre—sat down, and having written the first words of "Let not rage thy bosom firing" composed an air to them in the same character as "Water parted," though it is inferior in other respects: This he presented to Miss Brent, who being struck with the application of the first line to her own violence of temper, told the Doctor "that she was appeased, and would sing to the utmost of her ability to serve him."[24]

The anecdote was designed to bring out Brent's difficult character, her excellent vocal capabilities, and her ultimate sense of humor in accepting not only the new aria but also the opportunity to laugh at herself. Brent was painted in the role by Westfield Webb in 1762 in a now lost picture showing "her dress very exact, her necklace and esclavauge very finely executed." The illustration of her in the print *The 1st Representation of Artaxerxes* is the only surviving illustration we have (Figure 2).[25]

Similar use of an aria from *Artaxerxes* is made in the following anecdote of another singer who performed the role of Mandane, Ann Catley. Commenting to a woman she encountered on a rough sea voyage who asked her what her singing meant, Catley replied, "Nothing, my dear Madam . . . you have no ear: 'Tis only a tender movement—'Water parted from the sea.'"[26] This is one of the few anecdotes in Haslewood's book that is given a date, in this case 1773, one I would suggest is supplied because it marked Catley's early death.

In both these cases, the humor of the anecdote turns on the title of the aria and relies on its audience knowing something of the piece,

Figure 2. Anonymous, *The 1st Representation of Artaxerxes with a portrait of Rich the Manager*, ca. 1763. Etching, 16.2×23.5 cm. London: Victoria and Albert Museum, S.3943-2009.

a frequent characteristic of the theatrical anecdote. *Artaxerxes* was one of the few operas performed in eighteenth-century London where any likely hearer of the story (or reader of Haslewood's book) would have known the opera and could probably have sung both the aforementioned tunes.

Gertrud Mara: The Singer with the Stiff Knee

So far, the anecdotes dealt with here may or may not be factual. The two based on *Artaxerxes*, for example, are almost too good to be true, and it is entirely possible that the texts from the opera inspired the anecdotes which may, in all other respects, be entirely fictitious. However, in the case of Gertrud Mara, her behavior in concerts is attested by numerous reports that caused many to accuse her of being unprofessional, and her career was blighted by anecdotes that had some foundation in fact. Some of the complaints, however, were trumped up and the product of misogyny; she was, for example,

Figure 3. Anonymous, *The Wapping Concert*, 1786. Published by S. W. Fores, February 28, 1786. Etching and aquatint, 30×35.2 cm. London: British Museum, 1868,0808.5478.

accused of acting like a man, and of laughing and joking with the male performers during rehearsals.[27]

The most notable incident—and the one upon which Haslewood fastened—was one that took place at a concert in Oxford; Mara's insistence on leaving the stage after she had sung her arias and her refusal to stand up during the choruses of the oratorio led to her being hissed and booed, and ordered to leave the Sheldonian Theatre by the university's vice-chancellor. She publicly apologized, offering a long-standing problem with her leg as an excuse.[28] But no one believed this reason was genuine, and the continued circulation of the anecdote further colored the apparent dishonesty of a difficult performer and was damaging to her career; the following year she was pilloried in a vicious caricature entitled *The Wapping Concert* (Figure 3).[29] Here,

Mara is shown sitting, and refers to her "Le Genou Inflexible, or (Stiff Knee)," which prevents her standing. Her "stiff knee" excuse continued to follow her; John Wolcot made use of the image in his poem on the king's cancellation of her oratorio performances in 1787 because they clashed with performances by the Academy of Antient Music. As Joseph Roach argues, the cult of celebrity, the construction of "It," requires the celebrated figure to strike a balance between charismata (the positives) and stigmata (the negatives); when the stigmata are in the ascendant, celebrity is "too available to the identification of the audience."[30] For them, Mara's stiff knee made her notorious rather than celebrated.

Oxford proved to be troublesome for other singers; another anecdote from Haslewood claims that Giuseppina Grassini was offered a hundred guineas for two nights' performance; if true, this must have been during 1804 or 1805 while the contralto—famed for her voice, her teaching, and her affairs with Napoleon and the Duke of Wellington—was singing at the King's Theatre. Her "laconic" reply (in Italian) was that the fee "would not buy soap sufficient to wash her while she was there."[31] As with many singers' anecdotes, money was to the fore, the suggestion always being that singers asked for too high a fee and were personally extravagant.

Like Susannah Cibber, Mara's actual life story was more exciting than any anecdote. She was financially ruined by imprudent—and well-publicized—love affairs with two obviously unsuitable, much younger singers. By 1786, she was having an affair with the twenty-six-year-old singer Samuel Harrison with whom she visited Margate and Paris. By 1794, she had eloped to Bath with Charles Florio, with whom she spent the rest of his life. She courted public censure by living openly with him in Brompton, and public disgrace by beating her cook in 1798; but, although she and Florio were both brought before the magistrate Sir Richard Ford, the matter was settled out of court. She left England with Florio in 1801, and after traveling to Paris and to Berlin in 1803, she settled with him in Moscow in 1807, only to be made destitute by the burning of the city by Napoleon in 1812; she lost two houses and all her worldly goods in the flames. Florio died in 1819, having starved himself for days, eventually hallucinating and becoming violent, insisting—apparently falsely—that Mara was attempting to poison him.

The Beggar's Opera: An Anecdote on an Opera

In many ways, an "old opera" is not unlike an old singer: the anecdotes swirl around a long-standing work, just as they do a long-standing personality. Works, though, tended to be those that were well known and beloved. The works that were disliked—and there were plenty of those—attracted some initial responses; but it is only with longevity and repeated performances that anecdotes attach themselves to both works and their characters, and, to none more so than John Gay's *The Beggar's Opera*, first staged in 1728. In one of the most famous theatrical quips of the age, the success of the opera was said to have made Rich gay and Gay rich; and Swift begged Rich to "be thrifty and learn to value a shilling."[32] The work's original popularity may have been partly due to Lavinia Fenton, who created the role of Polly Peachum, and although not included in *Green Room Gossip*, she and her namesake were the subject of stories and anecdotes. In 1728, after the opera had proved a resounding success, she was the subject of the biography *The Life of Lavinia Beswick, alias Fenton, alias Polly Peachum*, which was a "mixture of fact and fiction."[33] It claimed that she "bestow'd her first favours" on a Portuguese nobleman at the age of seventeen, an early bestowal which caused others to say she was "minted" for the role of Polly.[34] At the end of the season, she ran away with the Duke of Bolton, who had attended the opera night after night to watch her perform; he is pictured by Hogarth with a libretto his hand.[35] But the scandal-crammed title page of *The Life of Lavinia Beswick* also claims that: "The whole is interspers'd with convincing proofs of her ingenuity, wit, and smart repartees. And [it concludes] with some remarkable instances of her humanity to the distressed."[36] The "ingenuity, wit, and smart repartees" are the same positive characteristics detailed in the anecdotes discussed above and below, and as with Mary Porter, there is an emphasis on her good works as a symbol of virtue; whatever Fenton may have done, she is redeemed by the "remarkable instances of her humanity." And in her "alias" as Polly Peachum, she was the subject of her own jestbook—a book of anecdotes by another name—which similarly prized tales and repartee.[37]

The Beggar's Opera was said to undermine public morals, and it was Thomas Herring, later archbishop of Canterbury, who condemned not just the story—which was easy enough to do—but the music, claiming that "several Thieves and Street-robbers confessed in Newgate, that they raised their Courage at the Playhouse, by the Songs of their Hero *Macheath*, before they sallied forth on their desperate nocturnal Exploits."[38] This was a stance that was probably responsible for the anecdote which suggested that the opera improved the behavior of footpads: "Gibbon has an observation on the *Beggar's Opera*, which, whether just or not, is ingenious; 'It has,' said he, 'a beneficial effect in refining highwaymen, and making them less ferocious, more polite, in short, more like gentlemen.' Mr Courtenay, on hearing this, said, with his usual happiness '*Then Gay was the Orpheus of highwaymen.*'"[39] The amoral effect of the show—if it *was* amoral—was further ameliorated by the addition of a new scene in 1777. This addition is the subject of one of Haslewood's anecdotes, which suggests that the scene allowed the hero redemption at the end of the opera:

> When Mrs. Farel [*sic*] played the part of *Macheath*, in 1777, at Covent Garden, there was a curious alteration made, on the suggestion of the moral Lessingham, at the end of the Opera, by introducing a scene of Woolwich Reach, with the *Hulk*, and the Hero entered under sentence of three years' imprisonment to heave ballast, while the rival females were introduced to take leave, and a promise of marriage to *Polly* at the expiration of the sentence. A chorus song concluded, having for burthen,
> "The wicked to-day may be virtuous tomorrow."[40]

The work's popularity led to it being performed far and wide in less than ideal circumstances, as instanced by this performance in the 1790s: "Every species of performer have attempted the Beggar's Opera, from the Theatre Royal, to Barns and Puppet-shows. Not longer ago than the year 1790, it was played at Barnstable in Devonshire, when Macheath had but one eye—Polly but one arm—the singers supported in the orchestra by a man who whistled the tunes—whilst the manager could not read."[41] The combination of grotesque elements is scarcely credible, and yet a player working in the minor theaters or in the provinces probably encountered at least one, if not all, of these in ill-prepared performances.

Francesca Cuzzoni: An "Inept" Anecdote

It was of the Italian Francesca Cuzzoni, one of the greatest of Handel's sopranos, that the anecdote "a bellyful of nightingales" was told.[42] The singer was the stuff of legend: preparing for her first London show in 1723, *Ottone, re di Germania*, she refused to sing one of Handel's arias because it had originally been written for another singer (or so the anecdote goes!), to which we are told "he took her up by the waist, and, if she made any more words, swore that he would fling her out of the window" if she did not comply.[43] She was pitched first against the castrato Senesino, and then the soprano Faustina Bordoni, and their onstage antics resulted not only in the usual catcalls and ovations but the production of a large amount of published commentary, including the well-known *Contre Temps; or, Rival Queans* with the scene set at the Temple of Discord.[44]

Musical competition of this kind between performers was not unusual, and was frequently reported either as an anecdote or a short news item in the press. Haslewood retails an anecdote of this type which uses considerable play on musical terminology: "One of the men of cat-gut conceiving a man of rival note was not *playing him fair*, but endeavoring to make him *lose his time*, at length took a *crochet* in his head, and quite *con spirito*, or rather *con furioso*, let fly a volley of music at the head of the supposed offender, which 'struck with a horrid *crash* the strings' of his fiddle, and completely *disconcerted* him, so that he made a sudden *shift*, or *octave* movement, from the *orchestra* to the Green Room."[45] The anecdote, which is among the longer ones in the volume, ends with a reference to William Hogarth's *Enraged Musician*,[46] and it says much for his intended audience that Haslewood could be confident that his readership had the skills to appreciate such esoterica, although the printer's use of italics at important moments at least ensures that even the most ignorant users of the volume could work out where the laughs were supposed to occur. The supposed competition took place between J.M.C. Bianchi and Felix Janiewicz (Yaniewicz) in 1801 at a theater in Dublin.[47] Another of Haslewood's competition anecdotes has what we might call "a slap in the face" conclusion, which contained much of the humor of a jest. Here, two "comedians" had a wager on who was the best singer, and they asked the composer

Thomas Arne to arbitrate. After they had performed, Haslewood's story runs, Arne, judging, said: "'As for you, Sir (addressing himself to the first), you are by much the *worst* singer I ever heard in my life.' 'Ah,' said the other, exulting, 'I knew I should win my wager.'—'Stop, Sir,' says the arbitrator, 'I have a word to say to you, before you go on, which is this, *that as for you, you cannot sing at all.*'"[48] We emerge with not just a winner, but the complete annihilation of the loser. But Arne, too, is part of the anecdote, which trades on the composer's reputation for being difficult and arrogant; our response is not to laugh, but to feel that his behavior is objectionable. And because we respond negatively to the arbiter, the losers gain our sympathy, just as the writer intended.

The incidents involving Cuzzoni resulted in anecdotes being passed around the theater, the most prominent of which made it into *Green Room Gossip*.[49] On hearing her sing, a supposed gallery attendee called out, "Damme, she has a nest of nightingales in her belly." The bon mot was, of course, very entertaining, coupling the world's most famous songbird with London's most popular singer. But on closer examination, the story is rather odd. The nightingale was well known to have discreet plumage—a fact that Hans Christian Andersen exploited in his fairy tale on the theme of the nightingale and the Emperor—so while the anecdote is on one hand flattering, on the other it can be read as backhanded insult to the singer's appearance. And it was perhaps true; Horace Walpole, on seeing her in *Rodelinda* in 1725, commented that she was "short and squat, with a doughy cross face."[50] Further, the image of a nest of birds in a singer's belly is peculiar to say the least, the belly not being a part of the body that is usually regarded as the origin of the voice. Writing on this anecdote, Justin Grize suggests that "her voice had betrayed her nature as a thoughtless animal, perhaps, or a besouled machine."[51] She was mechanical, then, and perhaps unfeeling. However, the oft-quoted third line of "To Signora Cuzzoni," Ambrose Philips's ode on her departure, "Empty warbler, breathing lyre,"[52] is suggestive of a certain type of voice production. This is a theme taken up by Charles Burney who, using similar bird imagery, referred to her as having a "native warble,"[53] and it may be that this vocal trait was the one that became the most prominent when her voice declined. Her sad (and sadly, very public) attempts to sing in London in the early 1750s elicited Burney's comment that she was "almost deprived of her voice, by age and infirmities"[54] and emphasize the hopeless poverty that many singers of all genders endured once their fame and skills had declined. A final anecdote of great pathos has Cuzzoni living in extreme poverty in Bologna, either selling greens from a stall or eking out a living making buttons.[55]

Kitty Clive: A Search for Posterity

The singer and actress Kitty Clive joined Drury Lane in 1728, and apart from a short interval at Covent Garden starting in 1743, she spent her career there, retiring in 1769. Winton Dean commented that "in character she was generous and loyal but quick tempered and sharp tongued."[56] She was equally at home in comic roles, such as Polly in *The Beggar's Opera*, as she was in serious ones, including those in Arne's *Comus* and *Rosamond*, even if Charles Burney was less than complimentary about her vocal abilities.[57] Her biggest successes were in ballad operas, including Colley Cibber's *Love in a Riddle* and Charles Coffey's *The Devil to Pay*. And in this varied and successful career lie the roots of an anecdote out of which Westminster Abbey emerges with no credit:

> When application was made to the dean and chapter of Westminster, to obtain permission for Mrs Clive the actress, being buried in the Abbey, one of the Prebends said, "he had made no objection to burying Garrick and Henderson in Poets' Corner, because each of them had *talents* independent of their professions, nor did he see any particular objection to allow the same privilege to Mrs Clive; But," added he, "if we do not draw some line in this theatrical ambition for mortuary fame, we shall very soon make Westminster Abbey a kind of *Gothic Green-room*."[58]

Clive was not honored with an Abbey interment, and it is impossible not to feel the power of misogyny in the justification of the inclusion of men because they "had *talents* independent of their professions." Further, the term "Gothic," while wittily employed in relation to the Abbey, will have been read by many as a barbed reference to her well-known relationship with Horace Walpole, which lasted from

1754 until her death; she lived near Walpole's famous and much-discussed "gothick" Strawberry Hill House, started in 1749 and completed in 1776. And his version of Gothic, like the Green Room, was something of fascination, for it was never free of the suspicion of moral deviation.[59]

Clive's epitaph from the churchyard at Twickenham was included by Haslewood at the end of the volume in a section best thought of as a memento mori. The gossip stops flowing; he ends with a long text headed "THE ACTOR'S PRAYER. *Addressed to* MERCURY, *the God of Eloquence*"; and begins a closing section called "Grave Subjects."[60] The section has a headnote using an ancient verse, one attributed to Walter Raleigh:

> Our graves that hide us from the searching sun,
> Are like drawn curtains, when the play is done;
> Thus march we playing to our latest rest,
> Only we die in earnest—that's no jest.

But it is a misquotation: Raleigh's text offers "setting sun"; Haslewood's text suggests a life lived under the spotlight, one extinguished by the fall of the theater curtain for the last time. The original of the last two lines does not continue the theater metaphor: "Thus playing post we to our latest rest, / And then we die in earnest, not in jest."[61] By changing the meaning of the word "playing," Haslewood captures a theatrical reference to death, real rather than onstage. Whether or not it was Haslewood himself who altered the text is not known; this version also appeared in other sources, including *The Drama: Or, Theatrical Pocket Magazine* for 1822.[62] The text was already circulating in musical circles, for a setting of it was included in Orlando Gibbons's *First Set of Madrigals and Mottets*, works of five parts for voices and viols; these were published in 1612.[63] Unlike much "ancient music," Gibbons's music was considered among the "classics,"[64] and in 1711 was included by Arthur Bedford in his notion of English music of a golden age.[65]

Haslewood's text that follows Raleigh's verse consists of a whole spectrum of humors and meanings in verses, formal obituaries, and transcriptions of plaques and tombstones. The heterogeneous nature of the whole collection is writ large in this short section, with contributions on both the famous and unknown, from London to obscure corners of the kingdom. And the jest is certainly not abandoned, nor is the use of theatrical jargon to carry the humor; Anna Seward, writing on the death of Anne Oldfield in 1730, penned:

> When Oldfield dies, e'en Congreve's laurels fade
> And this we own, in justice to her shade,
> The first bad exit Oldfield ever made.[66]

Jest or not, epitaphs tend to make, as here, anecdotes of a piquant kind; an epitaph, defined as "an inscription upon a tomb," can also be "a brief composition characterizing a deceased person, and expressed *as if intended* [my italics] to be inscribed on his tombstone."[67] And like Kitty Clive, Anne Oldfield—a performer with whom Clive was often compared[68]—was snubbed by those in charge of interments at Westminster Abbey; the dean refused a proposal by her partner, Charles Churchill, to erect a monument there to her memory.[69]

Conclusion

The anecdotes of singers included by Haslewood have two things in common. They are (nearly) all about women singers; and the anecdotes are (mostly) retailed in such a way as to enhance their reputations. And as we have seen, this need not have been the case; Charlotte Brent is an example here. The anecdote was designed to bring out her difficult character, her excellent vocal capabilities, and her ultimate sense of humor in accepting the new aria; it offered her the opportunity to laugh at herself, suggesting that she was an equable personality, if tough. Nothing is made of the fact that Arne had abandoned his wife for her when she was his pupil, and that at the time the scene purportedly took place they were cohabiting.

Behind Haslewood's narrative there is an effort to establish singers as respectable professionals in the world of the theater, which was seen as anything but. His efforts can be summed up in his comment on Mary Porter's collection of cash for the highwayman's family: "Such an action, in a person of high rank, would have been celebrated as something great and heroick: the feeling mind will make no distinction between the generosity of an actress and that of a princess." As Belle Watling says in *Gone With the*

Wind, "It's good money, even if it *is* mine."[70] And the story about Porter presents her as a redoubtable personality, as indeed do the stories of Brent and Mara, suggesting that women of this type of character were those most likely to be subjects of such anecdotes. The origin of the anecdotes themselves is unknown, a characteristic that almost defines the genre. Nonetheless, what is clear is that if a singer so chose, they could create, use, and repeat an anecdote about themselves to the furtherance of their own ends. But, as we have seen, anecdotes were dangerous and could be two-edged; the example of Mara's "stiff-knee," industriously elaborated on by Haslewood, shows just how destructive the circulation of an anecdote could become, particularly when there was, as in her case, a grain of truth in the story.

Notes

Epigraph: Gridiron Gabble [Joseph Haslewood], *Green Room Gossip* (London: J. Barker, 1808), 117.

1. "anecdote, n." *Oxford English Dictionary*, prepared by J. A. Simpson and E. S. C. Weiner, 2nd ed., 20 vols. (Oxford: Clarendon Press, 1989), 1:454.

2. Judith Milhous and Robert D. Hume, "Construing and Misconstruing Farinelli in London," *British Journal of Eighteenth-Century Studies* 28, no. 3 (2005): 361–385.

3. Malina Stefanovska, "Exemplary or Singular? The Anecdote in Historical Narrative," *SubStance* 118, vol. 38, no. 1 (2009): 16–30.

4. Aoife Monks, "Collecting Ghosts: Actors, Anecdotes and Objects at the Theatre," *Contemporary Theatre Review* 23, no. 2 (2013): 148.

5. Carl Hentschel, after a watercolor by Thomas Rowlandson, "Rehearsing in the Green Room," 1789. Engraving, Harry R. Beard Collection, given by Isobel Beard. London, Victoria and Albert Museum, S.2434-2013.

6. John Ebers, *Seven Years of the King's Theatre* (London: William Harrison Ainsworth, 1828), 80.

7. Gravity Galliniput, colored engraving, 1781. Made by C. Bretherton Jr., Harry R. Beard Collection, given by Isobel Beard. London, Victoria and Albert Museum, S.529-2013.

8. Henry Angelo, *Reminiscences of Henry Angelo: with Memoirs of his late Father and Friends, including Numerous Original Anecdotes and Curious Traits of the most Celebrated Characters that have Flourished during the past Eighty Years*, 2 vols. (London: Colburn and Bentley, 1830), 2:50–52.

9. Thomas Rowlandson, *The Prospect Before Us*, 1791. Etching, published by Samuel William Fores, January 13, 1791. London, British Museum, J,2.86.

10. Thomas Rowlandson, *The Prospect Before Us*, 1791. Etching, inscribed: "Humanely incrib'd to all those Professors of Music and Dancing whom the cap may fit." Published by Samuel William Fores, January 13, 1791. Preparatory watercolor, London, British Museum, 1985,0608.31.

11. Alan Bell, "Haslewood, Joseph," in *The Oxford Dictionary of National Biography*, ed. H.C.G. Matthew and Brian Harrison, 60 vols. (Oxford: Oxford University Press, 2004), 25:174–175.

12. "gridiron, n." *OED Online*, December 2020. Oxford University Press.

13. See *The Gentleman's Magazine* 83 (1813): 217–221, 333–334, 437, 553–563; *The Gentleman's Magazine* 84 (1814): 9–12, 337–339.

14. Haslewood, *Green Room Gossip*, 4.

15. Haslewood, *Green Room Gossip*, 1.

16. Haslewood, *Green Room Gossip*, 3.

17. Haslewood, *Green Room Gossip*, 3.

18. "Porter, Mary," in *A Biographical Dictionary of Actors, Actresses, Musicians, Dancers, Managers & Other Stage Personnel in London, 1660–1800*, ed. Philip H. Highfill Jr., Kalman A. Burnim, and Edward A. Langhans, vol. 12, *Pinner to Rizzo* (Carbondale: Southern Illinois University Press, 1987), 91–96.

19. Michael Burden, "Casting Issues in Purcell's Opera *The Fairy-Queen*," *Music and Letters* 74, no. 4 (2003): 596–607.

20. Highfill, Burnim, and Langhans, *A Biographical Dictionary*, 323.

21. Haslewood, *Green Room Gossip*, 43–44.

22. Haslewood, *Green Room Gossip*, 41–42.

23. Anna Ambrose, dir., *Honour, Profit and Pleasure*, written by Anna Ambrose and Peter Luke, featuring Simon Callow, Alan Devlin, and Jean Rigby, aired 1985, on Channel 4.

24. Haslewood, *Green Room Gossip*, 120–121.

25. Anonymous, *The 1st Representation of Artaxerxes with a portrait of Rich the Manager*, ca. 1763. Etching, 16.2×23.5 cm., London, Victoria and Albert Museum, S.3943-2009.

26. Haslewood, *Green Room Gossip*, 68.

27. Michael Burden, "Mara, Gertrud," in *The Oxford Dictionary of National Biography*, 36:594–596.

28. Haslewood, *Green Room Gossip*, 137.

29. Anonymous, *The Wapping Concert*, 1786. Published by S. W. Fores, February 28, 1786. Etching and aquatint, 30×35.2 cm., London: British Museum, 1868,0808.5478.

30. Joseph Roach, "Public Intimacy: The Prior History of 'It,'" in *Theatre and Celebrity in Britain, 1660–2000*, ed. Mary Luckhurst and Jane Moody (Basingstoke, UK: Palgrave Macmillan, 2005), 15–30, 19, 26.

31. Haslewood, *Green Room Gossip*, 136.

32. Jonathan Swift, to John Gay, in *The Works of Alexander Pope*, 10 vols (London: J. and P. Knapton, 1754), 10:85.

33. Olive Baldwin, Thelma Wilson, "Fenton [*née* Besswick; *married name* Powlett or Paulet], Lavinia, duchess of Bolton," in *The Oxford Dictionary of National Biography*, 19:310–312.

34. Anonymous, *The Life of Lavinia Beswick, alias Fenton, alias Polly Peachum* (London: A. Moore, 1728), 16.

35. William Hogarth, *A Scene from "The Beggar's Opera" IV*, oil on canvas, 1761. London, Tate Britain, N02437.

36. Anonymous, *The Life of Lavinia Beswick*, title page.

37. Anonymous, *Polly Peachum's Jests* (London: J. Roberts, 1728).

38. Thomas Herring, preface to *Seven Sermons on Public Occasions* (London: for the editor, 1763), v–vi.

39. Haslewood, *Green Room Gossip*, 98.

40. Haslewood, *Green Room Gossip*, 139.

41. Haslewood, *Green Room Gossip*, 52.

42. Haslewood, *Green Room Gossip*, 127.

43. John Mainwaring, *Memoirs of the Life of the Late George Frederic Handel* (London: R. and J. Dodsley, 1760), 110–111.

44. There are many accounts of these events; for an eighteenth-century report, see Charles Burney, *A General History of Music*, vol. 4 (London: for the author, 1789), 325–326, and for some contemporary commentary, see Suzanne Aspden, "The 'Rival Queans' and the Play of Identity in Handel's 'Admeto,'" *Cambridge Opera Journal* 18, no. 3 (2006): 301–331.

45. Haslewood, *Green Room Gossip*, 56.

46. William Hogarth, *The Enraged Musician, 1741*, etching and engraving. London, British Museum, 1868,0822.1554.

47. For Bianchi, see John C. Greene, *Theatre in Dublin, 1745–1820: A Calendar of Performances*, vol. 4 (Lanham, MD: Lehigh University Press, 2011), 3083, and for Yaniewicz, see John W. Moore, *The Complete Encyclopaedia of Music* (Boston: John P. Jewett and Co, 1854), 998.

48. Haslewood, *Green Room Gossip*, 74–75.

49. For one of the many overviews of these responses, see James Wierzbicki, "Dethroning the Divas: Satire Directed at Cuzzoni and Faustina," *Opera Quarterly* 17, no. 2 (2001): 175–196.

50. Like a number of Walpole anecdotes, the actual source is hard to pin down. As Aspden points out, this does not appear in the *Yale Edition of Walpole's Correspondence*: Suzanne Aspden, *The Rival Sirens: Performance and Identity on Handel's Operatic Stage* (Cambridge: Cambridge University Press, 2013), 74.

51. Justin Grize, "Singing Beasts: Opera and the Animal" (PhD diss.; University of Sussex, 2017), 43, https://www.proquest.com/dissertations-theses/singing-beasts-opera-animal/docview/2230917069/se-2?acccountid=6180.

52. Ambrose Philips, *Pastorals, Epistles, Odes, and Other Original Poems, With Translations from Pindar, Anacreon, and Sappho* (Tonson and Draper, 1748), 77.

53. Burney, *A General History of Music*, 316.

54. Burney, *A General History of Music*, 307.

55. Highfill, Burnim, and Langhans, *A Biographical Dictionary*, 1:118.

56. Winton Dean, "Clive, Kitty [Catherine]," in *The New Grove VII*, ed. Stanley Sadie, 29 vols. (London: Macmillan, 2001), 7:856–858.

57. Burney, *A General History of Music*, 654.

58. Haslewood, *Green Room Gossip*, 30.

59. See Matthew M. Reeve, "Gothic Architecture, Sexuality, and License at Horace Walpole's Strawberry Hill," *The Art Bulletin* 95, no. 3 (2013): 411–439.

60. Haslewood, *Green Room Gossip*, 153.

61. Walter Raleigh, "'What Is Our Life? The Play of Passion,'" in *Elizabethan Poetry: An Anthology*, ed. Bob Blaisdell (Mineola, NY: Dover, 2005), 122.

62. *The Drama: Or, Theatrical Pocket Magazine*, vol. 3 (London: T. and J. Elvey, 1822), 70–71.

63. Orlando Gibbons, *First Set of Madrigals and Mottets* (London: Thomas Snodham, 1612).

64. William Weber, *The Rise of Musical Classics in Eighteenth-Century England* (Oxford: Oxford University Press, 1992), 203.

65. Arthur Bedford, *The Great Abuses of Music* (London: printed by J. H. for John Wyatt, 1711), 219.

66. Anna Seward in Haslewood, *Green Room Gossip*, 153.

67. "epitaph, n." *OED*, 5:340.

68. See, for example, Berta Joncus's discussion of *The Theatre Turned Upside Down* (1733) in *Kitty Clive, or The Fair Songster* (Woodbridge: The Boydell Press, 2019), 152.

69. See https://www.westminster-abbey.org/abbey-commemorations/commemorations/ann-oldfield.

70. Victor Fleming, dir., *Gone With the Wind*, based on the novel by Margaret Mitchell (Los Angeles: Metro-Goldwyn-Mayer, 1939).

PART III

ACTING CAREERS AND THE PROFESSIONAL ANECDOTE

7

ANECDOTE AND THE REGIONAL ACTRESS

A History of the Farren Family in Several Anecdotes

FIONA RITCHIE

According to historian R. J. Broadbent, in 1773, James Whitley, manager of the theater at Manchester, wrote to Margaret Farren in response to her application for positions in his acting company for herself and her daughters:

> MADAM,—I have duly considered the subject of our late conversation, and do not think there is the least chance of your deriving any permanent benefit from theatrical pursuits. Inclination does not confer talent: for the sake of yourself and children I strenuously advise you to turn your attention to some other less dangerous and precarious line of life. I say less dangerous as applies to your daughters. I have passed a long career upon the stage, and where I have seen one person prosperous and happy, ten have failed, and many, particularly females, have been morally cast away. . . . Fix on some safe and certain occupation. Even a laundress, with tolerable plenty of work, is preferable to treading the stage as a *make-weight*. Do not feel offended at this bluntness. Nature has not endowed *you* with the qualities that are requisite to ensure success: as to Betsey, although she seems to possess every natural requisite, she is yet too young, and were she my daughter, I would sooner rear her up to go to service in a respectable family![1]

He closes the letter by pledging to lend Margaret some money and offering to help set her up in a trade. The Betsey mentioned here is

Elizabeth Farren, who became a well-known eighteenth-century actress who made her name on the London stage and went on to marry an earl, becoming Countess of Derby.[2] Broadbent reproduces this anecdote in a discussion of Farren's career, but more interesting to me than the light it sheds on the early years of the Countess of Derby is that the story reveals that Elizabeth was part of a family of theatrical women.

Biographical Gleanings of a Theatrical Family

The *Biographical Dictionary* documents that Elizabeth's parents, George and Margaret Farren, were performers, as were her sisters Catherine (Kitty) and Margaret (Peggy).[3] George Farren died around 1770, and Margaret was left to bring up three daughters. The letter from Whitley shows that she saw the theater as a viable means of making ends meet and raising her children. The implication of this missive is that the manager somehow recognized Elizabeth's innate nobility and tried to prevent her mother from allowing her to be "morally cast away" through a connection to the stage. The young woman would thus maintain the virtue and integrity deemed crucial in allowing her to move upward through the social ranks. This premise, however, is flawed, since Elizabeth only came to the Earl of Derby's attention as a result of her stage performances. The letter forms part of a pattern in early biographical accounts of Elizabeth Farren that emphasizes her inherent morality in order to demonstrate that she was a suitable partner for a member of the nobility, and indeed fit to marry the earl and become a countess rather than serve as his mistress, as many eighteenth-century actresses did with men of a higher social station.[4] Anecdotes abound that stress Farren's humble origins and emphasize her rags to riches story as she moved from strolling player to London celebrity and eventually aristocrat. In a particularly lurid example, John Doran recounts Farren's ascension to stardom through a series of vignettes contrasting her low provincial origins with her subsequent high social status.[5] The first of these anecdotes sees "Lizzy" taking sustenance to her father, who has been imprisoned in Salisbury as a strolling player (though Doran cites no sources for his account and no other biographies mention the imprisonment of George Farren). Suzanne Bloxam's biography of

Elizabeth refers to a nineteenth-century painting of this scene.[6] Although this image now seems to be lost, its existence suggests the appeal of such stories to audiences of the period.

Broadbent implies that he found the letter from Whitley quoted in "an anonymous and scarce pamphlet, entitled *Biographical Gleanings of the Countess of Derby, formerly Miss Farren*, published in the early part of the nineteenth century."[7] He notes that the author of this pamphlet doubts that the letter was in fact written by Whitley on the grounds that its tone is too delicate and refined for a regional theater manager.[8] However, we might rather be suspicious about the authenticity of this source because its intense nineteenth-century moralizing is a surprising reaction to eighteenth-century women trying to make a career on the stage. As a manager, Whitley must have encountered entreaties such as Farren's on a regular basis. Some commentators argued that the theater was "a seminary for intrigue and dissipation," and thus a particularly dangerous place for women, though its defenders countered that the playhouse could not "vitiate innate principals of virtue," and, of course, women were frequently seen on the stage.[9] The letter attempts to discipline Margaret and her daughters, but she disregarded its warnings, and her family made successful theatrical careers for themselves, as we shall see. In fact, Whitley did hire the Farrens to act at Manchester, which further suggests that this letter reveals more about attitudes toward the actress than it does about the details of the Farrens' situation. The *Biographical Dictionary* entry on Elizabeth Farren also quotes this letter, apparently directly from Broadbent. Thus, it is not only nineteenth-century historians who were susceptible to the lure of the anecdote; the leading contemporary source for biographical information on eighteenth-century performances (admittedly notably problematic for its failure to cite sources) included the letter as part of its biographical account of a major performer.[10]

The recent resurgence of interest in anecdote as a source for theater history has downplayed the genre's relationship to truth. Jacky Bratton has constructed the anecdote as a method of identity formation for theatrical communities but laments that anecdotes have previously been "trawled for 'factual' information that can be extracted and corroborated from other documentary sources" but less frequently "read for what their writers or their subjects seem to stress, or what their contemporary readership might have understood of theatre history from them."[11] Similarly, Paul Menzer has explored recurring Shakespearean anecdotes, arguing that they tell us something about the dramatist's plays that the plays themselves refuse to tell us. Like Bratton, he "is interested not in whether an anecdote is accurate but in what work it performs" and describes anecdotal history as "a vital sub-genre of theatre history, a history largely free of facts but not less full of truth."[12] The history of women's involvement in regional theater must also be sensitive to this complex relationship between anecdote and truth.

Elizabeth Farren's life generated a wide array of anecdotes not just because she was an actress but because she was an actress who married a peer and became a member of the English nobility. Her life, then, is well documented because of her exceptionality. But while trying to shed light on the origins and character of one particular star actress, these anecdotes often also gesture intriguingly to the theatrical careers of the rest of her family. For every London star, there were hundreds of performers working outside the capital in relative obscurity. It is these actors and actresses who make up the bulk of eighteenth-century theater history because they were more numerous; their experience is therefore more representative of the working life of theater professionals at the time. The careers of regional performers are less well documented (both in eighteenth-century records and in modern scholarship) than those of their counterparts in the capital, and the problem is even more acute for actresses in comparison with their male peers. In trying to write a history of women and regional theater, anecdote is often one of the few sources available. It therefore seems inevitable that these accounts must be read to some degree for the biographical information they can provide. Indeed, as Thomas Postlewait points out in his exploration of Shakespeare biography, what seem to be two distinct traditions of anecdote and documentary record are in fact "not just intertwined but mutually constitutive."[13] This mutually constitutive relationship between anecdote and record is explored in this chapter, which posits that anecdotes can be used as a starting point in reconstructing the lives and careers of regional actresses. Closer attention to female performers outside of London enables us to build a more detailed picture of the vibrant theatrical culture that existed across Britain in this period and also allows us to more fully recognize women's involvement in the eighteenth-century stage.

The Strolling Life

According to the *Memoirs of the Present Countess of Derby, (Late Miss Farren) . . . By Petronius Arbiter*, Elizabeth's father, George Farren, was an itinerant actor from Ireland with a penchant for drink. He met his wife in a tavern (she was the landlord's daughter) and Margaret was motivated to marry George by "an ambition to become an Actress herself," which she subsequently did, despite being "not very fortunate" in this profession.[14] During their "itinerant life . . . in different parts of England and Ireland," Margaret was able to support her children "by careful oeconomy on her part, notwithstanding Mr. FARREN's fondness for Ale," but George's death about ten or twelve years after the marriage "reduced Mrs. FARREN and her Children to the greatest distress."[15] Hence, Margaret's need to put her children on the stage, "that their exertions might contribute a small pittance to the general stock."[16] This biography, however, has the Farren family performing first of all in a strolling company so poor that its members had to carry scenery and costumes on their backs as they traveled from town to town, "nor were the Ladies excused on such occasions."[17] The author also relates that "it always fell to the lot of Lady DERBY [Elizabeth Farren] to carry the *Drum*" that was used to announce the company's arrival in each town, relishing this example of uncouth behavior again as a contrast to the actress's subsequent nobility.[18]

Doubtless, Margaret Farren struggled with the loss of income following her husband's death. But it is probable that her daughters were brought up in the acting profession and appeared onstage even before their father's decease. Acting families were very common in the provinces at this time. All theatergoers of the period would have known of the Kemble family: five of the children of provincial performers Sarah Ward and Roger Kemble became actors, Sarah Siddons and John Philip Kemble being the most famous.[19] Another biography of Farren, *The Memoirs of the Present Countess of Derby . . . By Scriptor Veritatis*, notes that "the children of players and musicians have a natural propensity to follow the track of their parents; they become very frequently proficient, without knowing how they have acquired merit; in their very infancy they sometimes surpass the veterans."[20] This work also reproduces a playbill for a performance at the theater in Ashton-under-Lyne on July 14, 1797, in which all the parts in the mainpiece and afterpiece were played by members of the Hillyard family.[21] The Hillyards do not appear in the *Biographical Dictionary*, but they seem to have been briefly synonymous with the idea of the theatrical family. The *Monthly Mirror* for July 1801 prints "for the entertainment of . . . readers" another playbill from 1797 in which the Hillyards took all the roles in *The School for Scandal* and *Barnaby Brittle*.[22]

In 1765, "Mr Farran's company of comedians, who far exceed all that ever acted here before" appeared in Southampton, and an actor named Farran (a common alternative spelling of the name) assisted a manager called Samuel Johnson in running a theater at Salisbury, where he and his wife were members of the company.[23] Although I have found no records of Elizabeth performing in Salisbury, the Farrens' connection with the theater there explains the claim made in the *County Magazine* for March 1787 that Elizabeth's first appearance was at the Salisbury Theatre.[24] James Winston's version of Elizabeth's discovery claims that she was found "when barely entering her teens, in a barn, where she was delivering GEORGE ALEXANDER STEEVENS'S Lecture upon Heads, to supply the necessities of herself, her mother, and her sister."[25] Whether or not this anecdote is true, it recalls William Hogarth's famous engraving "Strolling Actresses Dressing in a Barn" of 1738, a popular engraving of regional female performers that presented them as rustic and romanticized.

The author of the *Testimony of Truth to Exalted Merit*, another biographical pamphlet about Elizabeth, is at pains to assure the reader that "the manner in which she commenced her theatrical career, the companies with which she was connected, and the situation which she filled in them, were as respectable as an engagement out of London could possibly afford."[26] He further emphasizes that "Miss FARREN neither made her *debut* in a strolling party, nor associated with one afterwards."[27] The aim here is, of course, once more to downplay any whiff of scandal or indecorousness associated with Elizabeth's background in order to justify her ascension to the nobility. But such a rhetorical move has the unfortunate effect of downplaying or even obscuring the early regional careers of the other members of the Farren family. The distinction between "regular" (for want of a better word) and strolling companies is important in assessing the early careers of the Farren women. The performances of companies that appeared season after season at a fixed address are much better documented in the archives that remain to us. The official status of the Theatres Royal (which were established in many towns from the 1760s and 1770s onward) led to better record keeping. These regional performances have been privileged over the more itinerant kind by theater historians, and details of strolling companies are difficult to uncover.

When the Farren women joined Whitley's Manchester company it was in fact a step up for them. Although there was not yet a patent theater (or Theatre Royal) in the town, Whitley's company gained respectability by performing at a fixed address and in a purpose-built space. The earliest record of Elizabeth performing in the city is on February 2, 1774, and subsequent announcements in the *Manchester Mercury* show that she appeared regularly as an entr'acte singer and dancer in the following months. On April 8, 1774, a benefit performance took place for "the Widow Howard, Mrs Farran, and her three Children."[28] Elizabeth sang a new song and spoke an epilogue after a performance of *The Merchant of Venice* in which Catherine played Nerissa. Margaret sang "Sweet Willy O."[29] Catherine then appeared again as Maria in the afterpiece, Arthur Murphy's *The Citizen*. The evening concluded with "a poetic Address of Thanks to the Ladies and Gentlemen of *Manchester*, written by a Gentleman of the Town for the Occasion, and spoke by Miss E. Farran." Elizabeth's other roles that season included Ariel in *The Tempest* and Betty and Lucia in the farces *Cross Purposes* and *The Cheats of Scapin*.[30] Margaret appeared twice as Floriandus in a burlesque interlude entitled *The Fairy's Triumph Over Love*.[31]

Whitley subsequently "dispensed with the services of the Farrens," but he recommended Catherine (not Elizabeth, interestingly) to manager Joseph Younger.[32] Younger managed the Theatre Royal in Liverpool, and in 1775 took over the theater scene in Manchester when a patent theater opened there. His company performed in both towns. The Farrens therefore moved from Whitley's established, but not officially sanctioned, playhouse to employment at theaters with royal patents. However, this apparent upward trajectory from itinerant company to patent theaters is complicated by evidence that Margaret Farren and her oldest daughter had previously acted at the Bath Theatre Royal. A Mrs. Farran is listed as a member of the Bath company in 1759–1760, 1760–1761, and 1769–1770 in the performance calendar for that city. Miss Farran is listed for 1769–1770 and 1770–1771.[33] All of the Farren women acted for Younger at Liverpool and Manchester in the 1770s, but owing to contemporary writers' interest in Elizabeth's exceptionality, it is details of her performances that predominate in surviving accounts. *Walker's Hibernian Magazine* for July 1794 gives an anecdote about her Liverpool debut as Rosetta in *Love in a Village*: "Such was the poverty of her wardrobe, that the ladies in the company . . . were obliged to subscribe each a portion of apparel, before she could be properly equipped."[34] However, with Elizabeth's subsequent performance of Lady Townly, Younger was so pleased "that he procured credit with his tradesmen, for what clothes any of the family might stand in need of."[35] This account appeared at the height of speculation about the relationship between Derby and Farren (the author assures us it is "perfectly *Platonic*") and how it might develop should "*one event*" (that is, the death of the countess) take place.[36] Provincial poverty is therefore again emphasized in order to further elevate the social heights to which Farren eventually rose.[37] Eventually, Younger recommended Elizabeth to George Colman at the Haymarket Theatre in London. She made her first appearance there on June 9, 1777, as Miss Hardcastle in *She Stoops to Conquer*. She later made her way to Drury Lane, where she appeared regularly from 1778. The rest, as they say, is history: "Betsey" became "Eliza" and subsequently the Countess of Derby.

Margaret Farren: "Mrs Utility"

What, then, of the other Farren sisters? The *Biographical Dictionary* contains a short entry on Margaret, or "Peggy," the youngest.[38] She married the actor Thomas Knight in 1788, and in 1795 they were both performing in London at Covent Garden. The *Biographical Dictionary* recounts an anecdote about this engagement: "The press reported that Lord Derby, lover of Peggy's sister Elizabeth, had persuaded the management to article the Knights," that is, to give them a long-term contract in the capital.[39] No source is cited here for this statement, but in the entry on Margaret's husband, the authors claim that "the extent of Derby's assistance is reflected in the London press report on 1 August 1795 that Mr. and Mrs. Knight were said to have been engaged 'by Desire of their Majesties.'"[40] This claim, however, is not as straightforward as it might seem. If we are supposed to read this pressure from Derby as an instance of nepotism, it is odd that Covent Garden was encouraged to hire the Knights rather than Drury Lane, where Elizabeth Farren was working. Perhaps we should view the anecdote as evidence of Derby's concern that Elizabeth not be subjected to direct competition by having her sister in the same company. But I have found nothing in the documentary record to suggest that relations between the sisters were in any way strained. In any case, the authors of the *Biographical Dictionary* inferred that Derby was involved in the Knights' engagement from the press report about the royal family rather than from any direct evidence.

It is unlikely that the Knights would have needed the intervention of Derby to encourage the Covent Garden management to hire them as they were already seasoned professional actors. A brief survey of Margaret's early career makes clear the breadth of her experience. Like her sister, she first performed with her family in strolling companies and then acted under Whitley and Younger.[41] She was also employed for a summer season with Elizabeth at the Haymarket in London in 1777 before they both returned to the provinces.[42] Margaret joined Tate Wilkinson's Yorkshire circuit in 1782, then went to Edinburgh and Dublin before returning to Wilkinson's company "greatly improved" in 1786, where she stayed until 1788.[43] Wilkinson named her "Mrs Utility," presumably for the wide variety of parts she was able to play and her usefulness to the company.[44] Already an established actress, it was at York that she met Thomas Knight. They spent several years acting at Bath and Bristol before moving to London. Following their debut at Covent Garden, the *Morning Chronicle* pronounced the Knights "a valuable acquisition to the Theatre" and noted that they were well received by the audience.[45] Margaret left Covent Garden in 1798 after three seasons. The *Biographical Dictionary* claims that she was not reengaged at the playhouse, implying that she was dismissed, but Thomas Harral notes that she was "of essential service to the theatre" at this time.[46] The reason for her departure is therefore a mystery.

In a piece on Elizabeth's retirement from the stage on her marriage to the Earl of Derby, the *Sporting Magazine* for April 1797 reports that "Mrs. KNIGHT, of Covent Garden Theatre, sister to Miss Farren, retires from the stage after the present season, at the request of the Earl of Derby, who has settled an annuity on her."[47] Some commentators apparently believed that Margaret should leave the stage when her sister did, and the implication of the press report is that Derby's annuity would replace the actress's professional income. Margaret in fact continued to act in London during the following season and regularly appeared outside the capital, including in Edinburgh and Newcastle, until near the time of her death in 1804.[48] The annuity may have been insufficient or nonexistent, Margaret might simply have disregarded her brother-in-law's wishes, or perhaps, despite what the press claimed, Derby did not actually care whether she continued to act or not. The obsession of biographers with Elizabeth's rags to riches narrative obscures Margaret's independent success.

There is limited documentation of Margaret's regional performances, however. Wilkinson reports in his *Wandering Patentee* that during her time in Bath, Margaret was well known "and respected as a gentlewoman off the stage, and a great favourite on," and that the benefit nights she shared with her husband in Bath and Bristol were "crowded and fashionable";[49] in Edinburgh she was considered "a very sprightly actress."[50] According to the *Biographical Dictionary*, she played Desdemona in Edinburgh on January 11, 1783, and Peggy in *The Country Girl* in Bath on April 22, 1788, which gives some sense of her range.[51] Margaret's three seasons in London appear unsuccessful only in comparison with her sister's nineteen-year career in the capital, and only if we consider London performance as the gold standard by which success should be measured.

"Unpolished" Catherine Farren

Broadbent's account of the Farren women constantly and contemptuously compares Margaret and Catherine to their more famous sister, depicting them as unrefined and untalented in comparison with

Elizabeth. Margaret, he tells us, "had no claims to admiration, either as regarded her person or her temper, save that she was occasionally witty, but too often the shafts of her wit were barbed with malignity."[52] Again, no sources are cited for his evaluation, which is contradicted by Margaret's popularity at Bath and elsewhere, as well as surviving comments by John Colls (himself later married to an actress), who wrote to a correspondent that "she is very great. There is in her an awkward simplicity bordering on cunning—that spreads the sunshine of laughter" and compared her to Dorothy Jordan.[53] Broadbent makes a similarly scornful evaluation of the other Farren sister, Kitty: "Catherine had no particular pretensions to beauty, and was less polished in her manners. She died at Manchester on Friday, January 10, 1777, of consumption."[54] In this anecdote, written over a hundred years after Catherine's death, the actress is dismissed as "less polished" than Elizabeth, who was, according to Broadbent, "born to be a lady" (a destiny that she of course fulfilled, which makes the historian's comment easy to make, with the benefit of hindsight from his early twentieth-century vantage point).[55] Catherine's early death (if she was younger than Elizabeth, she must have been in her mid-teens) is made to seem inconsequential because she did not excel as an actress or match her sister Elizabeth's grace and beauty. Catherine's short life does not warrant an entry in the *Biographical Dictionary*, but its authors echo Broadbent's assessment of her in their account of Elizabeth, claiming that Kitty "had no special beauty or polish."[56] Such biographical treatment breaks apart this theatrical family, whereas the documentary record clearly shows that the Farren women consistently worked together.

In fact, we know that Catherine acted with her sisters until her death. In the benefit performance for the Farren family at Manchester in April 1774, Elizabeth and Margaret sang songs and delivered a prologue and address while Catherine had speaking roles in both the mainpiece and the afterpiece.[57] Catherine was at this point, therefore, the acting star of the family. The *Derby Mercury* records an even earlier appearance by the Farrens in which Kitty took the lead. On February 12, 1773, *Love in a Village* and *The Lyar* were performed by Carleton's company at the County Hall in Derby.[58] Miss Farren is billed as Rosetta and Miss E. Farren as Lucinda, with Mrs. Farren as Deborah Woodcock. The *Biographical Dictionary* assumes that it was Margaret who played Rosetta, but given that she was the youngest sister, it is more likely to have been Catherine, particularly given that she later took the major speaking roles in the benefit performance in Manchester.[59] In this case, pursuing information about Catherine's performances leads us to more information about Elizabeth's early career. Around this time, Whitley was constructing a theater in Derby, and in the following season the Farren family appeared there, perhaps poached by Whitley from Carleton. The *Derby Mercury* contains several performance announcements for 1774 that feature the Farrens.[60] A playbill reproduced in Wilkinson's *Wandering Patentee* (see Figure 4) shows that the Farrens also acted with Whitley at Wakefield in 1774 in the afterpiece *Old Mother Red-Cap*: Margaret as Hymen, Catherine as a Servant Maid, and Elizabeth as Columbine, with their mother as one of the masquers.[61]

Broadbent claims that it was Catherine whom Whitley specifically recommended to Younger, although he did engage the whole family.[62] According to the performance announcements for this period, Catherine played roles such as Audrey in *As You Like It* (at Birmingham on September 20, 1775, and Manchester on December 13, 1775), a speaking witch in *Macbeth* (on October 18, 1775, at Manchester), Columbine (in the pantomime *The Royal Chace* on December 13, 1775, at Manchester), Mrs. Peachum in *The Beggar's Opera* with Elizabeth as Lucy and Mrs. Farren as Diana Trapes (on November 6, 1776, at Liverpool), and various servant characters (Lucy in *The London Merchant* to Elizabeth's Maria on November 22, 1775, Lucy in *The Recruiting Officer* with Elizabeth as Rose on February 16, 1776, and Laura in *The Man's the Master* on May 22, 1776, all at Manchester).[63] This list of parts demonstrates that Catherine could sing and dance and that she was equally at home in Shakespeare as in contemporary drama. The last announcement I have found for Catherine appears in the *Manchester Mercury* for December 17, 1776. The performance advertised for the following day features Catherine as Mrs. Willoughby with Elizabeth as Miss Willoughby in *A Word to the Wise*, and all of the Farren women in the afterpiece, *A Trip to Scotland*: Miss P. Farren as Cupid, Mrs. Farren as Fillagree, Miss K. Farren as Miss Flack, and Miss Farren as Miss Griskin. Elizabeth eventually eclipsed Catherine as the family's leading actress, but this may have been a question of Catherine

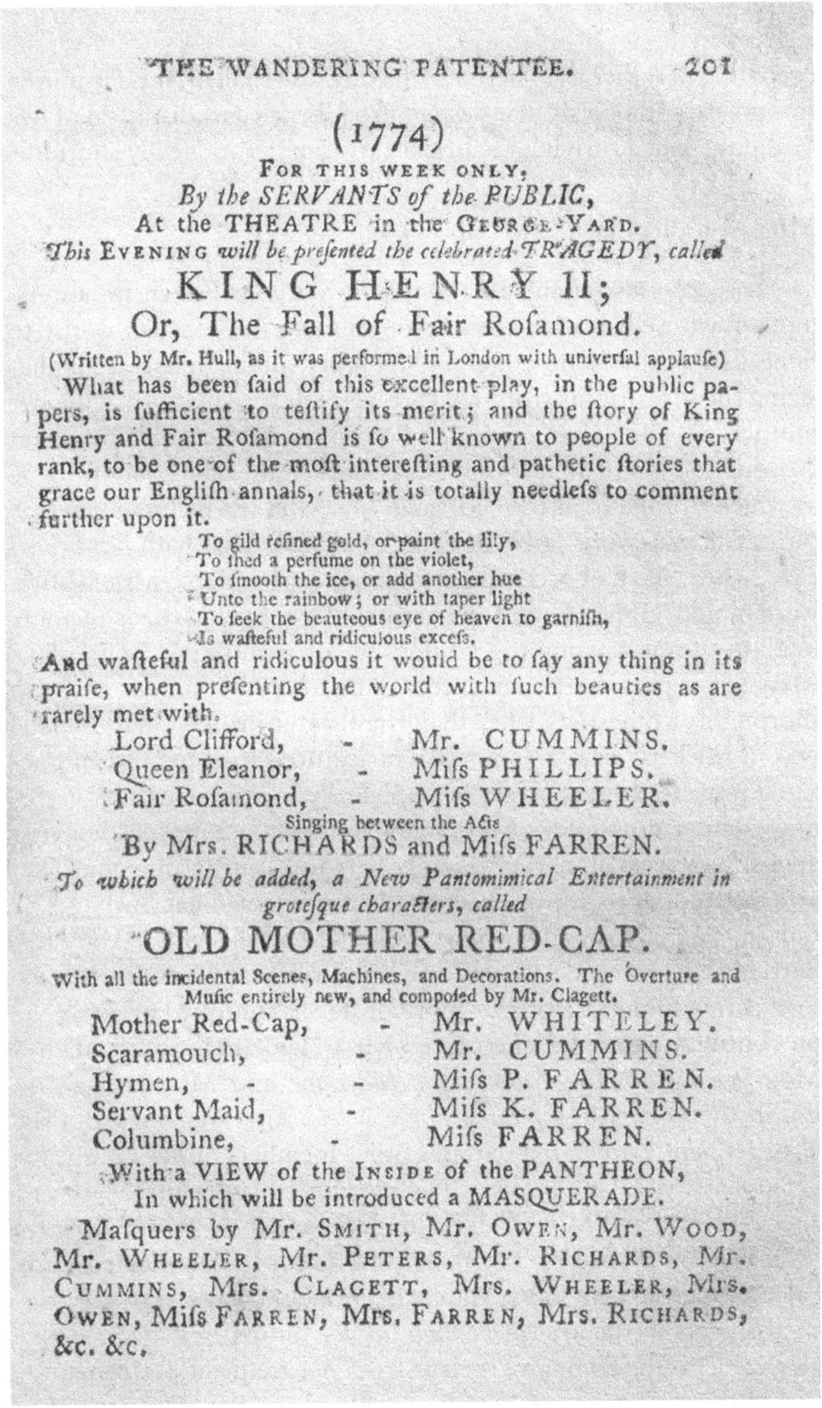

(1774)

FOR THIS WEEK ONLY,

By the SERVANTS of the PUBLIC,

At the THEATRE in the GEORGE-YARD.

This EVENING *will be preſented the celebrated TRAGEDY, called*

KING HENRY II;

Or, The Fall of Fair Roſamond.

(Written by Mr. Hull, as it was performed in London with univerſal applauſe)

What has been ſaid of this excellent play, in the public papers, is ſufficient to teſtify its merit; and the ſtory of King Henry and Fair Roſamond is ſo well known to people of every rank, to be one of the moſt intereſting and pathetic ſtories that grace our Engliſh annals, that it is totally needleſs to comment further upon it.

To gild refined gold, or paint the lily,
To ſhed a perfume on the violet,
To ſmooth the ice, or add another hue
Unto the rainbow; or with taper light
To ſeek the beauteous eye of heaven to garniſh,
Is waſteful and ridiculous exceſs.

And waſteful and ridiculous it would be to ſay any thing in its praiſe, when preſenting the world with ſuch beauties as are rarely met with.

Lord Clifford, - Mr. CUMMINS.
Queen Eleanor, - Miſs PHILLIPS.
Fair Roſamond, - Miſs WHEELER.

Singing between the Acts

By Mrs. RICHARDS and Miſs FARREN.

To which will be added, a New Pantomimical Entertainment in groteſque characters, called

OLD MOTHER RED-CAP.

With all the incidental Scenes, Machines, and Decorations. The Overture and Muſic entirely new, and compoſed by Mr. Clagett.

Mother Red-Cap, - Mr. WHITELEY.
Scaramouch, - Mr. CUMMINS.
Hymen, - - Miſs P. FARREN.
Servant Maid, - Miſs K. FARREN.
Columbine, - Miſs FARREN.

With a VIEW of the INSIDE of the PANTHEON,
In which will be introduced a MASQUERADE.

Maſquers by Mr. SMITH, Mr. OWEN, Mr. WOOD, Mr. WHEELER, Mr. PETERS, Mr. RICHARDS, Mr. CUMMINS, Mrs. CLAGETT, Mrs. WHEELER, Mrs. OWEN, Miſs FARREN, Mrs. FARREN, Mrs. RICHARDS, &c. &c.

Figure 4. Playbill for a 1774 performance featuring all of the Farren women (from Tate Wilkinson's *Wandering Patentee*). Courtesy of Rare Books and Special Collections, McGill University Library, Montreal.

becoming ill rather than her sister having more talent. It is clear even from the scant records that despite Broadbent's curt dismissal of her, Catherine had a thriving theatrical career in her tragically short life.

Mrs. Margaret Farren's "Tin Pocket"

Anecdotes also circulated about Mrs. Margaret Farren, the sisters' mother, whose behavior attracted attention after Elizabeth's rise to fame. These stories are not complimentary, aiming again at emphasizing the low origins from which Elizabeth rose by portraying her mother as somewhat uncouth. Petronius Arbiter recounts that George Colman (manager of the Haymarket, the first London venue at which Elizabeth performed) gave Margaret the nickname of "tin pocket" as she wore "a Pocket lined with *Tin*, filled with *hot boiled Beef*, which she had procured at a Shop near hand. . . . Mrs. F afterwards told COLMAN that she had the Pocket made so, as the only method of not wasting the *Gravy* she got with the *Meat*."[64] Thus Margaret is presented as an eccentric figure, parsimonious and also thoroughly domestic, rather than the theater professional that she was in her early career. Colman's caricature seems to be manufactured in order to embarrass her upwardly mobile daughter. Petronius Arbiter downplays Margaret's acting, claiming that her first appearance was "in a very humble part in Comedy on some Theatre in Lancashire, to which she had accompanied her husband."[65] But in Younger's company at Manchester, the elder Margaret Farren played a wide variety of comic roles and could often be seen acting alongside one or more of her daughters. For example, on February 19, 1777, she played Mrs. Heidelberg to Elizabeth's Miss Sterling in *The Clandestine Marriage* and Mrs. Drugget to Elizabeth's Dimity in the farce *Three Weeks After Marriage*. But she also frequently appeared without other members of her family, for example as Mrs. Credulous in *The Scheming Lieutenant* (March 17 and 21, 1777) and Miss Bridget Pumpkin in *All the World's a Stage* (March 6 and April 1, 1778). Furthermore, she also acted Lady Falconbridge in *King John* (March 8, 1776) and was one of the principal singers in the afterpiece *The Jubilee* on multiple occasions.[66] Her value to the company is clear from her frequent performances and range of parts.

Figure 5. Matthias Darly, *Miss^s. Dumplin Ducktail and Tittup Return'd From Watering*, 1778. Courtesy of The Lewis Walpole Library, Yale University.

Because of her connection with the Earl of Derby, Elizabeth Farren was a frequent subject of graphic satire; as well as offering a view of Elizabeth, these images can also be read for what they tell us about her family. Although these visual representations of the other Farren women have hitherto not been of interest to theater historians, they in fact offer us a somewhat rare glimpse of regional actresses. A 1778 caricature, *Miss^s. Dumplin Ducktail and Tittup Return'd From Watering* by Matthias Darly (Figure 5), depicts three women, one of whom has been tentatively identified as Elizabeth Farren since Miss Tittup was a character in Garrick's *Bon Ton* that she frequently played.[67] The other women have so far remained anonymous, but their facial features bear some resemblance to each other, suggesting that they are a family. One of the women is visibly older than the other two and therefore might well be Mrs. Margaret Farren. The third woman would then be the younger Margaret Farren, who appeared at the Haymarket with Elizabeth in 1777 (although not in 1778, when this image was published). This image provides a rare glimpse of the Farren women together, although a satirical one, and shows how these regional actresses were regarded by Londoners. The satire on the women's acutely fashionable dress is amplified by knowledge that these three women had recently been transplanted to the capital from the backwaters of the provinces and might be seen to be trying too hard to fit in by adopting London fashions to the extreme.[68]

Another caricature in which Mrs. Margaret Farren appears provides a visual anecdote about her. *The Platonic Lovers* of 1784 depicts "Lord Doodle" (that is, the Earl of Derby) and "Miss Tittup" (Elizabeth Farren) in a box, "with her Mamma at an humble distance."[69] This image refers to the long period before the death of Derby's wife in which his apparently platonic relationship with Elizabeth was perpetually chaperoned by the actress's mother, often to society's amusement, in order to avoid any accusations of impropriety.[70] Margaret here appears again in the context of Elizabeth's life, her own acting career obscured by her daughter's social rise. Like textual anecdotes, the visual ones found in caricature can also be used to shape the public's image of their subjects, often by means of personal insult and classist critique of the figure of the regional actress.

This chapter's exploration of the multiple anecdotes surrounding the Farren family highlights how problematic this type of source can be but also reveals the possibilities this material offers for reconstructing the history of women's involvement in regional theater. Elizabeth Farren's story is often told as a tale of her overcoming her low origins (her alcoholic father and her unsophisticated early performances in the regions) to become a London star, which subsequently allowed her to marry into the nobility. But placing Elizabeth in the context of her family reveals a different story. Her mother, Margaret, was highly professional, as were her sisters, Catherine and Margaret. Rather than being an inconvenience to overcome, Elizabeth's regional origins contributed greatly to her success in the capital, as it was in towns such as Bath, Derby, Manchester, and Liverpool that Elizabeth learned her craft. Anecdotes about the Farren sisters occasionally attempt to obscure this fact but ultimately reinforce its importance by emphasizing the women's careers outside the capital. Anecdote and record are indeed mutually constitutive in significant and interesting ways.

Notes

Financial support for the archival research used in this chapter was provided by the Social Sciences and Humanities Research Council of Canada. An early version of this material was presented at the Canadian Society for Eighteenth-Century Studies annual meeting in October 2016. I am grateful to Lisa Freeman for presenting the paper on my behalf when I was unable to attend.

1. I first encountered this letter in R. J. Broadbent, "Annals of the Manchester Stage, 1735–1845," 3 vols., unpublished manuscript, Manchester Library Theatre Collection, 1:35–36. It also appears in R. J. Broadbent, "Elizabeth Farren, Countess of Derby," *Transactions of the Historic Society of Lancashire and Cheshire*, n.s., 25 (1910): 83–96. References in this chapter are to the latter as it is more easily accessible. The published version quotes another letter from "J. R.," apparently a friend of Margaret's, which similarly warns Margaret away from the theater and expresses the opposition of the writer's husband to association with anyone connected with the stage (88–91).

2. For details of Farren's life and career, see "Farren, Elizabeth, later Countess of Derby," in *A Biographical Dictionary of Actors, Actresses, Musicians, Dancers, Managers & Other Stage Personnel in London, 1660–1800*, ed. Philip H. Highfill Jr., Kalman A. Burnim, and Edward A. Langhans, vol. 5, *Eagan to Garrett* (Carbondale: Southern Illinois University Press, 1978), 160–175; Peter Thomson, "Farren [Farran], Elizabeth [married name Elizabeth Smith Stanley, Countess of Derby] (1759–1829), actress," *Oxford Dictionary of National Biography* online, Oxford University Press, 2004; Suzanne Bloxam, *Walpole's Queen of Comedy: A Biography of Elizabeth Farren, Countess of Derby* (Ashford, UK: Published privately by the author, 1988).

3. "Farren, Elizabeth," in *A Biographical Dictionary*, 160–161.

4. Mary Robinson's connection with the Prince of Wales and Dorothy Jordan's with the Duke of Clarence (later William IV) are the most famous contemporary examples of such relationships. Three pamphlets about Farren were published in 1797, the year of her marriage to Derby and retirement from the stage. Although presented as biographical, their full titles reveal other agendas. Petronius Arbiter's *Memoirs of the Present Countess of Derby, (Late Miss Farren); Including Anecdotes of Several Distinguished Persons . . . With a Postscript Extraordinary!* (London: H. D. Symonds, 1797) hints at scandal; Scriptor Veritatis's *Memoirs of the Present Countess of Derby, Rescued by Truth from the Assassinating Pen of Petronius Arbiter; and Proving the Stage, from the Patronage of the Most Exalted Personages, to Have Been Always Considered as a School for Morality* (London: Lee and Hurst, 1797) positions itself as an attempt to emphasize Elizabeth's virtue in response to the previous biographer's claims; and the anonymous *Testimony of Truth to Exalted Merit: Or, A Biographical Sketch of the Right Honourable The Countess of Derby; in Refutation of a False and Scandalous Libel* (London: George Cawthorn, 1797) also stresses the actress's innate purity.

5. "Lizzy Farren's Christmas Eves," *Gentleman's Magazine* (March 1855): 241–247.

6. Bloxam, *Walpole's Queen of Comedy*, 14.

7. Broadbent, "Elizabeth Farren," 86. I have been unable to trace this pamphlet in any library catalogue.

8. Broadbent, "Elizabeth Farren," 88.

9. Veritatis, *Memoirs of the Present Countess of Derby*, 1.

10. "Farren, Elizabeth," in *A Biographical Dictionary*, 162. The *Oxford Dictionary of National Biography*, however, does not reference this source.

11. Jacky Bratton, "Anecdote and Mimicry as History," in *New Readings in Theatre History* (Cambridge: Cambridge University Press, 2003), 95.

12. Paul Menzer, *Anecdotal Shakespeare: A New Performance History* (London: Bloomsbury Arden Shakespeare, 2015), 6, 3.

13. Thomas Postlewait, "The Criteria for Evidence: Anecdotes in Shakespearean Biography, 1709–2000," in *Theorizing Practice: Redefining Theatre History*, ed. W. B. Worthen and Peter Holland (Basingstoke, UK: Palgrave Macmillan, 2003), 65.

14. Arbiter, *Memoirs of the Present Countess of Derby*, 10, 11.

15. Arbiter, *Memoirs of the Present Countess of Derby*, 10–11.

16. Arbiter, *Memoirs of the Present Countess of Derby*, 11.

17. Arbiter, *Memoirs of the Present Countess of Derby*, 12.

18. Arbiter, *Memoirs of the Present Countess of Derby*, 12.

19. Scriptor Veritatis in fact complains about the Kembles "monopolizing every claim to public favor in the Theatrical Line," Veritatis, *Memoirs of the Present Countess of Derby*, 33.

20. Veritatis, *Memoirs of the Present Countess of Derby*, 20.

21. Veritatis, *Memoirs of the Present Countess of Derby*, 34.

22. *Monthly Mirror: Reflecting Men and Manners. With Strictures on their Epitome, the Stage*, (July 1801): 57.

23. *Salisbury and Winchester Journal* (July 29, 1765). See also James Winston, *The Theatric Tourist*, facsimile of the first edition of 1805, ed. Iain Mackintosh, introduction by Marcus Risdell (London: Society for Theatre Research and the British Library, 2008), 64; Arnold Hare, *The Georgian Theatre in Wessex* (London: Phoenix House, 1958), 61–62.

24. *County Magazine* (March 1787): 239. The *Biographical Dictionary* erroneously gives the title of the source as the *Country Magazine* ("Farren, Elizabeth," 161). The entry on Joseph Younger, a manager with whom Elizabeth was later associated, claims that Elizabeth had appeared at Salisbury in 1773, but no further details are given and I have been unable to trace this performance. "Younger, Joseph," in Highfill, Burnim, and Langhans, *A Biographical Dictionary of Actors, Actresses, Musicians, Dancers, Managers & Other Stage Personnel in London, 1660–1800*, vol. 16, *West to Zwingman*, 366.

25. Winston, *The Theatric Tourist*, 51. He goes on to claim that Liverpool manager Joseph Younger employed the whole family and then "brought [Elizabeth] out at *Covent Garden*, at which Theatre he was Prompter." This account neglects the Farrens' early performances with Carleton and Whitley in Derby and Manchester (which will be discussed later) and skips over Elizabeth's time at the Haymarket. However, the *Derby Mercury* for June 24, 1774, attests that George Alexander Stevens did perform his *Lecture Upon Heads* (a satire on the current

interest in physiognomy) in Derby. The Farrens may have seen this performance while they were in that area.

26. *Testimony of Truth*, 15.

27. *Testimony of Truth*, 16.

28. *Manchester Mercury* (April 5, 1774. All details of the performance given here are taken from this announcement. The identity of the Widow Howard is unknown, but the fact that the Farrens' benefit performance was linked with hers suggests that it was designed to relieve the financial distresses of Mrs. Farren, also a widow. Nevertheless, Margaret Farren had been raising her daughters alone for about three years by this point.

29. This is probably the song in praise of Shakespeare by Charles Dibdin that was sung at David Garrick's 1769 Jubilee and in the afterpiece of that name that became popular on the London stage. See *Songs, Chorusses, &c. Which Are Introduced in the New Entertainment of the Jubilee, at the Theatre Royal, in Drury Lane* (London: T. Becket and P. A. De Hondt, 1769), 9–10.

30. *Manchester Mercury* (April 12, April 19, April 26, 1774).

31. *Manchester Mercury* (April 19, 26 April 26, 1774.

32. Broadbent, "Elizabeth Farren," 92.

33. See Arnold Hare, ed., *Theatre Royal Bath: A Calendar of Performances at the Orchard Street Theatre 1750–1805* (Bath: Kingsmead Press, 1977). Newspaper records suggest that these actresses were Margaret Farren and her daughter Elizabeth. See the *Bath and Bristol Chronicle*, November 9 and December 28, 1769; *Bath Chronicle*, January 31, 1771. There is, however, no mention of George Farren in the Bath calendar, although he does not seem to have died until around 1770. The Orchard Street Theatre in Bath was awarded a royal patent in 1768, one of the first playhouses outside London to be so designated.

34. *Walker's Hibernian Magazine* (July 1794): 1.

35. *Walker's Hibernian Magazine* (July 1794): 2.

36. *Walker's Hibernian Magazine* (July 1794): 2.

37. Scriptor Veritatis reminds us that the borrowing of stage properties from other performers was in fact "a thing practised every day in the Green-room." Veritatis, *Memoirs of the Present Countess of Derby*, 15.

38. "Knight, Mrs. Thomas, Margaret, née Farren," in Highfill, Burnim, and Langhans, *A Biographical Dictionary of Actors, Actresses, Musicians, Dancers, Managers & Other Stage Personnel in London, 1660–1800*, vol. 9, *Kickill to Machin*, 67–68.

39. "Knight, Mrs. Thomas, Margaret, née Farren," in *A Biographical Dictionary*, 68.

40. "Knight, Thomas," in *A Biographical Dictionary*, 63. The *Whitehall Evening Post* for August 1, 1795, does indeed make a brief report of this nature.

41. Performance announcements in the *Manchester Mercury* cast Margaret as various fantastical characters including Cupid in *A Trip to Scotland* (November 21, 1775; December 17, 1776) and Sylph in *Harlequin Dr Faustus* (January 7, 1777; January 14, 1777; February 11, 1777; January 6, 1778). The paper also announced her in various young boy roles such as Edward the Black Prince in *The Installation; or, The Institution of the Knights of the Garter* (March 4,

1777), Robin in *The Merry Wives of Windsor* (December 16, 1777), Lucius in *Julius Caesar* (March 3, 1778), and the Duke of York in *The Royal Martyr* (March 24, 1778).

42. Margaret is listed several times both as a Lilliputian in David Garrick's *Lilliput* and as Titania in George Colman's *The Fairy Tale* in the summer of 1777. London performance information is taken from the *London Stage* ,*Database* https://londonstagedatabase.uoregon.edu/.

43. Tate Wilkinson, *The Wandering Patentee*, 4 vols (York: Wilson, Spence, and Mawman, 1795), 2:267.

44. Wilkinson, *The Wandering Patentee*, 3:202.

45. *Morning Chronicle* (September 26, 1795).

46. Highfill, Burnim, and Langhans, "Knight, Mrs. Thomas," 68; T[homas] Harral, *A Monody on the Death of John Palmer* (London: George Cawthorn, 1798), 11. The *Biographical Dictionary* entry also quotes Harral's assessment, making it puzzling that the authors assume Margaret was dismissed from the theater.

47. *Sporting Magazine* (April 1797): 382.

48. Margaret's husband remained at Covent Garden until 1804, when he departed to become the manager of the Theatre Royal Liverpool. He sometimes acted in the provinces during the summer seasons, including with his wife. The *Biographical Dictionary* posits that they may have temporarily separated. Highfill, Burnim, and Langhans, "Knight, Mrs. Thomas," 68.

49. Wilkinson, *The Wandering Patentee*, 2:126.

50. *The Monthly Mirror* (September 1799): 181.

51. Highfill, Burnim, and Langhans, "Knight, Mrs. Thomas," 67, 68. The entry also lists many other roles that she played over the course of her career.

52. Broadbent, "Elizabeth Farren," 84.

53. Quoted in Highfill, Burnim, and Langhans, "Knight, Mrs. Thomas," 68, from a letter to Edward Jerningham of May 4, 1788, held at the Huntington Library.

54. Broadbent, "Elizabeth Farren," 84.

55. Broadbent, "Elizabeth Farren," 84. Broadbent puts these words in quotation marks but does not cite a source. Perhaps he is presenting this opinion as a popular piece of wisdom.

56. Highfill, Burnim, and Langhans, "Farren, Elizabeth," 161.

57. *Manchester Mercury* (April 5, 1774).

58. *Derby Mercury* (February 12, 1773). This Carleton was apparently John Boles Watson, later manager of an impressive theatrical circuit centered on Cheltenham. Lesley Phillips, *The Eccentric Mr Whitley* (N.p.: Independently published, 2017), 93.

59. Elizabeth Farren's year of birth is variously given as 1759, 1761, and 1762 (Thomson, "Farren [Farran], Elizabeth"). Thus in 1773 Elizabeth would have been between eleven and fourteen years old, Catherine necessarily a year or two younger, and Margaret younger than that. None of the sources I have consulted give birthdates for Catherine or Margaret, and there is often confusion between the sisters. Petronius Arbiter states that Catherine was the oldest sister, but he is

unreliable as he also confuses her with Margaret, claiming that it was Kitty who married Thomas Knight (*Memoirs of the Present Countess of Derby*, 11). It is therefore unclear whether his comment that "Miss KITTY FARREN's (now Mrs. Knight) chief merit lay in the performance of pert Chambermaids and giddy Girls" is about Catherine or Margaret (14). Petronius Arbiter seems to have taken these details, along with others, from an earlier biographical account of Elizabeth. See Joseph Haslewood, *The Secret History of the Green Room*, 2nd ed., 3 vols. (London: H. D. Symonds, 1792), 1:274–281.

60. *Derby Mercury* (August 26, September 30, October 7, October 28, November 25, and December 23, 1774).

61. Wilkinson, *The Wandering Patentee*, 1:201.

62. Broadbent, "Elizabeth Farren," 92.

63. Sources for details of these performances are as follows: Victor J. Price, *Birmingham Theatres: Concert and Music Halls, 1740–1988* (Studley, Warwickshire: Brewin Books, 1988), 1; *Manchester Mercury* (December 12, October 17, November 21, 1775; February 13, May 19, 1776); "Liverpool Playbills: Drury Lane 1767–71, Theatre Royal 1773–77," Liverpool Record Office.

64. Arbiter, *Memoirs of the Present Countess of Derby*, 16.

65. Arbiter, *Memoirs of the Present Countess of Derby*, 10.

66. See the performance announcements in the *Manchester Mercury* (March 5, 1776; February 18, March 11, March 18, 1777; March 3, March 31, 1778).

67. Mary Dorothy George, *Catalogue of Political and Personal Satires Preserved in the Department of Prints and Drawings in The British Museum*, vol. 5, *1771–1783* (Printed by order of the trustees, 1935), #5518. Elizabeth Farren first acted the part at the Haymarket on August 18, 1777, and performed the role a further sixty times in London until October 17, 1796, just before her retirement. Miss Tittup was, then, a character particularly identified with the actress.

68. George details the fashionable elements of the Farrens' dress in this image and suggests that they are exaggerated for satiric effect. George, *Catalogue of Political and Personal Satires*, vol. 5, #5518.

69. Mary Dorothy George, *Catalogue of Political and Personal Satires Preserved in the Department of Prints and Drawings in The British Museum*, vol. 6, *1784–1792* (Printed by Order of the Trustees, 1938), #6714.

70. The author of the *Testimony of Truth* assures the reader that "it is an indisputed fact, that she [Elizabeth] never admitted her Lordship to any interview, unless Mrs. FARREN was present" (31).

8

NEITHER CONFIRMED NOR REFUTED

The Anecdotal Elizabeth Barry

SETH WILSON

According to a quotation in *The Dictionary of Modern Proverbs*, "The plural of the word anecdote is not data."[1] Despite its suspect nature as hard evidence, many scholars have effectively argued for the anecdote's value as a vessel for establishing ideological or socio-cultural context for a given period.[2] As Diana Solomon has pointed out, anecdotal evidence can be a valuable source for figures that have been marginalized in the archival record. She warns, however, that historians must be extremely careful in drawing on anecdotes, which could contribute to further marginalization.[3] Scholars of the Restoration era are all too familiar with the sweeping generalizations that can come from reliance on anecdotal evidence.

The long-standing image of the period is that of a theater staging suggestive, licentious plays offered for the delectation of a debased, aristocratic audience. Positioned at the center of this debauched carnival is the nascent English actress, the most visible symbol of the supposed corruption of the age. With the introduction of women to the public stage, so the story goes, the high-minded drama of the previous age collapsed into sex-fueled romps, mirrored by a riotous crowd enjoying these women onstage and off. The early English actress has regularly been described as mercenary, sexually rapacious, and vain.[4]

As Laura Rosenthal has pointed out, the actress represented a threat to established values about gender and class.[5] Despite this, in relatively short order, the new class of professional actresses displaced the boy players from the previous generation and became a permanent feature of the English stage.[6] In this chapter, I argue that the pervasiveness of salacious anecdotes in histories of the stage framed actresses, individually and collectively, as possessing undesirable, unfeminine qualities. To make this case, I look at three anecdotes that have followed Elizabeth Barry, the first star actress of the English stage, in historiographical sources on her life: first, that she was trained for the stage by her lover, the Earl of Rochester; second, that she jealously stabbed a rival actress onstage one night to settle an offstage dispute; and third, that she died of rabies contracted from her lapdog. Each of these anecdotes shows Barry, variously, as exhibiting sexual voraciousness, greed, violence, and pretense to undue class privilege.

By equating the image of the actress with defective femininity, anecdotes curbed the potential of the actress to completely disrupt societal norms about class and gender.[7] Even if middle- and lower-class women attained fame and economic independence through acting, ribald anecdotes prevented them from thoroughly destabilizing traditional categories because they were pilloried as inherently incapable of decorous femininity.

Barry was a prime target for these kinds of attacks: as a woman from a modest background who rose to unprecedented levels of fame and fortune through her acting, she was a model of how profitable a stage career could prove. Moreover, she remained unmarried but carried on multiple high-profile romantic relationships during her life with men from both the aristocratic and common ranks. Barry was exactly the type of woman who constituted a threat to the traditional social order. She was independently wealthy, famous, respected for her mastery of her craft, and she engaged in nonmarital sexual liaisons across class lines.

Anecdotes that depicted Barry in an unflattering light could prevent her from becoming an aspirational figure. By branding the first highly successful actress as corrupt, these anecdotes showed the moral cost of her profession's material benefits. No matter how respected professionally, actresses could always be attacked through salacious details about their personal lives. Furthermore, anecdotes are effective vehicles for this kind of character assassination. Joseph

Roach notes that performance historiography has evinced a long-standing interest in the prurient, observing that "theatre history [is] usually supine before the lurid charms of anecdote."[8] Similarly, Malina Stefanovska has argued that anecdotes tend to remain in circulation because they are interesting; they manage to capture the imagination of a reader even as they resist easy interpretation.[9]

Before looking at the specific examples pertaining to Barry, I want to establish a definition of "anecdote" for the present discussion. Lionel Gossman has pointed out that anecdotes have a three-act structure, making them compelling micronarratives.[10] Moreover, they function "as particular instances exemplifying and confirming a general rule or trend or epitomizing a larger general situation."[11] The anecdotal is often marshaled inductively to support broad conclusions about a given era. Similarly, Joel Fineman argues that they are a hybridized literary-historical genre that "uniquely *lets history happen* by virtue of the way it introduces an opening into the teleological . . . narration of beginning, middle, and end."[12] By providing a digestible data point, an anecdote allows a reader entry into the ideological worldview of a historical period. In work focusing on the Restoration era, Kirsten Pullen has shown that anecdotes, through repetition in historical sources, acquire archival authority though they begin as orally circulated ephemera.[13] The more often a case is repeated, the more it gains the veneer of fact. Solomon has similarly noted that, although anecdotes are interesting, "when the purpose of sharing theatrical anecdotes is entertainment, then the line can blur between anecdote and gossip."[14] The interest that Stefanovska identifies as a key part of the anecdote is also its danger if the only purpose in its transmission is titillation.

To these observations, I add that anecdotes remain unverifiable as a part of their nature. Despite their unverifiability, they must be plausible in order to become accepted. Therefore, these accounts cannot be confirmed, but they also cannot be definitively refuted. I argue that because of their salacious intrigue, they have gained a historical traction that has given them the weight of fact when they may represent something far closer to gossip. Because they are not strictly factual statements, I see them as performative in the sense of an Austinian speech act.[15] All of the anecdotes I examine here play on transgressive behavior and perform the action of establishing

Barry as aberrant and without virtue. They do not quite "let history happen," as Fineman says, but rather establish a historical narrative performatively, by inscribing on Barry the larger cultural position she was presumed a priori to represent. Further, in each case, the narrative quality of the anecdote is underscored by a symbolic, metaphorical detail.

For each case, I will point to the anecdote in its earliest traceable source, and then chart a history of its recurrence. I will then offer factual reasons for skepticism about it, and end by arguing for its symbolic and performative action. Their frequent recurrence inseparably integrates them into Barry's biography. Each repetition that does not identify the original source obscures the fact that these anecdotes were added to her life story well after her death. Existing in sources alongside archivally verifiable information like her salary and the roles she played, these anecdotes present superficially as factual. In actuality, the anecdotal information frames Barry's transgression of boundaries without revealing factually true information about her work or life. In doing so, anecdotes circumscribe a cultural position for her that is inherently in violation of traditional values.

Barry and Rochester

Elizabeth Barry was likely born sometime between 1656 and 1658. Her father appears to have been a lawyer who lost his fortune fighting for the Royalist forces in the English Civil Wars, forcing him to abandon his children. The young Elizabeth was adopted by the Davenant family, which led to William Davenant introducing her to the stage with the Duke's Company in the mid-1670s. Her early forays into the acting profession were apparently disastrous, as she was fired at the end of her first season. She eventually overcame her early deficiencies to become the first great English actress, both artistically and economically. She played major roles in both comedy and tragedy—her forte—from 1677 to her retirement in 1710. Many of the great tragic roles of the era were written for her, including Belvidera in *Venice Preserv'd* and Isabella in *The Fatal Marriage*. She was a massive star whose work as a performer not only reshaped the theatrical landscape of her day but also exerted an influence on the genre of drama as well. Given her unparalleled skill at tragedy, she was the motivating force behind the development of the she-tragedy subgenre, as writers sought to create roles that would capitalize on her abilities.[16] By the mid-1690s, she had a weekly income of fifty shillings and an annual benefit performance that guaranteed her a minimum of seventy pounds.[17] In 1693, she was well enough off from her stage career to lend Alexander Davenant four hundred pounds in exchange for a share in the United Company, making her the first woman to achieve shareholder status. In the early 1700s, after she and Thomas Betterton led the secession from Christopher Rich's management of the United Company, her annual salary was approximately one hundred and fifty pounds, second only to Betterton himself. Moreover, she was Betterton's second-in-command in the management of the company. For a woman from an impoverished family, Barry rose to an incredible level of fame and wealth.[18]

Offstage, she remained unmarried throughout her life, though she carried on multiple affairs. She was probably the mistress of George Etherege and possibly Sir Henry St. John, among others. Among her earliest and most well documented relationships, however, was her liaison with John Wilmot, the Earl of Rochester. As their correspondence indicates, the two of them were romantically involved, and she had a daughter with him in 1677.[19] Though Rochester died in 1680 before Barry reached the apex of her fame, he found his way into her biography as not just her lover but the author of her success.[20]

Well after both Barry and Rochester were dead, the bookseller Edmund Curll wrote *The History of the English Stage* (1741). The book, purportedly Thomas Betterton's autobiography and featuring descriptions of many of his contemporaries, is really more a collection of unsubstantiated rumors and anecdotes.[21] In his *History*, Curll claims that Barry was fired not just once but three times, but each time Mrs. Davenant intervened on her behalf to have her try again. He says Barry finally broke through thanks to the interventions of Rochester. According to the anecdote, the earl's friends saw Barry act, and they all remarked that she would never succeed onstage. In order "to shew them he had a Judgment superiour," Rochester made a wager that he could make her the greatest English actress within six months of training.[22] As Barry's principal problem was allegedly a bad ear and an inability to speak verse properly, audiences and even other company members thought she was unintelligent. Rochester, however, could tell his pupil "was Mistress of a very good Understanding" despite her poor versifying.[23] To combat her weakness, the earl invented a new style of acting for Barry: "he made her Rehearse near 30 times on the Stage, and about 12 in the Dress she was to Act it in. He took such extraordinary Pains with her, as not to omit the least Look or Motion . . . he made her enter into the Nature of each Sentiment; perfectly changing herself, as it were, into the Person, not merely by the proper Stress or Sounding of the Voice, but feeling really, and being in the Humour, the Person she represented, was supposed to be in."[24]

The anecdote is persuasive, as it offers a clear, concise explanation for Barry's command of emotion. Further adding to its believability is the high degree of specificity Curll offers. The numerical details—rehearsing almost thirty times onstage and about a dozen in her costume—lend credence to the account. Rather than a general account of Rochester's methods, the anecdote persuades the reader by offering concrete detail.

Not only is the anecdote highly detailed, it also contains a compelling, titillating narrative: Curll suggests that the two of them began their romantic relationship while Rochester trained Barry, a secret the earl kept from his friends. After refashioning Barry, the anecdote says that Rochester invited not only his friends with whom he had laid the wager but also the Duke and Duchess of York (later James II and his wife Mary of Modena) to the theater to see her play Isabelle in Orrery's *Mustapha*. To the surprise of everyone except the earl, Barry was triumphant. Curll reports that "these Passions were so finely expressed by her, that the whole Theatre resounded with Applauses."[25] The duchess was so impressed that she gave Barry her wedding dress for future performances.[26] Thus, according to Curll, the Earl of Rochester is supposed to have launched the first great English actress by shaping her raw ability into a finely wrought power.

The legend of Rochester's training has doggedly followed Barry in almost every source concerning her, even by authors who seem to respect her achievement as an actress. Although the anecdote does not appear in Colley Cibber's writing on Barry in his *Apology*, Anthony Aston added it to the supplement he published around

1747, saying that "Lord Rochester took her on the stage, where for some time they could make nothing of her."[27] Roughly forty years later, Thomas Davies reiterated the anecdote in his stage history, *Dramatic Miscellanies*, nearly verbatim from Curll.[28] John Genest's comprehensive study *Some Account of the English Stage from the Restoration in 1660 to 1830* also repeats it, though he notes that Curll is somewhat unreliable as a source. Genest further points out that Curll must be mistaken about the timeline of events, as he claimed that Rochester used the role of Hellena in *The Rover* as a part of Barry's training, though Barry almost certainly created that role herself when the play debuted in 1677.[29] Edmund Bellchamber, in his biographical notes from the 1822 edition of Colley Cibber's *Apology*, agrees that Barry had a "criminal intimacy with the Earl of Rochester," but says, "I am not inclined, while doubting the precise anecdote of his assistance, to deny that much advantage might have been derived from his general instructions."[30] Genest's and Bellchamber's small objections offer the only resistance to the anecdote of Rochester's formative tutelage of Barry.

By the late nineteenth and early twentieth centuries, stage historians had taken to editorializing about Barry based on the anecdote. John Doran contradicts Curll's claims about her native intelligence in his reportage: "While the flash of her light eyes beneath her dark hair and brows was as yet mere girlish spirit it was not intelligence. *That* was given her by Rochester."[31] John Fyvie, acknowledging that Barry's accomplishments as an actress are unimpeachable, tells the reader that "in her private life she carried on the licentious tradition of the Restoration."[32] Fyvie later notes that Cibber's account does not mention Rochester but says that is "by no means inconsistent" with Curll's without fully explaining why.[33] He then proceeds to draw on her involvement with Rochester to say of Barry that "her shameless immorality was notoriously of the most mercenary character."[34] Henry Wysham Lanier's book on the early English actresses, a project that seems sympathetic to its subjects, nevertheless repeats the anecdote wholesale, likening it to a mythic story: "It was at first another Pygmalion trying to carve responsiveness, or at least the appearance of it, out of a human block."[35]

Modern scholars have treated the Rochester anecdote with varying levels of skepticism. In the first attempt at a programmatic, scholarly analysis of the first English actresses, John Harold Wilson recounts it as true with no further analysis, attributing her success to the earl.[36] The *Biographical Dictionary* says "this may be partly true" when recounting the anecdote, but also notes that she might have received some of her training from William Davenant's son Charles.[37] The entry on Barry in the *Oxford Dictionary of National Biography* repeats the anecdote with no commentary encouraging skepticism.[38] In her book on historical rehearsal practices, Tiffany Stern repeats the anecdote in a fairly straightforward way but notes that individual instruction of that type would have been unusual in the period.[39] Elizabeth Howe's book on English actresses, the best historical analysis of their impact, cites Curll on the legend of Barry's training but qualifies the reliability of the account by saying, "Curll's biographical facts, supposedly culled from Betterton's notes, may be shaky in that they seem to be based largely on hearsay and gossip."[40] A recent article by Kate C. Hamilton points out the numerous inconsistencies in the anecdote, essentially debunking it, but arguing that Barry found it useful professionally to play on her well-known connection to Rochester.[41] Robert D. Hume and Judith Milhous dismiss it outright as "anecdotal tarradiddle."[42]

Ample reasons exist for such a dismissal. Hume has also noted that Curll's list of training roles for her would have been impossible, and he and Treglown both agree that the timeline makes it highly implausible that Rochester would have been available and in London for the six months of the alleged training.[43] Curll's support for the anecdote's truth is not particularly convincing. He describes the source for his information on Barry vaguely as "some particular Memoirs, relating to her, we have been favoured with by a Gentlewoman, her most intimate Friend."[44] Moreover, although Rochester was a playwright and theatergoer, that does not mean that he had enough command over the highly technical period acting style to instruct a beginner.[45] Curll was an extremely unreliable hack writer, known for making up details wholesale and falsely attributing them to his subjects.[46] Crucially, the Rochester anecdote is not in Cibber's *Apology*. His description of her early difficulties is as follows: "I take it for granted that the Objection to Mrs. Barry at that time must have been a defective Ear, or some unskillful Dissonance in her manner of pronouncing: But where there is a proper Voice and Person, with the

Addition of a good Understanding, Experience tells us that such Defect is not always invincible."[47] Cibber tells us that Barry succeeded because of her natural intelligence and perseverance. As he knew her personally and worked alongside her for some time, I take his account to be far more reliable than Curll's, which was written nearly thirty years after Barry's death. While the anecdote cannot be disproven definitively, it is highly unlikely that Rochester had much of anything to do with Barry's successes.[48]

Notably, biographies of Rochester accept the anecdote uncritically and depict Barry in explicitly degrading terms, often making hay from the class difference between the two. James William Jonson returns to the mythical metaphor, arguing, "The gauche and seemingly untalented girl became a Galatea to his Pygmalion; during their first months of cohabitating, he coached her in the tricks of acting, imparting to her the secrets of feminine charm and coquetry he instinctively knew."[49] R. E. Pritchard calls Barry a predatory drain on the poor earl: "Convalescing and away from Barry, he was lax in providing her with what she wanted: money."[50] The most aggressively anti-Barry line is taken up by Jeremy Lamb. Drawing on Curll's claim that Rochester never loved anyone as much as he did Barry, Lamb says, "That such a dangerous-sounding woman was the object of his greatest passion was peculiarly apt and characteristically self-punitive."[51] When Rochester is centered in the narrative, Barry's training is construed as an exploitation of the earl's largesse, with the actress taking his tutelage and his money before leaving him to waste away. As she ascended to fame and fortune and he died, these accounts suggest she usurped his social position. Rochester was nearly a decade older than Barry and from a radically different level of privilege; their relationship had an inherent power imbalance. In biographies of the earl, however, the actress is depicted as a parasite looking to exploit his class prerogatives for her own gain.

Obviously, the alleged training mitigates Barry's agency by attributing her remarkable career to the intervention of a male genius.[52] I suggest, however, that it does not completely deprive Barry of agency but rather shows that sexuality was her primary form of power. Whether Rochester made the alleged wager to train her because he saw potential in her or out of a supreme confidence in his ability to mold even the most rank amateur into a star, the two eventually became romantically involved. Their affair is historically verifiable, but the training anecdote allows readers sympathetic to Rochester or inclined to disdain Barry to cast the relationship as transactional for Barry. In the readings offered by Fyvie and Rochester's biographers, Barry uses her wiles in an acquisitive way to gain the dramatic training necessary for fame. She exploits her sexuality for economic gain, which figures her as a glorified prostitute. Thus, while she was not here the author of her own artistic success, she was able to influence even a well-educated aristocrat with her sexual power.

Further, Johnson's reading of the anecdote and Rochester's imparting "the secrets of feminine charm and coquetry he instinctively knew" show that the actress lacked an inherent femininity.[53] Though she drew the earl in, he had to teach her appropriate behavior. Barry's inability to act well, especially in a theater that was dominated by upper-class characters and romantic plots, was a failure of her ability to conform to societal ideals about what constituted womanhood. Only through Rochester's intervention was she able to transform herself. In her later career, Barry was renowned for her passionate and evocative emotional mastery. That virtuosity was allegedly the product of Rochester bypassing her inability to versify properly by stressing passion during her training. Barry's Galatean qualities marked her not as a guileless young woman but rather as an unschooled force of nature in need of shaping. Ultimately, the anecdote allows for the interpretation that her sublime and explosive nature subsumed Rochester himself.

Finally, Curll's remark about Barry receiving Mary of Modena's wedding clothes is an apt metaphor for the actress's designs on seizing aristocratic privilege that the anecdote implies. By the time Barry re-entered the theatrical world, she had so mastered the art of acting that her performance merited a prize. The reward—a royal set of wedding clothes—would obscure her lower-class origins. Though the anecdote asserts that she would not have received the dress without Rochester's assistance, Barry alone enjoyed the fruits of victory. Within the framework of the anecdote, then, the dress serves as a symbol of her striving to escape her own class as well as usurping Rochester's. The dress symbolically underscores the anecdote's presentation of Barry as a pretentious, calculating manipulator whose success was not her own doing. The story's close association with her throughout history has served as a check on her accomplishments as a professional performer.

Barry and Boutell

Curll's book was also responsible for another of the most enduring stories about Barry, alleging that she nearly murdered her fellow actress Elizabeth Boutell onstage during a performance of Nathaniel Lee's *The Rival Queens* (1677). He reports that the actresses had a backstage quarrel over a veil that the prop master had given Boutell. Barry felt that the veil was due to her instead. The conflict between the two infiltrated the drama when Barry, as Roxana, was supposed to stab Boutell's Statira. Curll says that "Roxana hastening the designed Blow, struck with such Force, that tho' the Point of the Dagger was blunted, it made way through Mrs. Boutel's [*sic*] Stayes, and entered about a Quarter of an Inch in the Flesh."[54] He then mentions that audiences gossiped that the actresses' quarrel had actually concerned Rochester before assuring the reader that "it was only the Veil these two Ladies contended for, and Mrs. Barry being warmed with anger, in her Part, she struck the Dagger with less Caution, than at other times."[55]

Although the stabbing has not been as frequently linked with Barry as the Rochester anecdote, it still turns up in a number of sources. Davies recounts it, playing up its sexual nature: "As it was well known these ladies were not vestals, it was reported jealousy gave force to the blow."[56] Doran embellishes it in his retelling, claiming that Boutell stirred Barry's anger up by gloating: "The lady was not moderate in her victory . . . flaunting the trophy too frequently before the eyes of the rival queen."[57] He does insist, like Curll, that the veil was the sole cause of the incident, as Rochester was dead by the time the play was performed and Barry would never have stooped to jealousy over Boutell's flirtations with the property man.[58] Fyvie also reprints the anecdote, noting the irony that Curll takes the role of Roxana to be emblematic of Barry's ability to control her "passions, for it was when acting as Roxana in *The Rival Queens* that she once so gave way to her own naturally violent passions as to come within an ace of murdering one of her rivals."[59] Allardyce

Nicoll uses the incident, which he describes as a "nearly fatal struggle," as evidence of the basely violent nature of the Restoration theater atmosphere, though he misidentifies Boutell as Bracegirdle.[60] Rosamond Gilder also repeats it, though she doesn't name the actresses. She does, however, claim that "the Court and Town gossiped for weeks over the latest scandal in the playhouse."[61] Wilson cites the anecdote as well, though he describes the coveted item as a "scarf," and it also appears in the *Biographical Dictionary*.[62]

The Barry–Boutell feud is likelier than the Rochester anecdote, but it still lacks definitive factual corroboration. Barry and Boutell are billed together only once in *The London Stage*, appearing in a revival of *Rule a Wife and Have a Wife* staged in 1696. This was Boutell's last recorded role.[63] Boutell had originated the part of Statira in the 1677 premiere of *The Rival Queens*. Barry could not have appeared opposite her at that time, as the play belonged to the King's Company, and Barry was a member of the Duke's. By 1690, Statira no longer belonged to Boutell, as Bracegirdle had taken the role over for the United Company.[64] Presumably, Barry and Boutell must have played opposite each other sometime between the formation of the United Company in 1682 and Bracegirdle's assumption of the role in 1690. Only one public performance of *The Rival Queens* is recorded during that span, however; it was performed in December of 1685 at Drury Lane. No cast list has survived for that performance. Of course, the records from this period are incomplete, and many performances that took place have been lost to history.[65] Perhaps Barry and Boutell squared off in the 1685 performance, or perhaps their battle took place on another night that escaped cataloguing. Still, the anecdote is unverifiable with our current records.

Felicity Nussbaum has argued that *The Rival Queens* is particularly generative of anecdotes because the plot, two women competing for the affections of Alexander the Great, allows the audience to draw parallels with the real-life actresses playing the roles.[66] In this case, the anecdote confirms the presumed arrogant pretensions of the actress. Particularly meaningful is Curll's positioning of Barry against Boutell. While Barry's life is comparatively well documented, Boutell's biographical details are far more obscure. Even her death date is unclear—the last documentary reference to her is in November of

1697 when she was given permission to join her soldier husband on campaign in the Netherlands.[67] Though Barry and Bracegirdle certainly played the two roles against one another (likely the source of Nicoll's confusion), the anecdote is less about historical accuracy than about characterizing Barry as overwhelmingly petty. Curll praises Barry's performance rapturously, noting that she ennobled the play. Before she played Roxana, he says, the character was a "perfect burlesque on the Dignity of Majesty."[68] Despite her ability to elevate the drama, however, he insists that she debased the theater with her violent act. She was not content to capture the admiration of the audience; she allegedly needed the veil as well.

To establish that Barry's attack on Boutell was particularly cruel and capricious, Curll emphasizes the latter's vulnerability. He describes Boutell as "a very considerable Actress," but said she was "low of Stature" with "a Childish Look. Her Voice was weak . . . she generally acted the young Innocent Lady."[69] Barry is characterized as grandiose and majestic, Boutell as weak and childlike. The diminution of Boutell makes Barry seem all the more villainous. Based on this description, Boutell could never have threatened Barry's position as a performer or a sex symbol.

The Boutell stabbing anecdote performatively marks Barry as vain and dangerous. When the star is denied some small trinket, she responds by violently punishing her hapless rival. Here again, she represents nothing like decorous behavior. As with the wedding dress, the veil becomes a metaphor for Barry's foibles. It represents her desire for complete superiority, especially in terms of sex appeal. Having exploited her sexuality to achieve stardom, Barry then jealously defended her position. Moreover, Curll claimed Boutell allegedly got the veil because the property man had feelings for her. As Barry rose to her powerful position through sexual allure, she apparently wanted to stamp out any competition for that type of attention. Not only was Curll's version of the actress sexually profligate for material gain—she would defend her territory against any rival, no matter how insignificant. Although the stabbing anecdote seems like a bit of juicy backstage gossip, it performs a noxious action on Barry's historical image, making her out to be a jealous psychopath.

Barry's Death

One final anecdote concerning Barry deserves mention, one that originated not with Curll but with Davies. He reports that, although Colley Cibber said she died of a fever, "her death was owing to the bite of a favourite lap-dog, who, unknown to her, had been seized with madness."[70] This anecdote is far less pervasive than the previous two, though it does recur. Bellchamber repeats it and says that there "seems to be no grounds for disturbing [Davies's] supposition."[71] Fyvie also relays the dog anecdote, specifying that the madness was rabies.[72] The authors of the *Biographical Dictionary* also mention that her death was attributed to the sick pet.[73]

The dog anecdote is the least plausible of the three, as there is concrete archival evidence against it. Davies contradicts not only Cibber's *Apology* but also Barry's official obituary in the *Post-Boy*, which corroborates that the actress "died lately of a fever."[74] As support for his own version of her death, Davies cites an anonymous "actress, who was in London when Mrs. Barry died."[75] The evidence to support Barry's rabid dog biting her is quite weak. Davies was born in 1712, one year before Barry passed.[76] He could not possibly have acquired this information firsthand, making it mere hearsay, as he himself admits.

At the time the *Dramatic Miscellanies* was published, debate flourished in England regarding the ethics of dog ownership. Those opposed to keeping pets argued against it on moral grounds, saying that a dog was a waste of resources that should properly be used on humans. Dogs were a symbol for wasteful luxury and aristocratic excess. Lapdogs specifically were argued to be symbolic of a disordered female sexuality. Women were supposed to bestow their affections on men, so the argument went, and giving attention to a pet lessened the affection available for suitors and husbands. Thus, dogs were regarded as a waste of both material and emotional resources, and a sign of aristocratic, feminine corruption that presented a challenge to the proper order of society.[77] The dog anecdote, then, recasts Barry's death as another example of her intransigence.

Davies's anecdote drops a dog into Barry's life story as a potent symbol of her pretension to aristocratic privilege. Drawing on a contemporary debate about feminine propriety, he retroactively depicts

Barry as engaging in all the worst aristocratic excesses. Moreover, as she had no husband or surviving children, the lapdog was the only object of affection in her life. A never-married woman living in economic comfort was inherently suspect, invoking the contemporary debate surrounding pets would have exacerbated the suspicion with which a reader might regard the retired actress.

In this anecdote, Barry suffers rather than inflicts harm. Although she was able to radically transform herself throughout her life into a famous, respected, and wealthy woman independent of masculine control, Davies's dog anecdote served as a warning about that type of transformation. By rewriting the account of her death to include a rabid dog, Davies shows that her actions had fatal consequences. The illness and death that she allegedly suffered from the dog bite enact a boundary on class-jumping. Barry became wealthy and famous, but ultimately those things undid her. The dog bite anecdote serves as a warning about unseemly behavior.

The dog anecdote, while not as obviously pernicious as that pertaining to Rochester's training or as violent as that concerning the stabbing, illustrates that anecdotes are not about history so much as narrative. The goal of anecdote was not to add accurate information to the body of knowledge about Barry but to use her as an example to delimit the social influence of the actress by inscribing boundaries on acceptable behavior. Although Barry rose to unprecedented heights of success during her life, her historiographical image has been shaped to serve ideological rather than historical ends. In the archival record, we can see Barry influencing drama, the craft of acting, and the economic possibilities of a stage career. The salacious anecdotes about her, while entertaining, tell us little about Barry or her work. They do, however, tell us a great deal about the world in which she worked and how hard it tried, even after her death, to demean her.

Notes

1. Wolfgang Mieder, Fred R. Shapiro, and Charles Clay Doyle, *The Dictionary of Modern Proverbs* (New Haven, CT: Yale University Press, 2012), 202.

2. For instance, anecdotes figure prominently in New Historicist criticism. For discussions of their usefulness in writing theater history, see Jacky Bratton, *New Readings in Theatre History* (Cambridge: Cambridge University Press, 2003), 95–132, and Thomas Postlewait, "The Criteria for Evidence: Anecdotes in

Shakespearean Biography, 1709–2000," in *Theorizing Practice: Redefining Theatre History*, ed. W. B. Worthen and Peter Holland (Basingstoke, UK: Palgrave Macmillan, 2003), 47–70.

3. Diana Solomon, "Anecdotes and Restoration Actresses: The Cases of Elizabeth Barry and Anne Bracegirdle," *Restoration and Eighteenth-Century Theatre Research* 31, no. 2 (Winter 2016): 20.

4. By way of example, consider Allardyce Nicoll's commentary on the first actresses: "Very few of those actresses lived chaste lives . . . we must be careful not to assume that they always aided unselfishly in the interpretation of the works of dramatic art. The majority must have thought more of a fine gown, or maybe a coach and pair, than of a fine play." Allardyce Nicoll, *A History of English Drama, 1660–1900*, 4th ed. (Cambridge: Cambridge University Press, 1967), 1:72. This assertion is made without any supporting evidence. Even more sympathetic studies promote this construction. In *Enter the Actress: The First Women in the Theatre* (Boston: Houghton Mifflin Company, 1931), Rosamond Gilder suggests that "the actresses were particularly difficult to control. They were forever dashing off on private business, handing over their parts to some more stolid sister who at the moment had no lover to divert her from her duties" (147).

5. Laura J. Rosenthal, "'Counterfeit Scrubbado': Women Actors in the Restoration," *Eighteenth Century: Theory and Interpretation* 34, no. 1 (Spring 1993): 3–22.

6. Elizabeth Howe, *The First English Actresses: Women and Drama, 1660–1700* (Cambridge: Cambridge University Press, 1992), 19–26.

7. Kathleen Wilson has argued that eighteenth-century British society regarded vulgarity, not masculinity, as the opposite of femininity. See *The Island Race: Englishness, Empire, and Gender in the Eighteenth Century* (New York: Routledge, 2003), 25–26.

8. Joseph Roach, "Power's Body: The Inscription of Morality as Style," in *Interpreting the Theatrical Past: Essays in the Historiography of Performance*, ed. Thomas Postlewait and Bruce A. McConachie (Iowa City: University of Iowa Press, 1989), 103.

9. Malina Stefanovska, "Exemplary or Singular? The Anecdote in Historical Narrative," *SubStance* 118, vol. 38, no. 1 (2009): 26–27.

10. Lionel Gossman, "Anecdote and History," *History and Theory* 42 (May 2003): 149.

11. Gossman, "Anecdote and History," 155.

12. Joel Fineman, "The History of the Anecdote: Fiction and Fiction," in *The New Historicism*, ed. H. Aram Veeser (New York: Routledge, 1989), 56–61.

13. Kirsten Pullen, *Actresses and Whores: On Stage and in Society* (Cambridge: Cambridge University Press, 2005), 25–26.

14. Solomon, "Anecdotes and Restoration Actresses," 22.

15. J. L. Austin, *How to Do Things with Words* (Cambridge, MA: Harvard University Press, 1975). Austin argues that certain types of speech function not just as utterances, but as performative acts that have real-world consequences. Examples include marriage ceremonies and christenings. In this case, the performative action is naming Barry's femininity as defective.

16. Howe, *The First English Actresses*, chapter 5. See also Jean Marsden, *Fatal Desire: Women, Sexuality, and the English Stage, 1660–1720* (Ithaca, NY: Cornell University Press, 2006).

17. For comparison, a laborer in the period might average about twenty-five pence for more than a day's work. See Judy Z. Stephenson, "'Real' Wages? Contractors, Workers, and Pay in London Building Trades, 1650–1800," *The Economic History Review* 71, no. 1 (February 2018): 124. Based on these numbers, Barry made roughly three-and-a-half times more per week than the mean income of a laborer in the era.

18. "Barry, Elizabeth," in *A Biographical Dictionary of Actors, Actresses, Musicians, Dancers, Managers & Other Stage Personnel in London, 1660–1800,* ed. Philip H. Highfill Jr., Kalman A. Burnim, and Edward A. Langhans, vol. 1 (Carbondale: Southern Illinois University Press, 1973), 313–325.

19. Highfill, Burnim, and Langhans, *A Biographical Dictionary*, 313. See also *The Letters of John Wilmot, Earl of Rochester*, ed. Jeremy Treglown (Chicago: University of Chicago Press, 1980).

20. Solomon treats this anecdote at length in her article "Anecdotes and Restoration Actresses," noting that it serves to disempower Barry and ascribe her career to Rochester. She also notes that it is highly unlikely it is true, for a variety of reasons, including that a similar story had circulated previously about Rochester and an actress named Sarah Cooke. See Solomon, "Anecdotes and Restoration Actresses," 23–29.

21. Edmund Curll, *The History of the English Stage* (E. Curll, 1741). Authorship is variably attributed to Betterton, William Oldys, and Curll in scholarly bibliographies. In the present chapter, I attribute it to Curll.

22. Curll, *The History of the English Stage*, 14.

23. Curll, *The History of the English Stage*, 16.

24. Curll, *The History of the English Stage*, 16.

25. Curll, *The History of the English Stage*, 17.

26. Curll, *The History of the English* Stage, 17.

27. Anthony Aston's Supplement to Cibber (ca. 1747) in *An Apology for the Life of Mr. Colley Cibber, Written by Himself*, ed. Robert W. Lowe, vol. 2 (London: John C. Nimmo, 1889), 303.

28. Thomas Davies, *Dramatic Miscellanies*, vol. 3 (London: Printed for the author, 1785), 209–211.

29. William Van Lennep, Emmett L. Avery, and Arthur H. Scouten, eds., *The London Stage, 1660–1800; A Calendar of Plays, Entertainments & Afterpieces, Together with Casts, Box-Receipts and Contemporary Comment Compiled from the Playbills, Newspapers and Theatrical Diaries of the Period, Part 1: 1660–1700* (Carbondale: Southern Illinois University Press, 1965), 1:256. The editorial notes on this production, given March 24, 1677, at Dorset Garden, indicate that the archival sources are unclear on whether it was the premiere, although there is no known earlier production of it. The first printed edition, published by John Amery, came out in 1677. The title page indicates the play was licensed on July 2, 1677. A copy of the first edition is in the special collections of the University of London Senate House library, shelfmark D.-L.L. (XVII) Bc [Behn]. See also

Howe, *The First English Actresses*, 178, who credits Barry with originating the role.

30. Edmund Bellchamber's "Memoirs of the Actors and Actresses" from his 1822 edition, published in Cibber's *An Apology for the Life of Mr. Colley Cibber*, 358.

31. John Doran, *"Their Majesties' Servants." Annals of the English Stage from Thomas Betterton to Edmund Kean*, vol. 1 (Philadelphia: David McKay, 1890). Emphasis in original.

32. John Fyvie, *Tragedy Queens of the Georgian Era* (New York: E. P. Dutton and Company, 1909), 1.

33. Fyvie, *Tragedy Queens*, 3.

34. Fyvie, *Tragedy Queens*, 3–4.

35. Henry Wysham Lanier, *The First English Actresses from the Initial Appearance of Women on the Stage in 1660 Till 1700* (New York: The Players, 1930), 65.

36. John Harold Wilson, *All the King's Ladies: Actresses of the Restoration* (Chicago: University of Chicago Press, 1958), 111.

37. Highfill, Burnim, and Langhans, *A Biographical Dictionary*, 1:313.

38. Paula R. Backscheider, "Barry, Elizabeth," *Oxford Dictionary of National Biography* (Oxford: Oxford University Press, 2014).

39. Tiffany Stern, *Rehearsal from Shakespeare to Sheridan* (Oxford: Oxford University Press, 2000), 156.

40. Howe, *The First English Actresses*, 10, 115, 202.

41. Kate C. Hamilton, "The 'Famous Mrs. Barry': Elizabeth Barry and Restoration Celebrity," *Studies in Eighteenth-Century Culture* 42 (Autumn 2013): 294–295.

42. Robert D. Hume and Judith Milhous, "Murder in Elizabeth Barry's Dressing Room," *The Yale University Library Gazette* 79, no. 3/4 (April 2005): 167.

43. Robert D. Hume, "Elizabeth Barry's First Roles and the Cast of *The Man of Mode*," *Theatre History Studies* 5 (January 1985): 16–19; Treglown, *Letters*, 29.

44. Curll, *History of the English Stage*, 12.

45. Susan M. Martin, "Actresses on the London Stage, 1660–1755: A Prosopographical Study," (PhD diss., Pennsylvania State University, 2008), 35–36. On period style, see John H. Wilson, "Rant, Cant, and Tone on the Restoration Stage," *Studies in Philology* 52 (October 1955): 592–598; Joseph Roach, *The Player's Passion: Studies in the Science of Acting* (Newark: University of Delaware Press, 1985), chapter 1; and Alan S. Downer, "Nature to Advantage Dressed: Eighteenth-Century Acting," *PMLA* 58, no. 4 (December 1943): 1002–1037.

46. Paul Baines and Pat Rogers, *Edmund Curll, Bookseller* (Oxford: Oxford University Press, 2007), 26–27.

47. Cibber, *An Apology for the Life of Mr. Colley Cibber*, 159.

48. Far more influential, no doubt, was the fact that she was raised in the family of a theatrical impresario. Gilli Bush-Bailey argues that the Davenants' tutelage and the ability to mix with the upper class through them was the source of Barry's training. Gilli Bush-Bailey, *Treading the Bawds: Actresses and*

Playwrights on the Late Stuart Stage (Manchester: Manchester University Press, 2006), 45–46.

49. James William Johnson, *A Profane Wit: The Life of John Wilmot, Earl of Rochester* (Rochester, NY: University of Rochester Press, 2004), 178.

50. R. E. Pritchard, *Passion for Living: John Wilmot, Earl of Rochester* (Cambridge: Lutterworth Press, 2012), 67, 98.

51. Jeremy Lamb, *So Idle a Rogue: The Life and Death of Lord Rochester* (London: Allison & Busby, 1993), 152. The source of her "dangerous-sounding" reputation for Lamb seems to be mostly the satirical verses about her by Tom Brown, Robert Gould, and several anonymous authors. On the same page he describes her as "bad-tempered, demanding and hard-natured. Her mercenary nature eventually gained her a widespread reputation for using any man who could advance her career and prospects," an image supported by the satires on her.

52. Solomon, "Anecdotes and Restoration Actresses," 23–29.

53. Johnson, *A Profane Wit*, 178.

54. Curll, *History of the English Stage*, 21.

55. Curll, *History of the English Stage*, 22.

56. Davies, *Dramatic Miscellanies*, 298.

57. Doran, "*Their Majesties' Servants*," 109.

58. The *Biographical Dictionary* points out that, contrary to Curll's insinuation about Rochester, it was impossible that the two women could have argued over him. He was dead by 1690 when Barry debuted as Roxana, and in 1677, when Boutell created the role of Statira, the play belonged to the King's Company and Barry could not have appeared in it. See Highfill, Burnim, and Langhans, *A Biographical Dictionary*, 1:318.

59. Fyvie, *Tragedy Queens*, 11.

60. Nicoll, *A History of English Drama*, 18. Barry and Bracegirdle actually had a long and fruitful partnership onstage. See Howe, *The First English Actresses*, 156–172.

61. Gilder, *Enter the Actress*, 148.

62. Wilson, *All the King's Ladies*, 61; Highfill, Burnim, and Langhans, *A Biographical Dictionary*, 1:318.

63. Lennep et al., *The London Stage*, 1:468.

64. Howe, *The First English Actresses*, 153.

65. Robert D. Hume, "Theatre History 1660–1800: Aims, Materials, Methodology," in *Players, Playwrights, Playhouses: Investigating Performance, 1660–1800*, ed. Michael Cordner and Peter Holland (London: Palgrave Macmillan, 2007), 13–14.

66. Felicity Nussbaum, *Rival Queens: Actresses, Performance, and the Eighteenth-Century British Theater* (Philadelphia: University of Pennsylvania Press, 2010), 78.

67. Highfill, Burnim, and Langhans, *A Biographical Dictionary*, 4:261.

68. Curll, *History of the English Stage*, 19.

69. Curll, *History of the English Stage*, 21.

70. Davies, *Dramatic Miscellanies*, 217.

71. Bellchamber, "Memoirs of the Actors and Actresses," 359.

72. Fyvie, *Tragedy Queens*, 13.

73. Highfill, Burnim, and Langhans, *A Biographical Dictionary*, 1:323.

74. *Post-Boy* (November 14–17, 1713).

75. Davies, *Dramatic Miscellanies*, 216.

76. Highfill, Burnim, and Langhans, *A Biographical Dictionary*, 4:203.

77. Ingrid H. Tague, *Animal Companions: Pets and Social Change in Eighteenth-Century Britain* (University Park: Pennsylvania State University Press, 2015), 105–112, 139–147.

PART IV
ANECDOTES' AFTERLIVES
Scholarly Encounters

9
ANECDOTAL ORIGIN STORIES
Mary Ann Yates's Trip to Drury Lane

ELAINE MCGIRR

In April 1783, the *British Magazine and Review; or Universal Miscellany* published a "modern biography" of the actress-manageress Mary Ann Graham Yates, who was still living, and indeed, still performing, although near the end of her stellar career. This lengthy text—six double-column magazine pages plus a full-page engraving of *Mrs Yates, in the Character of the Tragic Muse, Reciting the Monody to the Memory of Mr Garrick* (Figure 6)—is a conventional periodical biography, carefully following the formula for describing the life of an "interesting" woman.[1] Frances Brooke's 1787 biographical obituary of Yates, published in the *Gentleman's Magazine*, is an extension and elaboration of the earlier text, strongly indicating that Brooke also wrote the unsigned and unattributed 1783 biography.[2] While the two biographies contain much of the same text, there are a few telling differences. The most salient is the compelling theatrical anecdote Brooke includes in the 1783 biography to create an "origin story" for her subject:

> As her father was a man of plain and primitive manners, our celebrated actress had never seen a play, till, at the age of sixteen, a lady took her to Romeo and Juliet; when the impassioned performance of Mrs. Cibber opened a new day on her delighted imagination. Fired by that enthusiastic impulse which so often decides the fate of genius, absorbed in admiration of

Figure 6. James Heath, after Thomas Stothard, *Mrs Yates, in the Character of the Tragic Muse, Reciting the Monody to the Memory of Mr Garrick*, 1783. London: National Portrait Gallery.

> those astonishing powers of which report had given her only a faint idea, she instantly recognised something congenial in her own mind: the spark mounted into a blaze; she melted into tears, not only of sympathy, but of emulation; and, just to herself, as well as to the consummate pattern of excellence before her, she felt, amidst the confusion of ideas in which she was enveloped, the celebrated sentiment of Corregio, on first seeing the works of Raphael—*Ed io son anche pittore!* From that moment, her passion for the theatre became unconquerable.[3]

Although it may seem innocuous at first glance, this remarkable anecdote about a young girl's first trip to the theater eschews all the conventional tropes of anecdotes about women in the theater. While most anecdotes merely display the woman as an object to be consumed, this imagined encounter offers a remarkable insight into Yates's career and character while also highlighting the centrality of women, female friendship, and female collaboration to Yates's professional success. This anecdote rewrites the "actress discovery" genre, creating a space for self-discovery rather than objectification. In rewriting the actress origin story, Brooke and Yates collaborate to rewrite the actress's place in theater history, placing her center stage and granting her both agency and authority.

Biographical vs. Anecdotal Truths

The 1783 periodical biography of Mary Ann Yates is a testament to this actress's significance. As Hannah Hudson demonstrates, biographies of female subjects were rare, and often "anecdotal, fictional, or merely so brief as to provide virtually no useful information."[4] The lengthy biography, which included not only the text and engraving of Yates but also a large table identifying ninety of her most popular roles, is the magazine's main focus: the prologue Yates spoke in Edinburgh is also reprinted as the magazine's "poetical article of this month."[5] Yates unites the muses, standing in for art and poetry as well as theater. Her stage work makes her worthy of a biography, but the print and the poem remind readers of her cultural authority. She is not just an actress; she is art itself. The biography appears to provide significant detail about Yates's life and career, but it is short on biographical fact, preferring to give "our celebrated actress" a history worthy of the celebrity she would become, rather than the childhood and novitiate she experienced. The biography shaves nine years off the actress's age, relocates her birth and childhood to London from Birmingham, and erases her early attempts at the stage.[6] These amendments to Yates's biography set up the anecdote of the actress's discovery and the beginning of her career at Drury Lane. It is important to stress that this anecdote has no grounding in biographical fact: there is simply no way that a sixteen-year-old Yates discovered the power of theater while watching Susannah Cibber's Juliet.

In biographical fact, Yates, née Graham, was born in Birmingham in 1728. In 1744, when she was sixteen, Susannah Cibber had not yet become Juliet. *Romeo and Juliet* was first revived that year with Jenny Cibber playing Juliet to her father's Romeo in the Haymarket; Susannah did not attempt the role for another four years. However, as the biography (and Yates herself) claimed that she was born in 1737 rather than 1728, perhaps we should be looking for a Cibberian Juliet in 1753. This initially looks more plausible, as Susannah Cibber did play Juliet several times in the winter of the 1752–1753 season and again in the autumn of the 1753–1754 season.[7] But even accepting this revised timeline for the sake of internal, rather than biographical, consistency, Yates could not have seen Mrs. Cibber perform in the winter of 1753. Nor could 1753 have been the first time she had ever seen a play, for Yates had already begun her theatrical career by then. She was a minor actress in Thomas Sheridan's company at Smock Alley in Dublin for the 1752–1753 season. Her first recorded appearance, under the name Miss Graham, was as Anna Bullen in *Henry VIII* on January 22, 1753.[8] She was released by Sheridan at the end of the season, but was hired immediately by David Garrick to begin her career at Drury Lane, meaning that if she did see Susannah Cibber perform Juliet in 1753, it was not as a naive audience member but as a junior colleague, watching from the wings.

Given the ease with which the anecdote can be disproven, what value can it have? What purpose does it serve? Hudson argues that the "biographer deploys authenticity and fictionality, revelation and concealment, strategically to hold readerly interest while deflecting potential critiques" of salacious or indecent content.[9] Jacky Bratton argues that the anecdote "purports to reveal the truths of the society, but not necessarily directly: its inner truth, its truth to some ineffable 'essence,' rather than to proven facts, is what matters most," while Jonathan Bate reminds us that "the point of the anecdote is not its factual but its representative truth."[10] The inclusion of the theatrical anecdote within a periodical biography, then, is not evidence of a dearth of verifiable information about the actress, but rather a narrative technique: the anecdote harnesses fictionality in order to achieve authenticity. Like many anecdotes about Nell Gwyn, it is true to her character even if it is utterly false to her biography; its truth is in its ability to highlight the "Yatesness" of Mary Ann Yates. The self-recognition recorded in the anecdote proves that Yates knows her own worth, a trait that managers deplored, as Yates demanded—and received—record fees for her appearances. However, the anecdote's evidentiary value lies not in its proximity to plausible historical or biographical truth. Its value does not even lie in its ability to limn Yates's "characteristic disposition," useful though that is. While Bratton argues that the theatrical anecdote "purports to reveal the truths of the society," this particular anecdote is, perhaps, less interested in exposing truths than in creating them.[11] Brooke not only gave Yates the history she deserved, but also used the anecdote to create a vision of a better theater: one that was open to talent rather than patronage, and that valued women for what they could do, not for who they knew or how they looked. The anecdote shows us a theater of women who work without rivalry and with personal and professional agency.

Thus, while the story of a teenaged Yates's trip to Drury Lane may not be true, it is telling. And perhaps it is most significant as a piece of feminist historiography, and as a testament to Brooke's admiration of Yates, her longtime friend and business partner. Brooke had already penned one fictional biography: Yates appears in *The Excursion* (1777) in her own character, and the novel's heroine, Maria Villiers, has been read as an avatar of the actress.[12] Given the close working relationship between Brooke and Yates, it is probable that Yates had some input into the content if not the structure of the periodical biography.[13] The anecdote may have been a creation of Brooke's or told to Brooke by Yates. We cannot know where the story originated, but the continued closeness of the two women strongly suggests that this theatrical anecdote tells the story of Yates's entry into the theater and theatrical profession the way she wanted it told.

This anecdote, and its place in a "modern biography" of Mary Ann Yates, is telling. It is a radical note smuggled into a conventional form in a conservative magazine. By using Yates's first trip to the theater to begin the story of her career, it initially seems to belong to a well-established genre of theatrical anecdotes: the discovery of a new (soon to be celebrity) actress. But it rewrites that genre. Other anecdotes in this genre describe a beautiful girl who is discovered and rushed to the stage for others to see. The classic in this genre is the discovery of Anne Oldfield:

> It was wholly owing to Captain *Farquhar*, that ever Mrs. *Oldfield* became an Actress, from the following Incident. Dining one Day at her Aunt's, who kept the Mitre Tavern in *St. James's-Market*, he heard Miss *Nanny* reading a Play behind the Bar with so proper an Emphasis, and such agreeable Turns suitable to each Character, that he swore the Girl was cut out for the Stage; to which she had before always expressed an Inclination, being very desirous to try her Fortune that Way. Her Mother, the next Time she saw Captain *Vanbrugh*, who had a great respect for the Family, told him what was Captain *Farquhar*'s Advice.[14]

Other versions of this anecdote leave out Oldfield's mother and Vanbrugh in order to focus on Farquhar's discovery and its effects: "The playwright George Farquhar was impressed when he heard Anne rehearsing passages from *The Scornful Lady* by Beaumont and Fletcher while she was working behind the bar; they subsequently became lovers."[15] There are countless other examples. For instance, Kitty Clive was similarly discovered while innocently demonstrating her histrionic talents:

> Mr. Watson, many years box-keeper at Drury Lane and Richmond, kept the Bell Tavern opposite to Mrs. Snell's [where Kitty lodged]. At this house was held the Beefsteak Club, instituted by Mr. Beard, Mr. Dunstall, Mr. Woodward, etc. Kitty Raftor, being one day *washing the steps of the house*, and singing, the windows of the club room being open, they were instantly crowded by the company, who were all enchanted

> with her natural grace and simplicity. This circumstance alone led her to the stage, under the auspices of Mr. Beard and Mr. Dunstall.[16]

In a slight variation on the theme, Peg Woffington is said to have been discovered by Madame Violante, who, struck by the young girl's beauty, followed her home and begged her mother to let her daughter perform.[17] In each of these anecdotes, the soon-to-be celebrity actress's beauty and erotic appeal is foregrounded, as is her desire to "try her fortune" on the stage. Woffington's childish beauty is fully realized when she arrives in London and approaches Rich, who reportedly confessed to Reynolds that "the amalgamated Calypso, Circe and Armida . . . dazzled my eyes. A more fascinating daughter of Eve never presented herself to a manager in search of rare commodities."[18] These discovered actresses are not artists, but the subjects, or objects, of others' art.

Again, what is important about these anecdotes is not their biographical truth but the way they introduce us to the celebrated actress: in the traditional actress discovery anecdote, the soon to be celebrity is seen and/or heard by someone with theatrical authority (usually a man) and then moved from this private viewing to the public stage. The actress is an object to be discovered, traded, and displayed: she is, in Rich's terms, "a rare commodity." Mary Ann Yates's origin story is different. Hers is a voyage of *self-discovery*. Where other actresses wait to be discovered while longing for the stage, "our celebrated actress" has no prior theatrical ambition and no need of male intervention. She is not looking for a lucrative career; rather, she becomes an actress when she views a performer at the peak of her powers and "instantly recognized something congenial in her own mind."[19] In this moment, Yates does not just experience sympathy. Her affective response to Cibber's pathos engenders fellow-being as well as fellow-feeling.[20]

Yates does not need to be found; she finds herself. Nor is she a spectacle or object for the male gaze. In contrast to the origin stories of Clive, Oldfield, and even Woffington, Yates's entry into the theater is feminocentric. The anecdote is carefully crafted to create a female-only theatrical space: Yates and her female friend in the audience watching Susannah Cibber onstage. In this anecdote, we have a Juliet without a Romeo, a Juliet, moreover, appreciated for her histrionic powers, not her beauty. Neither Yates nor Cibber is described within the anecdote, and the periodical biography gives scant attention to Yates's famous beauty. Yates is instead introduced as "this accomplished actress, whose superior talents make all which regards her interesting to the public."[21]

Men are notable in their absence from Yates's origin story and from the biography in general. The periodical biography walked a fine line that allowed it to bolster "the subject's celebrity without crossing the line into infamy,"[22] so it is not surprising that the theatrical anecdote it tells avoids the sexualized tropes of erotic tutelage so prevalent in actresses' biographies; there are no shades of Elizabeth Barry learning her craft under the Earl of Rochester here.[23] But it goes out of its way to remove men from the story of Yates's career and especially from positions of authority or control over her. Her father, the only man described at length, is rendered pitiable by his financial "reverses" and subsequent blindness. The opening paragraphs of the biography work hard to establish the father as the daughter's dependent: "Having the loss of sight added to these domestic misfortunes, [he] lived to have the evening of his days made happy by the filial gratitude of this his youngest child; who, as soon as success in her theatrical pursuits enabled her . . . took a small house in the King's Road, and afterwards a larger on Richmond Common, where those hours she could spare from her theatrical avocations were employed in soothing his declining years, by paying him those interesting attentions which duty and filial tenderness alone can dictate."[24] Yates is presented as both caregiver and main breadwinner, establishing her father in increasingly comfortable homes and devoting herself to his care in her free time. His poverty and blindness create an attractively desperate situation Yates can transcend while ensuring that her father cannot be credited with helping her on her road to stardom. Yates's father is the only man mentioned before the anecdote introduces us to Yates and her to the stage.

The men who were arguably integral to Yates's development as an actress are all signally absent, not just from the anecdote about Yates's trip to the theater but from the biography more generally. Thomas Sheridan, David Garrick, Arthur Murphy, and Richard Yates all could be—and have been—credited with giving Yates her start on the stage: Sheridan gave her a trial at Smock Alley; Garrick hired her for her first London season; Murphy wrote her first breakout lead role, Mandane in *The Orphan of China* (1759); and Richard Yates gave her his theatrical name and experience. Other biographical accounts of Yates stress these relationships to the exclusion of the women with whom Yates also worked. The *Biographical Dictionary of Actors* begins its entry on Yates by identifying her as "the second wife of the performer Richard Yates" and goes on to assert that "Arthur Murphy and Richard Yates helped to train her, and one must suppose that Garrick, since he took her back into the company in 1756–1757, also helped instruct her."[25] An early account, the 1772 *Theatrical Biography*, gives the credit to Richard Yates, averring that "under the direction of so veteran an instructor, she began to make improvements."[26] Yates's *ODNB* entry also identifies Richard Yates as the catalyst for Yates's rise, asserting that "when Mary Ann married him at some point in 1756, her theatrical status rose," but finds it was Murphy who made her a star: "Arthur Murphy . . . coached her privately as Mandane in his tragedy *The Orphan of China*. It was the success of this play . . . that confirmed her as a Drury Lane favourite."[27] Given this androcentric historiography, it is all the more significant that the 1783 biography dared to present a self-discovered, self-made actress. In stark contrast to the anecdotes and histories that preceded and followed, the "Miss Graham" anecdote is crafted to bring Yates to the stage through female hands, and to bring her to the stage fully formed. When she saw—and felt—Cibber's Juliet, Yates "instantly recognised something congenial in her own mind," and she self-identified as an actress from that moment. Yates made a positive decision to become—or rather, to profess to be—an actress. The biography continues: "From that moment, her passion for the theatre became unconquerable; and a friend, who had interest, having recommended her to Mr. Garrick, she came out the following Lent in the character of Virginia . . . when her youth, her uncommon beauty, and those rays of genius which broke through her untutored inexperience, like streams of light which precede the day, secured her the favour of the public."[28] Her self-discovery means that she did not require the mediating influence of male authority to recognize or validate her talent, nor did she require a male genius to coach, train, or champion her.

Role Play: Crafting the Perfect Anecdote

This theatrical anecdote—an anecdote about a trip to the theater and a celebrated actress's foray into the profession—is explicitly feminist. Not only does it rewrite the actress discovery trope, it also rewrites the misogynistic and ageist trope of ingenue versus aging diva. The trip to the theater fills Yates's heart with sympathy and emulation, and she is spurred onto the stage not by jealousy but admiration. The aspiring actress recognizes her own latent talent, but is not blind to Cibber's "consummate pattern of excellence."[29] The anecdote creates an environment in which women are not in competition but rather fellowship. Yates is moved out of the wings, where she presumably actually saw Cibber's Juliet, and into the audience so she could be struck by the power of Cibber's performance—so she could experience it rather than appraise it. "Miss Graham" learned her craft experientially: she strove to invoke the same passions, the same affective responses.

The choice of role here is significant in creating this narrative of emulation without rivalry. Given the fictionality of the anecdote, "Miss Graham" could have been made to go to the theater any night and witness any number of Cibberian performances. For instance, on March 26, 1753, Cibber chose Cleopatra in Dryden's *All for Love* for her benefit performance.[30] Cleopatra was not one of Cibber's successes—this benefit was the first time since 1738 in which we know she appeared in either Dryden's or Shakespeare's version of the story, and it was her last performance as the Egyptian queen—but Yates would become the nation's Cleopatra of choice, appearing regularly in both *All for Love* and *Antony and Cleopatra* from 1759 until 1779. Telling the story in this way would not only pin the anecdote to a particular time—March 1753—but also downplay Cibber's excellence while preordaining Yates's rise. For while Cibber chose Cleopatra for her benefit, it was not a role in her "line" of weepy, wronged wives. It did, however, fit Yates's "line" of passionate, fiery queens. Told this way, the anecdote shows Cleopatra inspiring Yates not to imitation but to revolutionary reinterpretation. It shows Yates as a radically new kind of actress—one who rejected the models of the previous generation and modernized the profession. In other words, it tells the story of a great actor's genius the way David

Garrick liked to tell it. But Cleopatra was not Yates's inspiration, nor Garrick her model.

A different anecdote would have had Yates attending the theater on a night in which Cibber performed one of the many roles, Shakespearean or other, in which both Cibber and Yates were celebrated: in Shakespearean tragedy alone, both actresses were acclaimed for their Constances, their Desdemonas, and their Cordelias. In this hypothetical version of the anecdote, Cibber's "consummate pattern of excellence" would have been fully acknowledged, and Yates would have figured as the worthy successor. Telling the anecdote this way would make a certain sense: Mary Ann Yates did indeed take over many of Susannah Cibber's signature roles, both comic and tragic. At the start of her career, Yates served as Cibber's official understudy and learned her craft from the elder tragedienne. However, this version of the anecdote places Yates firmly in the tradition, if not the shadow, of her predecessor. It would also misrepresent the stature and significance of both actresses. For while they did share a repertory, they did so in radically different postures: Yates may have learned her craft from Cibber, but she did not imitate or replicate Cibberian acting, choosing to play to her own vocal and physical strengths and developing a different stage persona. Yates was vertical where Cibber hewed to the serpentine line of beauty; Yates raged where Cibber sobbed.[31] The desire to be "just" but also to differentiate between the tragediennes, then, may explain why Brooke has the young Yates attend a play she could not have seen, and why Juliet is the perfect role to inspire Yates with admiration for Cibber's craft and simultaneous recognition of her own, equal but different powers.

The anecdote places "Miss Graham" at a performance of *Romeo and Juliet* for two reasons: because Juliet was one of Cibber's most popular roles—she performed it regularly from 1748 until 1763—and one of the few that Yates never attempted. The anecdote captures the moment in which Mary Ann Yates discovered her aptitude for acting, which she does in a moment of ecstatic connection to Cibber's Juliet, a part in which Cibber excelled and for which there is no Yatesean comparison. The anecdote thus stresses that Yates may have been "moved to emulation" by Cibber's performance, but not to direct competition, and certainly not to imitation: the second act does not see Yates taking up Juliet's dagger and displacing the older diva. The story of succession is less literal than that. It suggests that Mary Ann Yates is the rightful heir to, rather than a replacement for, Susannah Cibber. Indeed, the two actresses shared the stage from 1753 until Cibber's death in 1766. They frequently (and profitably) performed together in both comedy and tragedy.[32] By choosing Juliet as the catalyst for Yates's theatrical self-discovery, Brooke ensures that her anecdote does not set up an *All About Eve* plot but rather one of female collaboration; she tells a story of emulation without rivalry, of inspiration without imitation. Yates's singular genius is thus shaped neither by the years spent honing her skills (the biographical truth of the six years from 1753 to 1759 she spent as Cibber's understudy) nor by the fortuitously roving eye of a male champion who elevated her to the stage. The anecdote creates an alternative timeline that moves Yates effortlessly from audience member to lead actress, without displacing or deriding the talents of another performer.[33] Yates's early success comes not at Cibber's expense but by her grace—again, absence rather than competition or replacement creates a space in which both actresses can be excellent: "Mrs. Yates and Mr. Powell . . . drew such houses as, though in the absence of Mr. Garrick and Mrs. Cibber, rendered it the most lucrative season ever known."[34]

Having gone to great lengths to downplay any suggestion of rival queens, the 1783 biography writes a different narrative of succession. Rather than dwell on Yates's inheritance of Cibber's tragic mantle, the biography contrasts Yates's powers with those of her real rival: David Garrick. At several points the biography contrasts Yates and Garrick, repeatedly asserting that the actress-manageress was the actor-manager's equal—or better: "The greatness of her dramatic powers can only be equalled by their variety; that, Mr. Garrick excepted, no performer has done justice to such various and seemingly contradictory characters."[35] The biography of the "celebrated actress" also celebrates Yates's management of the opera, and in terms that were clearly designed to differentiate her from her male rivals:

> Of the direction of the Opera, it is not our business, or our intention, to speak very minutely; but thus much it would be unjust not to observe, that by the plain and obvious policy of treating the performers with kindness, paying them with punctuality,

> granting the most liberal salaries to superior merit, sparing no expense in whatever contributed to the beauty of the *spectacle*, and introducing the most exact order into the interior arrangements, the Italian theatre was raised from a stage of constant and ruinous loss, to that prosperous situation in which it was delivered to the gentlemen who succeeded in the undertaking.[36]

Yates's taste, tact, and appreciation of talent stand in implied contradiction to the practices of the male managers—Garrick, Colman, and Sheridan—with and for whom she worked. The biography's very structure suggests that Yates outperforms and outlasts her chief male rival. The choice of illustration for the biography completes this argument. Yates was a favorite model for artists; portraits and engravings of her as Tragedy and in characters from a dizzying range of tragedies and comedies abound. By choosing *Mrs Yates, in the Character of the Tragic Muse, Reciting the Monody to the Memory of Mr Garrick*, the biography places Yates on the stage, and David Garrick in the grave. For while the Monody ostensibly honored Garrick's memory, its effect was to impress audiences with Yates's majesty. The absent hero is easily forgotten in the presence of the awesome actress. Even Garrick recognized this, the biography hints, reminding readers that

> that exquisite judge and example of theatrical perfection, the late Mr. Garrick, paid Mrs. Yates the last compliment in his power, by selecting The Wonder, in which she performed Violante, the principal female character, to close the scene of his dramatic triumphs: a distinction she had, some years after, a melancholy opportunity of returning, by speaking at Drury Lane . . . the affecting Monody written by Mr. Sheridan to his memory; a production which, abounding with the most luxuriant poetic imagery, placed our admired actress in a new and striking point of view, by giving full scope to her unrivalled powers.[37]

From Juliet to the monody, Yates and Brooke collaborated to create a stage occupied by women, a theater in which women have agency, authority—and the last word.

Notes

1. For details on magazine biographies and gender, see Hannah Hudson, "'This Lady Is Descended from a Good Family': Women and Biography in British Magazines, 1770–1798," in *Women's Periodicals and Print Culture in Britain,*

1690–1820s: The Long Eighteenth Century, ed. Jennie Batchelor and Manushag N. Powell (Edinburgh: University of Edinburgh Press, 2018), 278–294.

2. F[rances] B[rooke], "Authentic Memoirs of Mrs. Yates," *Gentleman's Magazine* (July 1787): 585–589.

3. [Frances Brooke], *The British Magazine and Review* (April 1783): 250–255, 251.

4. Hudson, "'This Lady Is Descended from a Good Family,'" 280.

5. [Brooke], *The British Magazine and Review*, 252.

6. [Brooke], *The British Magazine and Review*, 250, 251.

7. Extant records in *The London Stage* record Susannah Cibber playing Juliet on January 1, February 5, and the 4th, 19th, and 26th of May in the 1752–53 season, and again on the 4th, 5th, and 19th of October at the start of the 1753–54 season.

8. Although Smock Alley was Yates's first confirmed professional stage appearance, she may have been the "Miss Graham" who appeared in drolls at "At Yates's (from the Theatre Royal in Drury Lane) Great Theatrical Booth facing the Hospital Gate" at Bartholomew Fair in 1748. George Winchester Stone, ed., *The London Stage 1660–1800; A Calendar of Plays, Entertainments & Afterpieces, Part 4: 1747–1776*, 3 vols. (Carbondale: Southern Illinois University Press, 1962), 1:58. A previous relationship with Yates would account both for Garrick's willingness to hire someone rejected by Sheridan and also her subsequent marriage to Richard Yates.

9. Hudson, "'This Lady Is Descended from a Good Family,'" 288.

10. Jacky Bratton, *New Readings in Theatre History* (Cambridge: Cambridge University Press, 2003), 103; Jonathan Bate, "A Life of Anecdote," in *The Genius of Shakespeare* (London: Picador, 1997), 3–33, b5.

11. Bratton, *New Readings in Theatre History*, 103.

12. See Paula Backscheider, "Frances Brooke: Becoming a Playwright," *Women's Writing* 23, no. 3 (2016): 325–338, and Katherine Charles, "Staging Sociability in *The Excursion*: Frances Brooke, David Garrick, and the King's Theatre Coterie," *Eighteenth-Century Fiction* 27, no. 2 (2014–15): 257–284.

13. Between 1773 and 1778, Yates and Brooke comanaged the King's Opera House in the Haymarket. While turning the fortunes of the opera house around and extracting significant profits, they also used their combined cultural authority to lobby for a license to perform spoken drama at King's, which would have created a formidable rival to the duopoly of Covent Garden and Drury Lane. For details, see Ian Woodfield, *Opera and Drama in Eighteenth-Century London* (Cambridge: Cambridge University Press, 2001).

14. [Curll], *Authentic Memoirs of the Life of that Justly Celebrated Actress, Mrs. Ann Oldfield* (London: Printed and sold by the booksellers and pamphleteers of London and Westminster, 1731), 55–56.

15. Jonathan Law, *Methuen Drama Dictionary of the Theatre* (London: Methuen, 2013), 334.

16. Lewis Melville, *Stage Favourites of the Eighteenth Century* (London: Hutchinson & Co., 1928), 54–55.

17. See, among others, Melville, who recites the anecdote at great length. Melville, *Stage Favourites of the Eighteenth Century*, 155–160.

18. Quoted in "Woffington, Margaret," in *A Biographical Dictionary of Actors, Actresses, Musicians, Dancers, Managers & Other Stage Personnel in London, 1660–1800*, ed. Philip H. Highfill Jr., Kalman A. Burnim, and Edward A. Langhans, vol. 16, *West to Zwingman* (Carbondale: Southern Illinois University Press, 1993), 201.

19. [Brooke], *The British Magazine and Review*, 251.

20. For more on the contagion of affect, see Jean Marsden, "Affect and the Problem of Theatre," *The Eighteenth Century* 58, no. 3 (2017): 297–307, and Helen Nicholson, "Emotion," *CTR* 23, no. 1 (2013): 20–22.

21. [Brooke], *The British Magazine and Review*, 250. In contrast, the obituary does praise Yates's beauty, although not until the third page, reminding readers that "she was beautiful, even to the most poetical ideas of beauty; she was tall, finely proportioned, and to the utmost degree graceful. Like Homer's Helen, 'She look'd a goddess, and she mov'd a queen'" (587).

22. Hudson, "'This Lady Is Descended from a Good Family,'" 281.

23. See Diana Solomon, "Anecdotes and Restoration Actresses: The Cases of Elizabeth Barry and Anne Bracegirdle," *RECTR* 31, no. 2 (2016): 19–36.

24. [Brooke], *The British Magazine and Review*, 205.

25. Highfill, Burnim, and Langhans, *A Biographical Dictionary*, 322, 325.

26. Anonymous, "Mrs. Yates," in *Theatrical Biography; or, Memoirs of the Principal Performers of the Three Theatres Royal*, 2 vols. (Dublin, 1772). (*ECCO*): 2:3–7, quotation vol. 2, 5.

27. Peter Thompson, "Yates [nee Graham], Mary Ann," in *The Oxford Dictionary of National Biography*, ed. H.C.G. Matthew and Brian Harrison, 60 vols. (Oxford: Oxford University Press, 2004).

28. [Brooke], *The British Magazine and Review*, 251.

29. [Brooke], *The British Magazine and Review*, 251.

30. Stone, *The London Stage 1660–1800*, 1:357.

31. For more on the different postures of tragedy adopted by Cibber and Yates, see my "New Lines: Mary Ann Yates, *The Orphan of China*, and the New She-Tragedy," *ABO: Interactive Journal for Women in the Arts, 1640–1830* 8, no. 2 (2018): 1.

32. See Stone, *The London Stage 1660–1800*, part 4, vol. 2, for performance statistics. See, for example, the performance of *Jane Shore* on January 8, 1761, "By His Majesty's Command" (836).

33. "Mr Hume's Agis being presented, and Mrs. Cibber, from illness, being unable to continue the part of Evanthe more than three nights, Mrs Yates succeeded her in the character, and with such success, as at once established her in the first line of her profession." [Brooke], *The British Magazine and Review*, 251.

34. [Brooke], *The British Magazine and Review*, 252.

35. [Brooke], *The British Magazine and Review*, 254.

36. [Brooke], *The British Magazine and Review*, 253.

37. [Brooke], *The British Magazine and Review*, 255.

10

THE VANISHING SUBJECT IN "ANECDOTAL" ABRIDGMENTS OF THEATRICAL BIOGRAPHIES

AMANDA WELDY BOYD

The inclusion of anecdote in theatrical biography often resulted in the supposed subject being obscured by the inclusion of every tired chestnut, anecdote, or anecdotal facsimile that the author could plausibly relate to the subject's life. Taking my cue from anecdote's original meaning of "a thing unpublished," I begin with a comparatively scarce anecdote about David Garrick. In the tradition of long-winded anecdote tellers, I will take my time in supplying this delightful anecdote in full:

> The last time that Garrick was at Paris, Preville [the most accomplished comedian in French theatre] invited him to his villa. . . . Our Roscius being in a gay humour, proposed to travel in one of the hired coaches that go to Versailles, on which road the villa of Preville was situated. When they got in, he ordered the coachman to drive on, who answered he would do so as soon as he got his complement of four passengers. A droll whim immediately seized Garrick, and he determined to give his brother player a specimen of his art. While the coachman, therefore, was attentively plying for passengers, Garrick slipped out of the door, went round the coach, and by his wonderful command of countenance, a power which he so happily displayed in [the role of] Abel Drugger, palmed himself upon the coachman as another passenger. This he did twice, and was admitted each time as a fresh passenger, to the astonishment and admiration of

> Preville. He whipped out a third time, and addressing himself to the coachman, was answered in a surly tone, "that he had already got his complement"—and would have driven off without him, had not Preville called out, that as the stranger appeared to be a very little man, they would, to accommodate the gentleman, contrive to make room.[1]

I tell this story not only to accommodate those readers who expect to read funny (and, ideally, new) anecdotes about stage celebrities from the long eighteenth century, but also because it is notable that I encountered the story not in Thomas Davies's 1780 biography of Garrick or Arthur Murphy's 1801 offering but in M. Lafayette Byrn's *Repository of Wit*, a cheap, popular production originating in 1853 that simply collected anecdotes, witticisms, and jokes by and about famous people with no pretense of sustained biographical analysis.[2] Scholars who have enjoyed Davies and toiled through Murphy may wonder why neither seized upon this memorable anecdote, if for no other reason than to increase the actual presence of Garrick in the narratives named for him. Additionally, in the context of my argument, I wish to use the above anecdote to establish what constitutes "anecdote": a brief and interesting or funny story, usually centering on our subject's interaction with another person, incorporating specific action that takes place in the realm of the everyday, frequently concluding with quoted speech (sometimes including dialect) that reveals the protagonist's wit or folly. These components are designed to showcase the essence of a character's personality.

S. Arthur Bent grandly describes the unifying power of anecdotes: "We are by anecdotes made more nearly contemporaneous with great men than were most of their contemporaries."[3] Anecdotes distill character; they illustrate and entertain. They are by no means the enemy of biography, but their inclusion can present obstacles for biographers. Although an anecdote's ostensible purpose is to reveal the character of its subject, this chapter suggests that anecdote, as an almost essential feature of life-writing in the eighteenth century, quite frequently served to conceal the actor it purported to display, trading sustained investigation of a main character for entertaining flashes of proximity. In the instances relayed here, Leslie Ritchie's idea of the *Anecdota obscura* as providing "a deceptive sense of representation" is highly applicable, but, within my texts, there is far less intention to obscure the subject or bear false witness. Here, the anecdotes that overshadow a subject-actor were initially added to assign more importance to him through association with other famous figures, and more prosaically, to swell the size of a volume about him.[4] However, in the process, the supporting cast of characters could unwittingly dominate the subject, especially as the vogue for anecdote in relation to a narrative through line of an actor's life intersected with the spatial restraints and consumer tastes of the medium used by a given biographer or editor.

The importance of anecdote to biography is undeniable. Famous biographer (and biographical subject) Samuel Johnson yearned for a time when anecdotes could be unfettered from a unifying biographical narrative. The daunting labor required to set anecdotes into a comprehensive biography, he reasoned, led to the loss of great material, which would be better served piecemeal than to remain unpublished.[5] History was on Johnson's side as well: as Gilbert Murray declared, "Biography in our [twentieth-century] sense—the complete writing of a life year by year with dates and document—was never practiced at all in antiquity . . . [ancient biography demonstrates] resolute indifference to anything like completeness. Ancient 'Lives' as a rule select a few great deeds, a few great sayings or discourses."[6] In some cases, biography was little more than a collection of anecdotes, closer to *The Repository of Wit* (from which came the Garrick–Préville anecdote above) than to Boswell's *Life of Johnson* (which itself has no scarcity of anecdote). But, in the eighteenth century, when theatrical biography was really just coming into its own as a (sub)genre, a complex consideration of the roles of sustained, sequential life-writing and anecdote, as well as of the balance of attention between the individual subject and the manifold members of his social circle, would be required.

A complete history of anecdote as a biographical tool is beyond the scope of this chapter. Instead, I offer a sampling of the strategies that eighteenth-century periodicals used when seeking to incorporate anecdote into biographical texts. The first example is the "Genuine Biographical Anecdotes of the Late Mr. Garrick," one of the first lengthy magazine obituaries, and notable in this instance for its foregrounding of "anecdote" in its title and approach. The next two examples are serialized, "anecdotal" abridgments of two book-length theatrical biographies—Thomas Davies's *Memoirs of Garrick* (1780) and James Kirkman's *Life of Charles Macklin* (1799), both of which accord different balances to anecdotes and narrative "connective tissue" (to call upon Helen Deutsch's fascinating conception of anecdote as autopsy, or "murderous fragmentation").[7] My final example is that of an article called "Anecdotes of Macklin" in *The Cabinet* magazine (1808), which was simply a string of anecdotes that, it turns out, came from William Cooke's 1804 "anecdotal" biography of Macklin. The play between chronological biography and nonsequential anecdote is particularly fascinating: in the first case, we see adjustments in the balance of the two features throughout four installments; in the latter three cases, we can juxtapose the periodical version with the book-length version of each work. In all instances, we see that the increasing primacy of anecdote in biography directly affected the development of generic expectations, and in turn, the position of the putative subject in relation to his or her story—even in obituary.

The "Genuine Biographical Anecdotes of the Late Mr. Garrick" appeared in the *Gentleman's Magazine*, starting in March 1779, in four installments (March through June) of several pages each. John Nichols assumed editorship in 1778 and almost immediately decided to expand the regularly occurring obituaries that began to run during the 1770s into longer memoirs, or "biographical anecdotes," when the deceased was considered extraordinary.[8] The "Anecdotes" represents an important development in theatrical biography, not just because of their vanguard position in magazine obituary but also because the words "Biographical Anecdotes" replaced the traditional "Memoirs of" or "Life of" form. Although Nichols's piece on Garrick gestures toward the shift in balance between a carefully chronological narrative (as in traditional obituary) and pure anecdote, which may be self-contained, this "Anecdotes" actually presents a unified narrative, situating anecdotes within the teleology of Garrick's life. For example, the May installment records the story of Dr. Hill, who once wrote a pamphlet accusing Garrick of frequently mispronouncing the letter "I" "as *furm* for *firm*, *vurtue* for *virtue*, and others."[9] Garrick responded with a witty epigram that the editor says "deserves to be preserved," in which the actor wishes that the letters "both have their due / And that *I* may never be mistaken for *U*."[10] The Hill episode occurs in the appropriate point in Garrick's life, and features Garrick as a key participant: it is as much an anecdote about Garrick as it is about Hill. It is also marked as one of the (comparatively few, apparently) significant moments of Garrick's life up until 1761, which may be a nod to his famously private personal life.

Strangely enough when the *Gentleman's Magazine* reports on a man who worked so hard to ensure his place in the popular press, the majority of the anecdotes in these issues are about other people, heavily skewed toward the first installment, and almost entirely in the form of footnotes. An epitaph for Gilbert Walmsley, registrar of the ecclesiastical court in Litchfield, and early patron of the school-aged Garrick, joins a letter supporting the job search of another companion of Garrick's life: the irrepressible Samuel Johnson. (Neither the epitaph nor the letter is, strictly, anecdotal, but they are clearly intended to be seen as such: the relationship between anecdote and -ana, or assorted documents about a person—i.e., "Garrickiana"—is worth further consideration.) Almost two entire columns of the five-column first installment are taken up by a discussion of Walmsley, and Johnson's footnotes on various subjects; the only truly novel piece of insight about Garrick himself in that same month's section is that he lost his voice during a play, but was restored by the juice of a Seville orange.[11] The second installment is even bolder in its preoccupation with characters other than Garrick, with the heading of the first page reading, paradoxically, "Biographical Anecdotes of Mr. Garrick—Fleetwood," followed by "Biographical Anecdotes of Mr. Garrick—Lacey." Garrick himself does not appear in the page that is devoted to Fleetwood: "The History of this Gentleman is very remarkable. It affords so striking a moral, and, at the same time, so important a lesson, that, though not *strictly connected* [my emphasis] with the Life of Mr. Garrick, we hope to be pardoned for inserting the following particulars concerning him," apologizes the editor, eventually offering a delightful anecdote about the genesis of the Drury Lane manager's gambling problem, namely, his mother's meddling in his love life.[12]

As the installments develop through the four-month run, we can see the magazine attempting to work out a system of incorporating anecdotes without overwhelming the main subject, evidently having perceived the proportion of stories focused on Garrick rather than other people in his orbit as needing adjustment. Although this "anecdotal biography" periodical obituary was limited by spatial constraints, the work is useful in considering the contents of theatrical biography and the distribution of those contents within the space allotted, and how the medium of any biographical work might lend itself more readily to some aspects of theatrical biography than others. We will see some striking differences between book-length and magazine-length biography with Thomas Davies's *Life of Garrick*, to which we will turn now.

Davies's project, the first widely successful eighteenth-century theatrical biography, underwent several distinct stages of composition, and its expansion and contraction clearly reflect shifting consumer interest in anecdotes. The full-length biography of 1780 was based on a three-page magazine article that Davies wrote in 1776 (under the pen name Leonato) on the occasion of Garrick's retirement that same year.[13] The article was a rather straightforward narrative of the key moments of Garrick's life, forming the barest outline for Davies's later two-volume biography, memoir, and history of the theater with David Garrick at its center. Davies's *Life* was almost immediately serialized—and drastically abridged into two installments totaling ten pages—for the *Universal Magazine* in 1780 under the title "Anecdotes of the Late David Garrick, Esq."

In reducing the two-volume *Life* into a series of articles, the editors of the *Universal Magazine* implicitly made a claim about which parts of the biography were most worthy of reproduction: the anecdotes. However, in practice, this early abridgment of a theatrical biography still included some connective tissue—a rough narrative of Garrick's life, incidentally peppered by anecdotes, but stripped of the lively cast of characters that threaten to overwhelm Nichols's biographical anecdote obituary. And while the magazine feature was a marketing device designed to sell copies of Davies's book—to give away all of the material would not only be unwise for the magazine but commercially preposterous for Davies—anecdotes, or at least the promise thereof, were clearly the means to attract a reading audience.

The *Universal Magazine* "Anecdotes" comes almost verbatim from Davies's *Life*, but without much of the context, character sketches, and incidental observations that make Davies's full text such a delightful read in the tradition of Colley Cibber's *Apology for the Life of Colley Cibber*. Indeed, this "Anecdotes" does not offer more than a handful of anecdotes in the true sense: instead, it is a narrative stripped of much of the action between Garrick and his contemporaries, and is all diverting stories of other people in which Garrick does not feature. Such small nuances form a large part of the portions from Davies's work that are more frequently in circulation today. Revealingly, while the "Anecdotes" was focused on the contours of Garrick's life, there were few *actual* anecdotes included, suggesting that the preponderance of Davies's anecdotes had been about other people rather than Garrick. Moreover, those anecdotes that featured Garrick were strangely truncated to deny him his signature wit and command: here, we see the threat of anecdote as biography in miniature compounded by the ability of an editor to decide when the anecdote has been completed, and thus, who the victor was in the anecdotal exchange. Anecdote, then, can obscure as much as it can enlighten.

Characteristic of the *Universal Magazine*'s strange editing tactics is the omission of what they considered an apparently frivolous sentence in a paragraph about Garrick's Dublin tour in the unseasonably hot summer of 1742, in which Davies (in the original, full-length text) claims that packed audiences experienced "epidemical distemper," nicknamed "the Garrick fever," a detail that proves irresistible to present-day scholars.[14] Similarly, while two excellent anecdotes of Quin and Cibber reacting to Garrick are included, sacrificed to the editorial pen is Garrick's excellent epigrammatic response to Quin's accusation that Garrickomania was a false religion.[15] Davies did record Quin's famous quip: "That Garrick was a new religion; Whitfield was followed for a time; but they would all come to church again."[16] Garrick's ensuing ten-line epigram, included in the full-length biography, captures his playful arrogance; the last four lines epitomize the characteristic sting and significance of Garrick's wit:

> Thou great infallible, forbear to roar,
> Thy bulls and errors are rever'd no more;
> When doctrines meet with gen'ral approbation,
> It is not heresy, but reformation.[17]

In the interest of space, perhaps, the *Universal Magazine* omits Garrick's retort, allowing Garrick's wit, unrepresented, to be eclipsed by his aggressor's.[18] This put the focus on Quin rather than Garrick, and, by downplaying Garrick's role, undermined the ostensible goal of anecdote in revealing the subject's character, with other participants functioning primarily to help illuminate the subject. In other instances, key events in Garrick's career that might appear to be canonical, such as his much-publicized rivalry with Spranger Barry, in which both men played Romeo in opposing playhouses on the same night, appear to have been judged as unimportant based on their absence in the abridged version.[19]

While the flavor of Davies's phrasing remains largely intact, including a beautiful critique of how Garrick delivered lines as Richard III, the reader of the serialized abridged version of the *Life* misses Davies's detailed examination of specifics and rich connections between Garrick and his world. Laudably, with the exception of the botched delivery of the Quin anecdotes, the abridged narrative's focus remains on Garrick; however, rather than emerging from the sea of detail intact, the actor seems to be playing to an empty stage. This phenomenon is not just a feature of the *Universal Magazine*'s editorial choices. Other excerpts of Davies's *Memoirs of Garrick* place the titular thespian firmly offstage, with the *London Magazine* offering "Memoirs of Mrs. Woffington, From the Life of David Garrick, Esq." and the *Universal Magazine* promoting the "Biographical Anecdotes of Mr. James Ralph, the political writer, From Davies's Life of Garrick." Such articles were predicated on the vogue for miniature biographies of the subject's contemporaries within a larger biography. In short, the generic demands for individual and group biography, or "stage history," within full-length memoirs almost ensured that some excerpts would have little to nothing to do with the supposed subject.

Acting as a double-edged sword, greatly abridged periodical versions of a longer text both publicize the work and, in the process of abridgment, allow the reader a seemingly much clearer, but often skewed, perspective from which to critique the entire work primarily sight unseen. Clearly, an author or editor had to walk a fine line when it came to the number of anecdotes and the proportion of anecdotes focused on people other than the main character, and that balance was especially tricky when navigating the spatial constraints of periodicals.

It seems that both presentations of the "anecdotal" lives of David Garrick in the periodical press struggled to find the appropriate balance between narrative and anecdote: the obituary provided anecdotes about other people at the expense of narrative about Garrick, and the Davies abridgment chose a more straightforward, chronological narrative at the expense of anecdote, despite presenting itself as "Anecdotes." The seeming failures of "anecdotal" abridgment in actually providing anecdotes would be replicated and rectified (respectively) by a serialized abridgment of Thomas Kirkman's 1799 biography of comedian Charles Macklin. The editors of the *Edinburgh Magazine* present the "Anecdotes of Charles Macklin," which lacks any sort of narrative tissue available in Kirkman's original (including Kirkman's signature philosophical and moral framing) in favor of displaying pure anecdotes. However, these anecdotes, almost entirely about people on the periphery of Macklin's life, served less to reveal anything about Macklin himself than to tour through a menagerie of loosely related characters engaged in anecdote-friendly activities.

Further examination reveals several light, but by no means codified, patterns, including that the title "Biographical Anecdotes" in magazine articles seems to indicate more narrative and less actual anecdote (what we may—erroneously, as noted earlier—think of as more "classical" biography than anecdotally driven material), and more exclusive focus on the thespian whose life is under examination. "Anecdotes of," however, indicates a focus on an actor, an actor and his circle, or the circle itself; this material is grouped within an overarching narrative framework or simply as disjointed paragraphs that allow the anecdotes to speak for themselves. We can see that authors (and editors) are still working through the relationship between anecdote and other biographical content in deciding what constitutes a *Life* worth reading.

The war between anecdote and sustained life-writing can be perceived clearly in three full-length biographies of the comedian Charles Macklin, all appearing within a five-year period immediately after Macklin's death in 1797: in brief, the first biographer refused to indulge in any anecdotes (not a well-received choice); the second indulged in a Fielding-esque style with plenty of anecdotal diversions (panned for its slapdash inclusion of everything even remotely related to Macklin); and the third, eminently practical biographer, who almost certainly took his cue from magazines, straightforwardly called his work an "anecdotal biography," by which he meant that his text contained a reasonably consistent but not overly intrusive narrative through line that provided a rough timeline for plenty of anecdotes.

As we can see in smaller biographical accounts that precede a full-length book, anecdotes often formed the first grains around which a larger narrative of a theatrical life developed into a publishable work. It is no coincidence that Macklin's anecdote-embracing second and third biographers, Kirkman and Cooke, serialized their memoirs of Macklin in magazines before presenting their work in whole as freestanding volumes. However, while Cooke's narrative (which was marketed explicitly as "a new species of biography") ran, unmolested by abridgment, Kirkman's more fanciful and novelistic rendering of his "protagonist's" life was reduced from a tissue of anecdote-driven narrative to a collection of anecdotes without the gathering membrane of a larger story. For example, one installation of Kirkman's memoirs appears in the *Universal Magazine* in May 1799 under the heading "Anecdotes of Charles Macklin" and is indicated as coming "from his Life, in 2 vols., by Kirkman." Like the collections of primarily unrelated anecdotes to which publications such as the *Theatrical Monitor, or the Green Room* belonged, the *Universal Magazine*'s presentation of Kirkman cherry-picked anecdotes from the narrative. Characteristic is one example of an anecdote centered on the manager of Covent Garden, John Rich, who, upon witnessing a patron tumble from the upper gallery of Covent Garden, "very generously ordered that he should have every possible assistance . . . at Mr. Rich's expence."[20] The story builds to this punch line: "Mr. Rich told him that he should be welcome to the freedom of the pit, provided he would never think of coming into it in that manner again!"[21] In the particular context of the magazine, the anecdotes were not used for the sake of illustrating anything particular about Macklin; instead, they strip Kirkman's attempts at philosophical or moral framing and frequently focus on secondary characters in Kirkman's narratives. These anecdotes are tangential to Macklin's story, suggesting something about these minor figures and their relationship with Macklin, if indeed the actor appeared at all.

In the dismembering of Kirkman's volumes, the magazine editors made headings of character names like "Anecdote of Rich, the Manager" to force crude divisions between anecdotes that, in Kirkman's work, appear many pages apart. The anecdote of Rich as manager, stripped of its embedded meaning in the narrative, stands out like a sore thumb in a smattering of anecdotes about Macklin; this suggests both the editor's disinterest in restricting the subject matter to the supposed subject, Macklin, and a desire to maximize Kirkman's writing as a source of brief, catchy stories at the expense of any greater purpose in telling Macklin's story.

What falls under the rubric of "anecdote" is worth considering, especially as anecdotes increasingly achieve greater ability to stand alone outside of a larger biographical narrative framework. In the same document where Rich, "the Manager," receives his own heading and a legitimate anecdote, of the other six items, only two of them are properly what we think of as anecdote. The fracas between James Quin and Macklin over the latter's "damned tricks" onstage, and Macklin's subsequent failure to appear on the dueling field ("at the Obelisk, in Covent-garden") was apparently a favorite chestnut of Macklin's, "often related [by himself] with that luxuriant force of description, which characterized his story telling."[22] The anecdote is doubly desirable for the story-revealing truths about Macklin (and Quin, of course) as characters, and also about Macklin's abilities as a narrator. Its weakness as an anecdote, the clear resistance to providing only bare essences, is at least partially absolvable because Macklin himself was not, generally speaking, pithy. The third entry in these "so-called "Anecdotes of Charles Macklin" is a rare example of true anecdote:

> There was one circumstance occurred during the rehearsal of this piece (The True Born Irishman, a farce, written by Macklin) which we shall take leave to mention here. One of the performers, to instruct whom Mr. Macklin had taken infinite pains, having occasion to announce "*Lady Kinnegad*," and not pronouncing the name as the veteran liked, he stepped up to him,

> and, in an angry tone, exclaimed, "What trade are you, sir?"—The performer replied, "Sir, I am a *gentleman*!" "Then," rejoined the stage Nestor, "stick to that, sir; for you will never be an *actor*!"

It is pithy, characteristic, focused entirely on Macklin, and wrought in his own words (though not to the extent of longer anecdotes in which Macklin is a participant and the narrator). It is the only such example offered in "Anecdotes of Charles Macklin, from his Life, by Kirkman" (but not in Kirkman's full-length *Life*).[23] Other items, including letters, criticism, and Macklin's infamous "character sketch" of Garrick, were all described by the editor as "the most remarkable [anecdotes] given [in Kirkman's work]."[24] However, the most accurate term for the type of material the *Universal Magazine* published was "Macklinana," where the "-ana" suffix indicated the record left behind of one's life, including letters, publications, musings, and oral contributions codified into print. A similar pattern is replicated in the *Weekly Entertainer*'s "Character and Anecdotes of the Late Celebrated Actor Charles Macklin" (1799), also based on excerpts from Kirkman's *Life*. Despite the title's promise of "anecdotes," character dominates in the *Weekly Entertainer*. A lone story of Macklin's participation in a subscription for the recently deceased poet Thomas Cooke is overwhelmed by the promised summative "character" of Macklin; the rest of the document is composed of the driest biographical facts to be found in Kirkman's original, a feat unto itself in such a flavorful work.

Should readers of excerpted biography be forced to choose between biographical detail about the subject or amusing anecdotes that are legitimately about the subject at hand? It would seem so, at least as represented in magazines. Consider the "Anecdotes of Macklin," from *The Cabinet* magazine, published in September 1808. The *Cabinet* piece is useful in undermining the possibility that Macklin just did not say anything witty, which would have otherwise explained the scarcity of good anecdotes about him in abridgments of Kirkman's work. The "Anecdotes of Macklin," accurately named, boasts eight sterling examples of anecdote, all of which conclude with Macklin making an observation in the form of a witty retort. Representative is this story: "A gentleman at a public dinner asking him, inconsiderately, whether he remembered Mrs. Barry, the celebrated Actress, who died about the latter end of Queen Ann's [*sic*] reign, he planted his countenance directly against him with great severity, and bawled out, 'No, Sir—nor Harry the Eighth either—They were both dead before my time.'"[25] This is the perfect essence of Macklin distilled into an anecdote: the other player in the story is practically irrelevant beyond being an impetus for Macklin's wit, Macklin's movement, speech patterns (including the condescending, characteristic "sir"), and attitude are all captured instantly, and his supposed exact words are repeated. Best of all, our hero gets the best of the transaction, and we are reminded that Macklin was cranky, ungracious, and hot-tempered, even in his dotage. All of this is done compactly and memorably, and points to the truth of Bent's earlier-quoted optimism about the power of anecdote to bring long-dead men directly into view with breathtaking clarity.

As it turns out, the Queen Anne anecdote and the rest of the material from the *Cabinet* magazine article are taken verbatim (and unheralded) from a third full-length biography of Macklin by William Cooke. Cooke's biography was unique to its time in capitalizing on the vogue for anecdotes and biography by straightforwardly writing an anecdotal biography that was heavy on anecdote without completely sacrificing narrative tissue. Cooke argues that anecdotes were central to Macklin's personal discourse and observes: "As to anecdotes, he [Macklin] was rich in [them] . . . which rendered his company, occasionally, very entertaining and improving . . . when he attempted to shew off his reading, [he] was tedious, and embarrassed beyond measure—but when he gave us his experience of life, he evidently shewed he did not live inattentively."[26] Thus, Cooke justified his own reliance on anecdote, and since he forthrightly subjugated connective narrative to anecdotes, it was easier to abridge his work without feeling the competing strain between factual matter and representative story.

But there is a darker implication to the sort of biography that Cooke produced, to magazine "anecdotal biographies" and even more purely anecdotal works like *The Repository of Wit*. The movement of anecdote into a single scene detached from a larger narrative evokes opportunistic and transgressive possibilities: unmoored from surrounding frameworks or assessments, anecdote can transition from being an integral part of a philosophical meditation on the character under discussion to being simply an easily traded, cheaply consumed commodity, with the very name "anecdote" used as a catchall for any easily excerpted fragment. After all, anecdotes took very little space to print and could mingle promiscuously in a hodgepodge that lacked organization even by the eighteenth century's remarkably loose standards. This combination of unmediated and disorganized snippets meant that such compilations did not take very much energy to edit and could largely be reused from edition to edition with some updated or new material supplanting the old chestnuts after several editions.

While the dynamics governing anecdote are undoubtedly complex, at its root, anecdote thrived in the rich soil of periodicals, where editors had precious little space and time, and where readers received a comparatively high bang for their buck, so to speak, in being able to trade anecdotes—being brief and memorable—about specific public players and thus seem to be "in the know." This trade, in turn, meant that complex lives were reduced to portable trifles—not a bad thing, perhaps, in the context of classical biography, except that often the moral lesson or implication was discarded for humor or novelty.

Ultimately, the most successful example of anecdotal writing in the four examples discussed here is the one that least resembles what contemporary audiences would recognize as true biography: the unmediated Macklin anecdotes from *The Cabinet*. When presented in the context of a larger biography, the anecdotes that formed a cornerstone of celebrity worship also distracted readers from sustained contemplation and understanding of the supposed central actor-subject. Clearly, the dominance of anecdote during this period profoundly impacted our impression of individual eighteenth-century actors in relation to their social milieu, while also affecting future life-writing practices and debates.

Notes

1. M. Lafayette Byrn, *Repository of Wit and Humor: Comprising More Than One Thousand Anecdotes, Odd Scraps, Off-hand Hits, and Humorous Sketches* (Boston: J. P. Jewett & Company, 1853), 25–26.

2. My attempts to locate the original source of this anecdote have been fruitless.

3. S. Arthur Bent, "The Illuminating Power of Anecdote," *The North American Review* 55, no. 430 (1892): 347.

4. See Leslie Ritchie's chapter in this volume, "Killing Delane; or, Mimickry and the *Anecdota obscura*."

5. James Boswell, *The Journal of a Tour to the Hebrides* (London: Henry Baldwin, 1785), 32.

6. Francis T. Glasson, "The Place of the Anecdote: A Note on Form Criticism," *The Journal of Theological Studies* 32, no. 1 (1981): 143.

7. Helen Deutsch, *Loving Dr. Johnson* (Chicago: University of Chicago Press, 2005), 65.

8. See N. D. Norman, "From a Record of Death to a Memory of Life: The Rise of the Biographical Obituary in the *Gentleman's Magazine*" (master's thesis, Virginia Tech, 2008).

9. "Genuine Biographical Anecdotes of David Garrick" (3), *The Gentleman's Magazine* 49 (May 1779): 226–228.

10. "Genuine Biographical Anecdotes of David Garrick" (3), 227.

11. "Genuine Biographical Anecdotes of David Garrick" (1), *The Gentleman's Magazine* 49 (March 1779): 117–119.

12. "Genuine Biographical Anecdotes of David Garrick" (2), *The Gentleman's Magazine* 49 (April 1779): 171–173, 171.

13. Leonato [Thomas Davies], "Eulogium on Mr. Garrick's Leaving the Stage," *Gentleman's Magazine* 46 (1776).

14. See, for instance, Heather Ladd, "Theatre, Celebrity, and Contagion: David Garrick's 1742 Dublin Visit and James R. Planché's *Garrick Fever*," *Theatre Notebook* 72, no. 2 (2018): 78–99.

15. Thomas Davies, "Anecdotes of the Late David Garrick" (1), *Universal Magazine* 66 (June 1780): 252–256, 255–256.

16. Thomas Davies, *Memoirs of the Life of David Garrick* (London: Printed for the author, 1780), 1:45.

17. Davies, *Memoirs of the Life of David Garrick*, 1:45.

18. In the editor's decision to remove Garrick's marvelous response to Quin's verbal attack, we see the more malevolent meaning of Ritchie's *Anecdota obscura*, in which the obsession with singularity results in a false sense of victor and victim of wit.

19. See, for instance, Elaine M. McGirr, "'What's in a Name?': Romeo and Juliet and the Cibber Brand," *Shakespeare* 14, no. 4 (October 2, 2018): 399–412, and Leslie Ritchie, "Pox on Both Your Houses: The Battle of the Romeos," *Eighteenth-Century Fiction* 27, no. 3 (2015): 373–393.

20. James Kirkman, "Anecdotes of Charles Macklin, from his Life, by Kirkman," *Universal Magazine* 104 (May 1799): 317–324, 318.

21. Kirkman, "Anecdotes of Charles Macklin," 318.

22. Kirkman, "Anecdotes of Charles Macklin," 318.

23. Kirkman, "Anecdotes of Charles Macklin," 318.

24. Kirkman, "Anecdotes of Charles Macklin," 317.

25. William Cooke, "Anecdotes of Charles Macklin," *The Cabinet* 4 (September 1808): 191–192, 192.

26. William Cooke [Cook], *Memoirs of Charles Macklin, Comedian* (1804; Charleston, SC: Nabu, 2011), 429.

11

QUEERING ROXANE FROM DAVENANT TO RICHARDSON

DANIELLE BOBKER

> "woman + woman is central to the question of modernity itself"
>
> —Susan Lanser

A theatrical anecdote recounted in Anthony Hamilton's secret history of the Restoration court, *Memoirs of Count Grammont* (1714), anchors a queer intertextual network that reaches back to William Davenant's two-part *Siege of Rhodes* (1656, 1661) and Nathaniel Lee's *The Rival Queens* (1677), and forward to Daniel Defoe's *Roxana* (1724) and, more obliquely, Samuel Richardson's *Pamela* (1740).[1] In the longest episode of Hamilton's *Memoirs*, an experienced maid of honor, Miss Hobart, shares a bit of gossip about an actress who, after an earl dupes her into a sham marriage, comes mockingly to be known only by the name of the Eastern queen character she had recently performed to acclaim. Versions of this story, which may refer to the actress Hester Davenport, circulated widely in and around the Restoration court—the epilogue to *The Rival Queens* mentions it, and in her *Memoirs of the Court of England* (1707), Marie d'Aulnoy turns it into a gripping gothic episode in which the deceived actress edges toward madness and self-destruction.[2] In Hamilton's *Memoirs*, the anecdote explicitly serves as a cautionary tale about the sexual double standard: Miss Hobart is warning her young protégée, Anne Temple, about the predatory sexuality of libertine men.[3] However, via its allusion to orientalist Restoration drama, Hamilton's version also slyly underscores the erotic designs of the female courtier who recounts it. At least two literary historians have noted in passing the *Memoirs*'s significance as a source for eighteenth-century novelists.[4] This chapter aims at once to flesh out and expand the scope of these proposed intertextual connections, showing how the *Memoirs*'s actress anecdote bridges gaps not only between the seventeenth and eighteenth centuries, fact and fiction, the court and the commercial sphere, and drama and the novel, but also, crucially—by bringing home the polymorphous perversity that English writers had typically projected Eastward in this period—between patriarchal heterosexuality and female–female desire.

Arguably, all anecdotes are queer in its broadest sense. From the Greek word meaning "unpublished things," "anecdote" came into English usage with the publication of the seventeenth-century translation of the sixth-century *Anecdota; or the Secret History*, which, unlike Procopius's eight military histories of Emperor Justinian, focused on tales of debauchery and excess at court, like the one about the Empress Theodora having geese peck barley grains from between her legs as she lay undressed onstage.[5] By definition, anecdotes tell the unofficial story, the quick and dirty chronicle of events that no one entirely believes, but everyone wants to hear. Yet, since inevitably anecdotes do find audiences, whether only by means of whispered conversations or in writing as well, the original meaning of the word underscores an essential paradox of the form. Moreover, because of this irresistible appeal, anecdotes—the original memes—have always been deceptively powerful media of cultural transmission and literary innovation. Thus, Helen Deutsch describes the anecdote as "the seed at the heart of narrative" that may engender any number of new stories, and, similarly, Andrea Loselle observes, "Just one can . . . be the kernel from which a whole novel grows."[6] As they pass through unpredictable, potentially viral circuits, anecdotes may quickly reproduce or remix not only the manifest elements of other narratives, such as character, setting, or plot, but also the latent elements as well—the affects, nuances, and subtexts. Channeling the many feelings generated and expressed in embodied performances, including, after the Restoration, those involving the new presence of women on the public stage—often in breeches roles that highlighted the fluidity of gender—anecdotes about goings-on in and around the theater were especially ripe with queer possibility.[7]

As we shall see, the general appeal of the duped actress anecdote had to do in part with how it reiterated a famous historical narrative about the Ottoman concubine who had deigned to set the terms of her own sexual contract with a sultan. But the special impact of Hamilton's version lay in how he nested this straight plot within another one—linked to the same historical figure—about navigating patriarchal sexuality by way of a significant attachment to another woman. With respect to form, this chapter will consider the processes of domestication that Hamilton initiates.[8] In his *Secret History of Domesticity*, Michael McKeon traces the eighteenth-century emergence of the English domestic novel from the older genre of secret history, showing how this literary evolution entailed the transfer of questions of sovereignty and sexuality from royal dynasties—where reproduction, marriage, and other close alliances had a self-evident political value—down the social ladder to nonelite couples and individuals. Significantly, Hamilton's *Memoirs* contributes to this broader English process of formal change by reversing a long tradition of cross-cultural projection: by eliciting comparisons between interpersonal dynamics at and around the Stuart court and the theater it sponsored, and those more often associated with Eastern despotism in this period, the text also makes these patterns of feeling available for further interrogation and transformation in local contexts.

With respect to affect and attachments, however, the focus here is not exclusively on heterosexuality, which has preoccupied literary historians accounting for the rise of the domestic novel, but also on homosocial desire, the patterns of identification, affection, competition, and erotic attraction that bond people of the same sex to one another, often most powerfully through their necessary engagement in heterosexual economies. When Eve Sedgwick coined the term "homosocial desire" in *Between Men*, she privileged the literary representation of male experience on the grounds that the patriarchal exchange of women has made men's bonds with one another more fraught and culturally charged than those of women.[9] Subsequently, Sharon Marcus has proposed that, while it is true that the borders between heterosexuality, homoeroticism, and hate have not been policed so rigorously for women as for men, women's relationships are (and were historically) no less complex and vital. Her *Between Women* shows how all kinds of intense female–female bonds were continuous with and even foundational to marriage and motherhood in nineteenth-century British writing.[10] Hamilton's actress anecdote opens up an earlier literary history in which female homosocial desire draws on and redirects sovereign power.

In early editions of Hamilton's *Memoirs*, the name of the character that the duped actress plays differs. In the original French publication, Hamilton gave Roxelane (Roxolana) as the actress's role. In the first English translation, Abel Boyer changed it to Roxana, a variation that was retained in some, but not all, subsequent translations. The alteration is unsurprising given that these similar names were often used interchangeably in the period. Indeed, several feminist literary historians, recognizing the extent to which Roxana and Roxolana characters overlapped in the European orientalist imagination, refer to the composite figure they formed as Roxane, a practice I continue here.[11] Although the original Roxana and the original Roxolana lived nearly two thousand years apart, both were foreign first wives of renowned Eastern conquerors with a reputation for murderous jealousy. In the fourth century B.C.E., Roxana, the Persian first wife of Alexander the Great, allegedly killed the emperor's second wife, Statira, with an eye to her own son's future as Alexander's successor. In the sixteenth century, Roxolana, a Ukrainian-born Turkish slave ("Russelana"), became the first woman to marry an Ottoman sultan, and later allegedly convinced him to kill his eldest son by another concubine.[12]

Feminist critics have already considered how seventeenth- and eighteenth-century European Roxane myths mingled fantasies and fears of Eastern excess with homegrown misogyny, arguing that, whether she appeared on the stage or the page, Roxane was conjured as the quintessential performer, possessing an uncanny ability—both mesmerizing and terrifying—not only to stir others' sexual desires but also to embody and exploit a wide range of passions while concealing her selfish motives and interests. Katie Trumpener proposes that Roxane came to symbolize "womanhood itself: mysterious, sensual, resentful."[13] Ros Ballaster points out how Roxane, eager to costume and display her own exotic appeal, came to personify "the vicious source of an incitement to luxury that wastes the manly powers of a nation."[14] Felicity Nussbaum explores Roxane's violent and duplicitous protectiveness of her children.[15] Attending to the homosocial shadow narrative running through Hamilton's ostensibly straight theatrical anecdote gives a new edge to the Eastern epithet as an index of the interplay between women's heterosexual ambitions and their potent relationships with one another.

Although the central plot of Hamilton's Roxane anecdote concerns heterosexual relations, it is arguably formally queer insofar as it twists the period's best-known historical Roxane narrative, a slave-to-sultaness tale in Richard Knolles's *Generall Historie of the Turkes* (1603), into an inverted allegory. That is, the full meaning of Hamilton's anecdote is gleaned only when readers compare the characters and events not (as with a typical allegory) to more recent or better-known English counterparts, but rather to temporally and geographically more distant—Eastern—ones. Hamilton's wry female courtier, Miss Hobart, explains that one of the highest-ranking men in England had become so infatuated with the brilliant Roxane actress that even gambling and smoking had lost their appeal. Yet, being "both very virtuous and very modest, or wonderfully obstinate," Hobart conjectures, the actress "proudly rejected" all of the earl's many propositions, promises, and gifts until he offered to marry her in a private ceremony—only to discover the morning after that the wedding was a fake, with the earl's own trumpeter and drummer in the roles of priest and witness. The earl provides the actress with a yearly maintenance but nothing more: she has not been made a lady but confirmed a whore. The actress looks to King Charles for amends for the earl's "infamous imposition," but "in vain did she throw herself at the king's feet . . . she had only to rise up again without redress" and told to think herself "happy . . . to receive an annuity of one thousand crowns, and to resume the name of [Roxane], instead of Countess of Oxford."[16]

Roxane's defeat in this battle of the sexes pointedly reverses the outcome of Richard Knolles's famous narrative, which accounts for Solyman the Magnificent's mid-sixteenth-century marriage to Roxolana—a first in the history of the Turkish empire. Traditionally, an Ottoman sultan did not marry. Instead, sultans afforded special privileges to those concubines—generally female prisoners of war—who gave birth to boys, particularly to the mothers of first-born or favorite sons in line for the throne. With no parliament and no hereditary nobility under him, authority was concentrated in the sultan's hands, and it was thought a wife—necessarily a free woman—could absorb and appropriate his power to a dangerous degree.[17] Knolles writes that the enslaved Roxolana orchestrated her own rise by feigning piety until Solyman agreed to release her from bondage, then by denying him sex on religious grounds until he agreed to formalize their union under Allah.[18] Knowing the unprecedented success of her Eastern namesake casts an ironic shadow around the English actress's fate. Like the Ottoman concubine, she tries to leverage her desirability to a prominent man. But she has overestimated the value placed on sex by the men at the English court.[19] While the actress does stand to benefit financially from the earl's deal, the notoriety she gains in place of a royal title effectively lowers her public position. Ultimately, her theatrical role as sultaness usurps her English identity, and the name Roxane, formerly a mark of recognition for her sublime performance, becomes an ironic sign of the audaciousness and spectacular failure of her off-stage ambitions. A fellow actor jokes that the actress's talent for suspending her disbelief might now help her cope with her real-life disgrace: "The Sultana [Roxane] . . . might have supposed, in some part or other of a play, that she was really married."[20] The sad truth is, the earl outperformed her.

Miss Hobart relays this anecdote to her protégée after having undressed her, as they lounge on a couch in the antechamber of a bathing closet. Ostensibly, Hobart means to warn Temple about men like the Earl of Rochester, who has recently begun toying with the ingenue's affections—to let her know what happens to women who inflate the value of their sex appeal. Yet the noblewoman, notorious at court for being "particularly attached to the fair sex," is, like the actress in her anecdote, a performer too, with her own hidden agenda.[21] Miss Hobart's previous female favorite recently jilted her for Rochester. Since Rochester now has his eye on Temple as well, through Temple Hobart has the chance to even the score with her rival. Given the events that occasion it, therefore, Hobart's story of sexual coercion is also part of her own strategic play for dominance. The actress's Eastern epithet undoubtedly serves to comment on the ruthlessness of men at the Restoration court. At the same time, the embedded allusion to orientalist English drama winks at the intricate homoerotic context in which the anecdote has been relayed.

Climactic discovery scenes in Davenant's and Lee's orientalist seventeenth-century plays explore how despotic male power inflames female–female intimacies in unexpected yet highly consequential ways. Numerous factors made the East a common screen for the erotic projections of seventeenth-century English and European writers. Classical notions of temperament, which held that warmer climates naturally made people more passionate, were reinforced by orientalist religious, political, and literary associations that linked Islam with polygamy and hot-water bathing (itself considered a source of libidinal fire), despotism with sexual slavery and sexual competition in the seraglio, and Eastern landscapes with pastoral sensuality. Homoerotic desires were thought to flourish in the sex-segregated spaces of harem and hammam as an almost inevitable outcome of bodies deprived of heterosexual outlets for their lust. Thus, sexual tensions between women formed a strong undercurrent within orientalist writing in all genres.[22] Exploiting these long-standing queer and exotic associations, Davenant's and Lee's plots also grapple, at the level of metatheater, with the new forms of theatrical intimacy afforded by the advent of the proscenium arch and shutter stage, and particularly of female players themselves.

In his two-part heroic drama, Davenant invents an idealized homosocial Roxane. Multiple plots in *The Siege of Rhodes* align Solyman's military victory over Rhodes with the resolution of a pair of parallel and interlocking conjugal disputes: that of Solyman and Roxolana and that of Alphonso, the Duke of Sicily and protector of Rhodes, and his bride-to-be, a woman-warrior named Ianthe. Roxolana has accompanied the sultan to the Mediterranean, but Solyman finds Roxolana cloying and demanding, a distraction from his serious man business. Ianthe, on the other hand, who sells the jewels in her dowry to pay for her passage to Rhodes, fights alongside her fiancé. While Alphonso admires her bravery, he worries about Ianthe's virtue. In part 1 of the play, the Turks capture Ianthe. But Solyman, captivated in turn by Ianthe's courage and sense of duty, allows her to return to Alphonso, his enemy. Upon hearing that Solyman has freed Ianthe after a private encounter, Roxolana and

Alphonso are both wracked with jealousy. In part II, as the European army collapses, Ianthe voluntarily puts her trust in Solyman, returning to the Ottoman camp to negotiate a truce. Rather than meeting with Ianthe himself, however, the sultan devises a test for Roxolana.

When the shutters open in act 4, scene 3, the space is "*wholy fill'd with ROXOLANA'S Rich Pavillion, wherein is discern'd at distance, IANTHE sleeping on a Couch; ROXOLANA at one End of it.*"[23] The "*Turkish Embroidered Handkerchief in* [Roxolana's] *left hand*" and "*naked Ponyard* [dagger] *in her right*" symbolize the sultaness's dilemma at this moment: she can lead Ianthe to Solyman's bed and thus seal the Ottoman victory or she can murder Ianthe and extend the war with Rhodes. Parting the curtains that surround the couch, Roxolana is so struck by Ianthe's beauty that at first she feels she has no choice but to surrender her marriage bed. "I am Conquer'd who came here to kill," she whispers.[24] Then Roxolana addresses Ianthe directly:

> I have a Present for you,
> ....
> And, though 'tis single now, it quickly can
> Be multipli'd; you shall have many more.
> It is this kiss—It comes from *Solyman*.[25]

When Ianthe is "amaz'd, and must go back," Roxolana laughs at her: "Are Christian Ladies so reserv'd and shy?"[26] But she soon softens:

> Draw near, and give me your fair hand.—
> I have another Present for you now;
> And such a Present as I know
> You will much better than the first allow;
> Though *Solyman* will not esteem it so.
> 'Tis from my self—of friendship such a Seal—[*Kisses her.*]
> As you to *Solyman* must ne'r reveal.—
> And that I may be more assur'd,
> By this agen you are conjur'd.—[27]

Roxolana's passions turn repeatedly throughout this scene. Before seeing Ianthe, she is enraged. On seeing her, Roxolana is sensually "conquered," as she says, and identifies with the sultan's desire, embracing Ianthe in her public role as his envoy. But Ianthe's resistance affects her again: her next kiss is "from my self" and a sign of

Roxolana's own "friendship." From the vantage of this direct connection, she comes to see both herself and her rival as independent moral agents, able to make an agreement of their own. So long as Ianthe remains loyal to Roxolana and refuses Solyman, she shall live—and Roxolana, for her part, will use her influence with him to end the war on different terms. In this way, Davenant attributes Roxolana's heroism to the force and fluidity of her feelings throughout this encounter—the way her aggression quickly transforms into an erotic attraction, and then a reciprocal political identification. Suddenly capable of thinking beyond patriarchal triangulation, Roxolana devises an original strategy for military and conjugal peace: together she and Ianthe transcend the sultan's double bind. Over the course of the two-part drama, Roxolana's feelings for Ianthe cover the whole homosocial spectrum, including a highly patriarchal form of competitiveness. Yet the play's resolution depends on an attachment to Ianthe in which the sultan is extraneous, serving neither as conduit nor obstacle to Roxane's desires.

The climactic scene of Nathaniel Lee's domestic tragedy, like that of Davenant's heroic drama, draws its intensity from female homosocial desire. But whereas Davenant celebrates the political yields of women's alliances, Lee revels in the spectacle of their violent collapse. War in the Indies has just ended, but it is when Alexander comes home to Babylon in triumph at the start of the play that his real troubles begin. Returning with him, Roxana gloats over a private victory. During the celebration in Susa, Alexander has broken his vow of loyalty to Statira, his milder-mannered second wife. The ensuing conjugal conflict parallels the mutiny brewing among the rival courtiers plotting Alexander's assassination. Statira first swears that to punish his infidelity, she will never see Alexander again. Later, however, in a confrontation with Roxana, Statira's anger at her female rival displaces her anger at her husband:

> What [the queen mother's] threats, objected fears,
> My sister's sighs, and Alexander's tears
> Could not effect, thy rival rage has done.
> . . . .
> I'll see the king in spite of all I swore,
> Though curst, that thou mayst never see him more.[28]

As in the *Siege of Rhodes*, the climax of *The Rival Queens* is a discovery scene. Statira is asleep in a bower, awaiting Alexander, when Roxana approaches her, dagger in hand:

ROXANA.
Come, give me back his heart,
And thou shalt live, live empress of the world.

STATIRA.
The world is less than Alexander's love,
Yet, could I give it, 'tis not in my power.
This I dare promise, if you spare my life,
Which I disdain to beg, he shall speak kindly.

ROXANA.
Speak! Is that all?

STATIRA.
Perhaps at my request,
And for a gift so noble as my life,
Bestow a kiss.

ROXANA.
A kiss! No more?

STATIRA
[*aside*]. O gods!
What shall I say to work her to my end?
Fain I would see him.[*Aloud.*] Yes, a little more,
Embrace you, and forever be your friend.

ROXANA.
O, the provoking word! Your friend! Thou di'st.
Your friend! What must I bring you then together?
Adorn your bed and see you softly laid?[29]

In *The Siege of Rhodes*, conjugal, erotic, and imperial matters are intricately interwoven: Roxolana's facility in transforming competition into erotic desire for and autonomous identification with her rival—sublimating her sexual jealousy—is her supreme heroic virtue. In *Rival Queens*, by contrast, both empresses privilege conjugal matters over affairs of state. In fact, Roxana is willing to exchange her political dominance as first lady for Statira's current dominance in the bedroom: "Give me back his heart, / And thou shalt . . . live empress of the world." Statira's reply—"'tis not in my power"—reflects the primary importance that she also attributes to Alexander's sexual favor. Statira taunts that even if she could negotiate a conjugal truce between the emperor and his first wife, the results would be forced—a mechanical kiss, a dutiful embrace, a polite "friendship" at arm's length. Significantly, Roxana is able to see Statira through Alexander's eyes, to imagine her as an object of his desire—"What must I . . . / Adorn your bed and see you softly laid?" But unlike Davenant's heroine, Lee's Roxane character does not use this flexible sexual imagination as the basis of a new autonomous bond. Her rival does, however. When the poisoned Alexander at last stumbles into the bower, Statira, dying from the wound Roxana has inflicted, instructs him: "Spare Roxana's life; / 'Twas love of you that caused her give me death."[30] Statira's last-minute diplomacy curses Roxana to live on, alone, as she and Alexander take their final breaths together.

In Davenant's and Lee's plays, despotic foreign courts provide grand mirrors of new channels of homosocial desire in Restoration England, including the tensions and tentative truces between the king's childless Catholic wife and his many fruitful live-in mistresses, the variety of closet alliances and rivalries between other female courtiers and courtesans at Whitehall Palace, and the new backstage dramas between women urged to compete for elite male attention and for their first professional roles in English theater. With her multiple triangulated motives, Hobart is made by Hamilton after the fashion of an orientalist Roxane. Hobart's attraction to Temple is not really separable from her desire to top Rochester or at least to channel his own presumed sexual prerogative. Moreover, since the favor of her mistress, the Duchess of York, has provided Hobart with access to the bathing closet in the first place, we must also consider that her preachy attempt to seduce Miss Temple there also extends from her obligation to please the duchess, whose own reputation depends on those of her maids of honor. The passions between women that Davenant and Lee portrayed as the key to Roxane's greatness and her hubris, respectively, are undoubtedly cooled and tamed, appearing more controllable and less consequential when

Hamilton transposes them to Miss Hobart's rational English heart. The implicit ironic distance between Hobart and the Roxanes on the Restoration stage suggests the diminishing intensity and political scope of relationships between women as absolutist structures of feeling—like Whitehall Palace itself, which had burned to the ground in 1698—were beginning to fade from collective memory. However, unlike his straight Roxane, Hamilton does give his queer Roxane some of the charisma of her predecessors. Although Hobart does not ultimately succeed in seducing Temple, neither does she fall from the Duchess's favor, even after the attempt becomes the latest scandal to entertain the court.[31]

And Roxane persisted, in all her complexity. Handwritten notes in Northrop Frye's personal copy show that, as he was reading the *Memoirs*, the influential critic intuited the afterlife of Hamilton's version of the theatrical anecdote in eighteenth-century novels. Obviously finding Miss Hobart's combination of seduction and didacticism telling, Frye wrote in the margins near the start of the bathing-closet episode, "A long improving moral lecture delivered to a naked woman, by a Lesbian: what a period!" Then, beside the anecdote itself, he speculated, "Source for Defoe? source for Richardson?"[32] David Blewett has also briefly made the case that Hamilton's interpolated anecdote was an important source for Daniel Defoe's novel *The Fortunate Mistress: or, a History of the Life of Mademoiselle de Beleau Known by the Name of Lady Roxana*, which, like Hamilton's actress and his own protagonist, also came to be widely known simply as *Roxana*.[33] The inspiration that Defoe took from the orientalist female figure of conjugal ambition is plainly signaled in the novel's title. Less immediately obvious is how Hamilton's interpolated theatrical anecdote also provided a valuable template for the novel's layered psychosexual dynamics.

The central straight plot of *Roxana* riffs on the formal and affective structure of the core of Hamilton's anecdote. Having followed Roxane from the Ottoman seraglio to the Restoration theater, Hamilton brought her into the backrooms at Whitehall Palace that he knew well, thanks to the endless reminiscing of his older sister and her husband, Count Grammont. Cued by and building on Hamilton's revision, the business-minded Defoe updates Knolles's Ottoman rags-to-riches story once again, spinning it into a fictional spiritual autobiography or what we might call a Puritan secret history, in which, retrospectively and with regret, Roxane reflects on her own remarkable success in navigating the newly thriving commercial sphere. Defoe's Roxane acquires the name mid-career when, deliberately stirring up orientalist fantasies, she dances for a party of English courtiers—and, it is implied, King Charles himself—in a magnificent Turkish dress. "One of the Gentlemen cry'd out *Roxana! Roxana!*, By —, with an Oath," she recalls, "upon which foolish Accident I had the Name of *Roxana* presently fix'd upon me all over the court End of Town, as Effectually as if I had been Christen'd *Roxana*."[34] In Hamilton's anecdote, the English actress, like her Ottoman namesake, pursues matrimonial legitimacy, but gets only economic compensation in the form of a sizable yearly pension. Defoe, with an eye to the growing cultural respect for private wealth, inverts the actress's hierarchy of value for his Roxane. When Defoe's protagonist assumes the identity of the Eastern queen, it signals her enthusiastic embrace of sex work and her conscious rejection of conjugal stasis and subjection. As she puts it, "I had a mortal aversion to marrying . . . but form'd a thousand wild Notions in my Head, that I was yet gay enough, and young, and handsome enough to please a Man of Quality."[35] Leveraging her desirability to two rich men has already earned her vast quantities of cash. She now determines actively to seek a private contract with a man as averse to matrimony as herself. "I thought of nothing less than of being Mistress to the King himself," she confesses.[36]

Defoe's protagonist eventually shares with Hamilton's Roxane an appreciation of the social capital of an elite title. Unlike the actress, Roxana succeeds, more or less, at fulfilling this desire when she finally agrees to marry the Dutch merchant after he purchases the title of count. Nevertheless, like Hamilton's Roxana, Defoe's protagonist is filled with regret. Whereas the actress directs her righteous anger at the earl and at the laws and patriarchal structures that condone sexual coercion, Defoe's Roxana, as penitent sinner, blames herself and the weakness of her faith. In Hamilton's *Memoirs*, Miss Hobart offers the story of the English actress's deception as a warning. Recognizing that in a protocapitalist age, the anecdote is susceptible to being read as a positive exemplum, Defoe plays up Roxana's psychic pain to ensure that readers do not miss his explicit Christian moral:

even officially sanctioned unions are spiritual whoredom if—like Roxolana with Solyman or Roxana with her newly minted nobleman—couples are motivated by anything other than mutual affection and concern.

As in the *Memoirs* and the dramas to which Hamilton alludes, an intricate homosocial subplot also undergirds Defoe's heterosexual Roxane narrative. Amy is Roxana's loyal maid and most regular bedmate. A friend (*amie*) and alter ego (a "me"), as Terry Castle has noted, Amy loves her mistress "to an Excess hardly to be describ'd," serving variously as her manager, counselor, bawd, emissary, and henchman.[37] Early in the novel, Roxana's married landlord saves both women from starvation. When it becomes clear to Amy that he is going to ask for sexual compensation for his "Goodness," Amy proposes to go to bed with him on her mistress's behalf.[38] Roxana initially refuses this offer, saying "I'd die before I would consent or you would consent for my sake."[39] But quite spontaneously one night, after having slept with the landlord herself for a year, Roxana decides that Amy should in fact be part of their arrangement. "I sat her down, pull'd off . . . all her Cloaths, Piece by Piece, and led her to the Bed to him: *Here*, says I, *try what you can do with your Maid Amy*: She pull'd back a little . . . at first, but . . . when she [saw] I was in earnest, she let me do what I wou'd; so I fairly stript her, and then I threw open the Bed, and thrust her in."[40] In Castle's Freudian analysis, this turn of events represents a queer version of the primal scene, with Amy in the role of mother. However, Defoe's debts to the Hamilton anecdote provide an older conceptual frame for Roxana's wish to consummate her bond with Amy sexually via the landlord. Like Hobart and the stage Roxanes to whom Hamilton implicitly compares her, Roxana experiences a wide range of feelings for her favorite over the course of the novel. By advancing this encounter with the man on whom she and Amy are both dependent, Defoe's protagonist embodies her homosocial desire more fully than do any of her literary precursors. Moreover, by transposing power dynamics formerly associated with the Ottoman seraglio to an ordinary English home, Defoe registers the distance between the protocapitalist English sexual economy and its older Eastern counterpart in which the emperor holds a singular power: it turns out that early eighteenth-century Europe provides not fewer but more vehicles for competition and vice. Thus, as Roxana and Amy together shift their attention from one man to the next, from one commercial sexual transaction to the next, the proliferation of opportunities to triangulate their attachment makes it not only the most complex but also the most resilient—and, not insignificantly, the most lucrative—one in the novel.

To this day, Roxane connotes the quintessential cis-femme heterosexual suspect, the consummate female performer who deploys sex or sex appeal with men as a means to material or social ends of her own. In the 1978 Police song, Roxanne "walk[s] the streets for money" and doesn't care "if it's wrong or if it's right." In the 2019 Arizona Zervas song, she "keep[s] running back . . . / Only 'cause I pay up." This chapter has aimed to nuance and complicate these enduring oppressive associations by illuminating the homosocial intensities that circulated within and alongside this eminently repeatable myth of heterosexual ambition from the late seventeenth through the early eighteenth century, raising questions about the manifold risks and rewards of women's relationships and their potential to divert patriarchal sexual power. In the long run, domestication—in English settings, in prose, in fiction—was not advantageous for queer Roxane's reputation, as evinced by her decline from a bona fide heroine (in Davenant) to a drama queen (in Lee) to a pragmatic female courtier (Hamilton) and then a hell-bound whore (Defoe). In fact, by way of conclusion, I propose that *Pamela*, which, as Frye observes, was also likely to have been inspired in part by Hamilton's actress anecdote, was the end of the line for queer Roxane. Although Richardson does not name Roxane in the novel, it is easy to hear echoes of the actress anecdote in Richardson's heroine's motivated resistance to her master's propositions and assaults throughout the first half of the novel. Emboldened by Hamilton's and Defoe's reinterpretations of Knolles's orientalist history, Richardson made the radical decision to take the captive servant at her word—to authenticate her spiritual devotion right from the start. Yet I hear vanishing echoes of the homosocial Roxane too in the fact that Pamela's appeal rests to a significant degree on the skills, style, and status that she has acquired through her dressing-room intimacy with Lady B, a relationship that ends, with her mistress's death, before the novel begins.[41]

Notes

Epigraph: Susan Lanser's *The Sexuality of History: Modernity and the Sapphic, 1565–1830* (Chicago: University of Chicago Press, 2014), 148, argues that "the struggle the novel enacts over the place of female agency in the social order turns out to be imbricated with the Sapphic."

1. Ruth Clark's *Anthony Hamilton: His Life and Works* (London: John Lane, 1921), 202–203, suggests that "Mémoires de Grammont," which Hamilton composed between 1704 and 1707, was intended only for manuscript circulation. However, a French publisher began selling *Mémoires de la vie du Comte de Grammont* with no named author in 1713. The following year, the London journalist Abel Boyer packaged his English translation as a roman à clef. In 1715, a new English edition of this translation with an appended key appeared.

2. See Rodney Baine, "Roxana's Georgian Setting," *Studies in English Literature* 15, no. 3 (1975): 459–471; Nathaniel Lee, "Epilogue," in *The Rival Queens* (Lincoln: University of Nebraska Press, 1970), lines 28–33; and Marie-Catherine d'Aulnoy, *Memoirs of the Court of England* (London: B. Bragg, 1707), 439–449. John Harold Wilson's "Lord Oxford's 'Roxolana,'" *Theatre Notebook* 12, no. 1 (Autumn 1957): 14, suggests that Hester Davenport was the leading performer who "left the stage to live with Lord Oxford."

3. The identity of the protagonist of this episode is a bit of a mystery. In the original French edition of *Mémoires de la Vie du Comte de Grammont, contenant particulièrement l'Histoire Amoureuse de la Cour d'Angleterre sous le Regne du Roi Charles II* ([Paris?], 1713), the character who tells the story is called Mademoiselle Hubert. The original English translation represents this character as "Miss H——t," which the subsequent key parses as "Mrs. Hobart." The 1719 English edition specifies "Mrs Hobart, sister to Sir John Hobart of Norfolk," who was a baronet and member of Parliament. Without naming them, Frederic Barlow in his *Complete English Peerage* (London: 1772–73), 2:45, mentions that one of John Hobart's two sisters "died unmarried." However, according to James William Johnson, *A Profane Wit: The Life of John Wilmot, Earl of Rochester* (Rochester, NY: University of Rochester Press, 2004), 87, the real-life "Miss H—t," who got between Rochester and Anne Temple, was Dorothy Howard, later libeled in a verse of Rochester's "Signor Dildo."

4. David Blewett and Northrop Frye both commented briefly on the *Memoirs*'s significance to eighteenth-century novelists; see Daniel Defoe, *Roxana*, ed. David Blewett (New York: Penguin, 1987), 349–350, and Frye's marginalia in *Memoirs of the Court of Charles the Second*, ed. Walter Scott (London: Henry G. Bohn, 1859), annotated no. 121, E. J. Pratt Library, Victoria University, University of Toronto, 230.

5. Procopius, *The Secret History*, translated by Richard Atwater (New York: Cosimo, 2007), 47–48.

6. Helen Deutsch, "Oranges, Anecdote and the Nature of Things," *SubStance* 38, no. 1 (2009): 31–55, 49; Andrea Loselle, "Introduction," *SubStance* 38, no. 1 (2009): 33.

7. See, for instance, Kristina Straub, *Sexual Suspects: Eighteenth-Century Players and Sexual Ideology* (Princeton, NJ: Princeton University Press, 1991).

8. Michael McKeon, *Secret History of Domesticity: Public, Private, and the Division of Knowledge* (Baltimore: Johns Hopkins University Press, 2005). See especially chapter 9, "Figures of Domestication," 436–466.

9. Eve Kosofsky Sedgwick, *Between Men: English Literature and Male Homosocial Desire* (New York: Columbia University Press, 1992).

10. Sharon Marcus, *Between Women: Friendship, Desire, and Marriage in Victorian England* (Princeton, NJ: Princeton University Press, 2007).

11. In "Performing Roxane: The Oriental Woman as the Sign of Luxury in Eighteenth-Century Fictions," in *Luxury in the Eighteenth Century: Debates, Desires and Delectable Goods*, ed. Maxine Berg and Elizabeth Eger (New York: Palgrave MacMillan, 2003), 165–177, Ros Ballaster refers to "Roxane" as "a composite figure of Orientalised femininity" (166).

12. For accounts of these historical narratives, see Ros Ballaster, "Performing Roxane," and her "Roxolana: The Loquacious Courtesan," in *Fabulous Orients: Fictions of the East in England, 1662–1785* (New York: Oxford University Press, 2005), 59–70, as well as Katie Trumpener, "Rewriting Roxane: Orientalism and Intertextuality in Montesquieu's *Lettres persanes* and Defoe's *The Fortunate Mistress*," *Stanford French Review* 11 (1987): 177–191.

13. Trumpener, "Rewriting Roxane," 178.

14. Ballaster, "Performing Roxane," 175.

15. Felicity Nussbaum, *Torrid Zones: Maternity, Sexuality, and Empire in Eighteenth-Century English Narratives* (Baltimore: Johns Hopkins University Press, 1995), 34, and notes.

16. Anthony Hamilton, *Memoirs of the Court of Charles the Second*, ed. Walter Scott (London: Henry G. Bohn, 1859), 230–231.

17. As Paul Rycaut, *Present State of the Ottoman Empire* (1686; repr., New York: Arno Press and the New York Times, 1971), understands it, sultans generally "take no feminine companion of their Empire in whom they may be more concerned than as in Slaves" because, they believe, were the custom of conjugal relations in use, "the chief Revenue of the Empire would be expended in the Chambers of Women, and diverted from the true Channels in which the Treasure ought to run for nourishment of the Politick body of the Common-wealth" (155).

18. Richard Knolles, *Generall Historie of the Turkes* (London: A. Islip, 1603), 719–767.

19. In an episode whose homosocial complexities would repay a longer analysis, Delarivier Manley, in *New Atalantis*, 6th ed., vol. 1 (London: John Morphew, 1720), 1:65–103, partly resists then reinscribes Knolles's fear and hatred of female sexual agency. A countess counsels her young friend to proceed cautiously and negotiate marriage with her lover, a duke, before his passion grows stale, advising her "to read the History of *Roxalana,* who by her wise Address . . . brought an imperious *Sultan* . . . to divide with her the Royal Throne" (1:93). But the girl succumbs too soon, and the countess ends up deploying the strategy and marrying the duke herself.

20. Hamilton, *Memoirs*, 276.

21. Hamilton, *Memoirs*, 221.

22. See, for instance, Susan Lanser, *The Sexuality of History* (Chicago: University of Chicago Press, 2014), 92.

23. William Davenant, *The Siege of Rhodes, Part* 2, ed. Ann-Mari Hedbäck (Stockholm: Uppsala, 1973), lines 249–251 (original italics). As Elizabeth Howe, *The First English Actresses: Women and Drama, 1660–1700* (Cambridge: Cambridge University Press, 1992), explains, "When a stage direction in a Restoration dramatic text reads '*the scene opens*,' this refers to the opening of a set of shutters onto something else; '*the scene shuts*' means the shutters were then closed at the end of the 'scene.' There were three and possibly even four sets of shutters to create different scenes. All were placed wide enough apart to allow players to act behind one set and in front of another" (3–4). Opening and closing three or four sets of painted panels along a succession of grooves created for viewers something like the experience of moving through a sequence of rooms in enfilade. It was Davenant who introduced the shutter stage to public theater. See Kevin Cope, "The Glory That Was Rome—and Grenada, and Rhodes, and Tenochtitlan: Pleasurable Conquests, Supernatural Liaisons, and Apparitional Drama in Interregnum Entertainments," *Studies in the Literary Imagination* 32, no. 2 (Fall 1999): 1–18.

24. Davenant, *Siege of Rhodes, Part* 2, 4.3.66.

25. Davenant, *Siege of Rhodes, Part* 2, 4.3.75, 84–86.

26. Davenant, *Siege of Rhodes, Part* 2, 4.3. 91, 93.

27. Davenant, *Siege of Rhodes, Part* 2, 4.3.131–139.

28. Lee, *The Rival Queens*, 3.1.264–266, 269–270.

29. Lee, *The Rival Queens*, 5.1.81–95.

30. Lee, *The Rival Queens*, 5.1.158–159.

31. I explore Miss Hobart and the Duchess of York's bond in *The Closet: The Eighteenth-Century Architecture of Intimacy* (Princeton, NJ: Princeton University Press, 2020), 45–75.

32. Northrop Frye's marginalia appear in Hamilton, *Memoirs of the Court of Charles the Second*, 230.

33. See David Blewett's notes in Defoe, *Roxana*, 349–350.

34. Daniel Defoe, *Roxana*, ed. Melissa Mowry (Peterborough, ON: Broadview Press, 2009), 195.

35. Defoe, *Roxana*, 181.

36. Defoe, *Roxana*, 181.

37. Defoe, *Roxana*, 69. Terry Castle, "'To Amy Who Knew My Disease,'" in *The Female Thermometer: Eighteenth-Century Culture and the Invention of the Uncanny* (New York: Oxford University Press, 1995), 44–55, 48, remarks that "virtually all the significant shifts in the plot—the manifest alterations in Roxana's 'fortune'—are occasioned . . . by [Amy's] facilitations."

38. Defoe, *Roxana*, 73, 67.

39. Defoe, *Roxana*, 68.

40. Defoe, *Roxana*, 82–83.

41. The residual effects of this relationship are indicated from the start of Samuel Richardson's *Pamela* (New York: Oxford University Press, 2008), 13, when, on reading Pamela's letter to her parents following Lady B's death, Mr. B says, "I see my good Mother's Care in your Learning has not been thown away upon you."

CODA

Whither Theatrical Anecdote?

HEATHER LADD AND LESLIE RITCHIE

As well as enjoying the immersive pleasure of reading a lengthy novel—the thrill of seeing characters' inner selves revealed in letters, thoughts, and conversation, as they careen through brisk plots bristling with incident—eighteenth-century readers also enjoyed the distinctly different pleasure of reading a volume of anecdotes. In such a collection, the reader was the picaro, and the adventures might begin anywhere. A volume of anecdotes is aleatoric, not taxonomic, not linear, not systems-into-systems-run, but "an Olio / Compiled from quarto and from folio; / From pamphlet, newspaper, and book," as the title page of William Oxberry's collection *The Flowers of Literature* (1821) boasts. Oxberry's preface tells readers how to read and enjoy anecdotes, with easy confidence in his ability to entertain with "old jokes, which are not a jot the worse for wear" and "old stories, which make you young again":

> When the air is nipping cold without, and the fire crackles and sparkles within, and the mulled wine is smoking on the table, and every foot is crowded on the fender . . . seat yourself in your easy chair, a glass of hot punch on one side of you, and your wife or mistress on the other, and my hat to a halfpenny you cry "bravo," to every other joke I venture . . . my easy chat will never put you to the trouble of thinking, and if now and then you should slip a page, depend upon it you'll never miss it—[1]

Eve Tavor Bannet's comprehensive survey of histories of reading in the eighteenth century identifies numerous directions in recent scholarship. These trends include the study of print's imbrication with conversation and its connections to orality; consideration of modes of reading, including reading aloud in settings ranging from private to public; and analysis of the effects of repeated reading, commonplacing, transcription, and marginalia upon texts' dissemination and reception. Cumulatively, such studies reveal changing attitudes toward the idea of print texts' centrality and fixity.[2] Yet anecdote, a mutable genre with intimate connections to all of these reading practices that are now the object of scholarly attention, has thus far largely escaped notice. In the last few pages of this collection, we would like to reflect on the scholarly contributions made by the chapters in this volume, which, we argue, exceed their applications to eighteenth-century theater history, and to suggest future directions for the study of anecdote.

Contributions of This Collection

Several contributions to *English Theatrical Anecdotes, 1660–1800* showcase anecdotes behaving badly—not just pithily recounting bad behavior, but operating in ways inimical to their historical subjects. In "Killing Delane; or, Mimickry and the *Anecdota obscura*," Leslie Ritchie posits the "*Anecdota obscura*," a pattern of elision and obfuscation within anecdotal biography that in this case reduces a complex individual with a full theatrical career to a single humiliating tale. She scrutinizes permutations of an anecdote about David Garrick imitating Dennis Delane to death: Garrick effectively ruins Delane's career and shortens his rival's life with his public mimicry of the other actor's outdated style. In uncovering the extent to which Garrick's biographers use anecdote to exalt their famous subject and manufacture his singularity, this chapter casts a fresh light on anecdotes that come to stand in for significant shifts in dramatic practices like the movement away from declamatory speech. Ritchie introduces two vital and interrelated strands that run throughout this volume: theatrical anecdote as a mechanism of celebrity and the ethical costs of anecdotal narrative.

Máire MacNeill's chapter, "Violent Afterlives: The Anecdote in Eighteenth-Century Theater Biographies," addresses the profusion of theatrical anecdotes featuring violence among professional performers. Cognizant of the period's equivocal views of the acting profession, she notes how the same story can be used for opposing ideological ends. As does Ritchie, MacNeill tracks variations of a ubiquitous anecdote, tracing accounts of Charles Macklin killing James Hallam backstage at Drury Lane from daily newspapers to later biographies and obituaries of the famous Irish actor. She reviews how this incident, filtered through different media and authorial agendas, was initially presented and how it was treated decades later in assessments of Macklin's character and career. MacNeill also presses the relationship between anecdote and gender, confirming and elaborating on the gendering of theatrical anecdotes now widely acknowledged among scholars of the eighteenth-century stage. She explicates how violence between women performers is represented as farce, and violence between men shown as a graver matter, albeit not necessarily a career-destroying one. MacNeill, as other contributors in this collection do, calls attention to the extent to which theatrical anecdotes were manipulated and recontextualized by writers of (in)famous lives.

The aim of the theatrical anecdote is to entertain, but a great many specifically aim to shame their targets while provoking laughter among knowing readers. Heather Ladd's "Samuel Foote, Esq.: Caricature, Class, and the Comic Theatrical Anecdote" focuses on theatrical anecdotes as a comic genre underwritten by conservative ideas of social and cultural hierarchy. Comedian Samuel Foote, whose genteel background enabled this brand of humor, is featured in many such classist anecdotes. Although Foote's self-presentation was that of a rebellious envelope-pusher, his afterlife in anecdotes published into the nineteenth century reveals a residual skepticism about middle-class participation in the acting profession. Ladd reads many anecdotes starring Foote as they enact forms of social and cultural policing of figures such as the social-climbing performer, both failed and successful. In so doing, this chapter articulates some of the underlying social constructions that enable the humor of anecdotes, including assumptions about the decorum appropriate to different social strata.

Theatrical anecdote, in keeping with the larger image-driven celebrity culture of the stage, is preoccupied with the bodies of eighteenth-century performers, especially female ones. In "Pregnancy and the Late Stuart Stage, 1661–1702," Chelsea Phillips engages in the important work of navigating anecdotal evidence about the reality and reception of performing women's pregnant bodies. Acknowledging the dubiety of this information, she explores the period's economic, artistic, and moral responses to the pregnant actress, as well as the ways in which theater scholars have interpreted these responses. Phillips uses actress Elizabeth Farley Weaver as a case study and carefully examines the circumstances of Weaver's departure from the King's Company and scholarly depictions of this event. She nuances accepted generalizations about the stigma of pregnancy in the playhouse and contrasts Weaver's career with that of Jane Rogers, highlighting illegitimacy as a determining factor in the reception of the performer's pregnancy. This chapter also considers anecdote as the locus of worries about the intersections between effective performance and dissembling. Crucially, Phillips models the thoughtful and responsible use of theatrical anecdotes when research materials such as repertory data prove slight.

Nevena Martinović's "'A High Treat to the Anecdote Hunters!': The Body of Mrs. Sophia Baddeley" likewise considers anecdotes about the female performer's highly visible and much contested body, studying what published descriptions of the aging female body have to say about the period's moral standards and the gendered construction and destruction of stage celebrity. Like Phillips, Martinović is sensitive to the misogynist dynamics of many theatrical anecdotes, and the way the anecdote itself serves as a stage for shaming female performers with irregular private lives. As in Ladd's chapter, Martinović—focusing on sexuality rather than class—explores the anecdote's social policing function. She notes how the young unmarried Baddeley (Miss Snow) is immortalized in printed panegyrics of her beauty, which pose a contrast to the fallen Baddeley, whose rough appearance purportedly reflects her blemished reputation. This chapter argues that anecdote enables the depiction of Sophia Baddeley's aged body as the product of her moral failings, and frames it as an exemplum in the periodicals and books that memorialize the actress's life and career.

Michael Burden's "A Bellyful of Nightingale: Seven Stories of Seven Singers" considers a body of anecdotes about professional singers that illuminates credible features of the careers of eighteenth-century entertainers. Burden uses the constructive metaphor of the cabinet of curiosities to discuss anecdotes, discursive pieces collected and embellished like physical objects of interest. Stressing the period's obsession with green room activity, Burden draws on published texts, including the two-volume *Secret History of the Green Room*, that purport to divulge these backstage goings-on. His chapter emphasizes and elaborates the range of anecdotes about musical performers like Mary Porter, Susanna Cibber, and Francesca Cuzzoni. Although some of these vignettes are colored by misogyny, many others present these women performers as respectable, even powerful, professionals. Significantly, Burden's chapter examines the noteworthy connection between prints and anecdotes, studying images like *The Prospect Before Us* that visually present "anecdotable" moments and entertainingly sketch characters from the theatrical world. Burden also makes the important observation—worthy of further scholarly investigation—that anecdotes collect around enduringly popular works like *The Beggar's Opera*.

Fiona Ritchie's "Anecdote and the Regional Actress: A History of the Farren Family in Several Anecdotes" turns to anecdotes about actress Eliza Farren and her lesser-known relations. Before Farren's socially elevating marriage, she and her family were active dramatic professionals in English theaters outside London. Like Phillips, Ritchie appraises the value and hazards of anecdotal evidence where other records of historical fact are scarce. Many anecdotes about the famous actress are cast in a stereotypical rags-to-riches narrative and either overemphasize her lowly origins or her innate gentility for contrast's sake; this formula likewise downplays the independent successes of the other Farren performers who sometimes appear as foils to the illustrious Eliza. Ritchie recovers the Farren theatrical family from an anecdotal tradition that privileges individual celebrity over the working lives of other dramatic professionals. Resituating Farren amid a larger familial saga and history of regional theater, Ritchie models a careful and balanced use of anecdote with an understanding of its mutually constitutive relationship with the documentary record.

Seth Wilson also weighs in on the actress's origin story as a site of historiographical dispute in "Neither Confirmed nor Refuted: The

Anecdotal Elizabeth Barry." Concentrating on three anecdotes involving Barry and her sexually and socially adventurous behavior, he analyzes how these entertaining microhistories seek to compromise the burgeoning professional status of Restoration actresses. The Barry on display in these vignettes is an unfeminine type, an unruly social climber who imperils the social order. The actress is simultaneously attractive and repellant, serving as an outlet for the desires and apprehensions of a stratified heteropatriarchy. Wilson, like Martinović, reads an anecdote about the actress's death as a cautionary tale illustrating the moral wages of an unconventional life. Alongside other contributors to this collection, Wilson attaches symbolic meaning to expressive details within the anecdote's brief fragments of celebrity and turns a critical eye on anecdotes that rehearse and capitalize on damaging stereotypes of actresses.

Clearly, stage debuts and other stories of nascent dramatic talent are a key subgenre of the theatrical anecdote. Elaine McGirr's "Anecdotal Origin Stories: Mary Ann Yates's Trip to Drury Lane" makes a convincing case for Frances Brooke's feminist reimagining of Mary Ann Yates's beginnings. Brooke writes about the actress-manageress's first trip to the theater when Yates's innate genius is revealed in her putative response to Susanna Cibber's performance. McGirr confirms that this compelling anecdote cannot have a basis in fact, but argues for the story's importance within a feminocentric historiography of the stage that refuses the tired template of men discovering and fostering female talent. Contrasting this potent story of self-discovery and female influence with traditional origin stories of actresses like Anne Oldfield, Kitty Clive, and Peg Woffington, McGirr argues that Brooke created an important, if fictional, narrative of female theatrical succession rather than competition, and in so doing, established (through anecdote) a valuable ideal for women's theatrical participation.

Continuing the collection's investigation of anecdotal afterlives, Amanda Weldy Boyd contributes "The Vanishing Subject in 'Anecdotal' Abridgments of Theatrical Biographies," a chapter adapted from her published monograph. Boyd's work illustrates a striking irony within eighteenth-century theatrical biographies, which often pushed their central subjects into the background. As in Leslie Ritchie's chapter, Boyd reflects on the power of anecdote to conceal rather than reveal celebrity personages. She narrows in on the intriguing play between chronological biography and nonsequential anecdotes, observing the increasing predominance of anecdotal content. Anecdotes attempt to distill personality, she explains, but ultimately trade sustained character study for amusing morsels of fabricated celebrity intimacy. Boyd's chapter underlines the commercial dimension of anecdote as a mode of writing theatrical lives.

Queer theatrical anecdotes have a long history, the playhouse arguably being an intrinsically queer space, a literal and metaphorical stage for play around gender and sexuality. In "Queering Roxane from Davenant to Richardson," Danielle Bobker builds her chapter around a suggestive anecdote from Anthony Hamilton's secret history of the Restoration court, which she uses to anchor a queer intertextual network involving the historical-theatrical figure of Roxane. Hamilton's vignette involves a woman telling her attractive young protégée a cautionary tale: the story of an actress known for playing Roxane who was duped into a false marriage. Bobker identifies the queer erotics of this seduction scene and shows how the Roxane allusion bridges patriarchal homosexuality and female homosocial desire as well as the English court and the exotic "East." Vis-à-vis this anecdote, she delves into the relationship between anecdotes, the secret history, dramatic performances, and finally, the novels of Defoe and Richardson. Tracking the figure of Roxane from distant history into Restoration drama and into eighteenth-century fiction, Bobker productively recognizes anecdotes—small, but formidable in their viral movements through culture—as "the original memes."

Future Directions

As our contributors demonstrate, theater scholars are using anecdotes with greater sensitivity to the historical inaccuracies and bigotries anecdotes can sometimes perpetuate. While chapters in *English Theatrical Anecdotes, 1660–1800* address various prejudices that saturate the anecdotal record, many of which fixate on the performer's body, there is much room for further scholarship on other societal biases that inform anecdotes about theater people. Theatrical anecdote about racial minorities is a topic in need of further exploration, especially given rapidly growing attention to the representation of Black and Indigenous lives, past and present. W. A. Hart makes note of an Irish-born Black singer, Rachael Baptist, who appeared on the English and Irish stage in the 1770s.[3] Hart draws on the theatrical memoirs of Irish actor and dramatist John O'Keefe, who recollects a Marlborough Gardens concert he attended as a boy, where Baptist "was heard by the applauding company with great delight, without remarks on her sables."[4] In this instance, appreciation for the racialized performer's musical talents trumps racism. Conversely, in *Staying Power: The History of Black People in Britain* (1984), Peter Fryer observes the presence of Black musicians who played in the English royal courts, and briefly discusses the Black French horn player known as Cato. Cato, he notes, was admired for his musical abilities, but was a "slave first to Sir Robert Walpole and then the Earl of Chesterfield, who gave him as a present to the Prince and Princess of Wales in 1738."[5] Here, anecdote operates problematically to objectify this musician and render his talent part of his exchange value.

Scholars have recovered materials concerning other Black artists active in London yet largely forgotten by mainstream history, and anecdote is often the genre that enables such recovery. In 1782, Joseph Jekyll published a posthumous biography of the Afro-British writer and composer Ignatius Sancho, including Sancho's letters.[6] The inclusion of documents by Sancho links this biography to the "-ana" concept of biography discussed elsewhere in this collection, and accords the subject a measure of self-representation. Sancho was subsequently the subject of a short biographical sketch in Abigail Mott's *Biographical Sketches and Interesting Anecdotes of Persons of Color* (1826).[7] In this case, an anecdote does not evolve into more expansive life-writing, but the reverse: Mott employs Sancho's previously established celebrity to construct condensed anecdotes that powerfully "advocate the cause of Universal emancipation," emphasizing Sancho's religious faith and his thoughts on slavery.[8]

There is considerable scholarly and popular interest in Joseph Bologne, Chevalier de Saint-Georges (still sometimes problematically termed the "Black Mozart"), a prolific French composer and musician who regularly visited England.[9] One anecdote about Saint-Georges relates his fierce physical and verbal retort to a stranger's racial epithet.[10] Yet another anecdote (titled "Effective Music!") about the violinist does not even mention his race, but rather shows his exquisite musical sensibility: "There is the incident attached to the name of the Chevalier St. George[s]. He was once rehearsing a symphony composed by his friend, Simon Leduc, who had recently died. In the middle of the adagio the Chevalier was so overcome by the expression of the music that he let fall his bow and burst into tears."[11] This anecdote, which celebrates Saint-Georges's sensitivity and musical skill, offers a counterpoint to racist, economically driven conceptions of Africans as objects rather than feeling human beings—views that justified slavery during and beyond Saint-Georges's lifetime.[12] Anecdotes such as this, interpreted with care and circumspection, can illuminate perceptions of performers and artists of color during the eighteenth century.

Looking forward, beyond the temporal scope of this collection, anecdotes about the first major Black actor on the London stage, Ira Aldridge (1807–1867), are revelatory as to how both racism and racial tolerance manifested within the early nineteenth-century theater. The actor is physically absent but imaginatively central in a disturbing anecdotal exchange between the manager of the Theatre Royal Dublin and the husband of an actress, Madame Celeste, on contract with this playhouse. This husband, "A Yankee of the genuine type," is irate that his wife's name will be associated with Aldridge's, although they will not likely be acting in the same plays, much less directly opposite each other.[13] Two kinds of racism emerge in this conversation: the Yankee's violent bigotry, and the milder prejudice of the Irish manager, who confirms that his own nation does not socialize with Africans. The Irish manager accepts Aldridge as a performer, averring that "he's a good actor and the public like him. His colour is nothing to me, though it were green, blue, or red."[14] This story is "passed off as a humorous anecdote," but is not funny to a contemporary reader aware of the psychological and professional costs of racism to Black artists.[15] Further work on race and anecdote would undoubtedly uncover more examples of supposedly amusing stories about racialized performers as they were subjected to variously expressed prejudices to which celebrity and artistry only granted partial immunity.

Another topic yet to be explored by scholars of anecdote is fatphobia's role in tales of the stage. Martinović touches on this issue in her chapter on ageism, as does Phillips in her account of pregnant actresses' bodies, but there is more work to be done on sizeism in celebrity culture and specifically in the anecdotal record. Weight discrimination, arguably one of the last frontiers of socially acceptable bigotry among educated, left-leaning people in the twenty-first century, is unsurprisingly also evident in theatrical anecdotes published in the eighteenth and nineteenth centuries. Charles Dignum (1765–1827), a multitalented musician who wrote and sang in London for several decades after his debut in 1784 in the Handel Memorial Concerts, was the subject of several anecdotes that insultingly drew attention to his weight. In the anecdotal biography of Dignum included in her *Anecdotes of Actors* (1884), Mrs. Matthews observes that he was "*fat*; and fat people are remarkable," she stereotypes, "for sweet temper."[16] Matthews calls him "the dumpling" and describes how he prepares for singing a piece, not just by warming up his voice but by preening and "looking in the glass, as if he had the face to think well of himself."[17] Discussing the expression of emotion through movement in eighteenth-century acting technique, Tiffany Stern relays an anecdote about Dignum from Haslewood's *Secret History*.[18] Apparently, Dignum was too large to comfortably place his right hand on his heart, "and 'wished to know if his left would not do as well.'"[19] The ableist anecdote concludes with the actor being talked out of this inaccurate gesture. Proving this story's veracity, as is the case with many other anecdotes referenced in this volume, is admittedly difficult. Regardless, its circulation impinges on the performer's dignity, turning his obesity and his physical limitations into a punch line.

Tracing the roles that English theatrical anecdotes play in constituting theater history, and more broadly, in the social formation of attitudes toward gender, race, age, and other categories of marginalization, would benefit immeasurably from two undertakings: first, an exhaustive bibliography of anecdote collections, theater histories, theatrical memoirs and biographies, and other anecdote-rich texts; and second, a large-scale, text-based digital archive of theatrical anecdotes about Restoration and eighteenth-century performers. This latter digital humanities project would be a huge undertaking, but one with significant benefits. Ideally, this archive of primary sources would include the kind of tag searches so helpful to users of

Orlando: Women's Writing in the British Isles from the Beginnings to the Present to allow scholars to track patterns within the anecdotal record. Metrics would aid in answering questions such as: What is the ratio of anecdotes about actors to those about actresses? What proportion of anecdotes are set in the green room or onstage, versus in the public realm outside the playhouse? How often do monarchs or other individuals with titles marking their class feature in theatrical anecdotes?[20] A searchable electronic archive would enable researchers to compare versions of the same story, tracking the "drift" of anecdotes across texts and periods. Such an archive could broaden work on theatrical anecdote, illuminating the transatlantic movements of these small-scale narratives and enabling researchers to transcend the research periodization that artificially separates work on the eighteenth and nineteenth centuries. As so many of the chapters of this book have shown, the afterlife of the eighteenth century in the nineteenth century is a topic ripe for continued research.

Finally, research on Restoration and eighteenth-century English theatrical anecdotes could enrich discussions of the spate of twenty-first-century plays set in this period and deeply interested in its protomodern celebrity culture. The 2015–2016 theater season alone saw runs of several plays in this vein: Claire van Kampen's *Farinelli and the King* (Duke of York), Ian Kelly's *Mr Foote's Other Leg* (Haymarket), Jessica Swale's *Nell Gwynn* (Apollo), and Lolita Chakrabarti's story of Ira Aldridge, *Red Velvet* (Garrick). Kelly, who adapted his own biography of Samuel Foote for the London stage, used theatrical anecdotes as fodder for countless lines and scenes in *Mr Foote's Other Leg* (2015), which was staged at the Haymarket, Foote's old stomping grounds.[21] For example, Kelly borrows an anecdote about Irish actress Peg Woffington in her celebrated breeches role of Sir Harry Wildair (from George Farquhar's *The Constant Couple*), which is told in W. R. Chetwood's 1749 *General History*: "This agreeable actress, in the part of Sir *Harry*, coming into the Green-Room, said pleasantly, *In my conscience! I believe Half the Men in the House take me for one of their own Sex*. Another actress reply'd, It may be so; but, in my Conscience! the other Half can convince them to the contrary."[22] Depending on the source, this punch line is attributed to John Rich, James Quin, or, by 1883, to Kitty Clive.[23]

Ian Kelly's play puts this joke about the actress's allegedly voracious sexual appetite in Foote's mouth, during an imagined falling-out between Foote and Woffington.[24] Kelly deploys this anecdote to stage Foote's much remarked-upon tendency to take a joke too far; Kelly's Foote becomes a tool for showing how anecdotal wit was weaponized for the judging and policing of the offstage sexual morality of the actress. Other modern plays set during this formative period of theater history likewise avail themselves of the enormous body of anecdotes about the eighteenth-century stage that *English Theatrical Anecdotes, 1660–1800* has made significant strides in illuminating.

The Celebrity Anecdote: Then and Now

Anecdotes, still one of the smallest units of print celebrity, possess an obvious and enduring commercial appeal. Then as now, anecdotes about entertainers are a lucrative genre that promises insider information about an exclusive set of interconnected people. Even when their behavior is worthy of neither imitation nor aspiration, (in)famous performers fascinate, their art rendered more interesting by the stories surrounding it. In the twenty-first century, anecdotes continue to exert the power to color, if not disrupt and taint, the reputations of contemporary celebrities. Anecdotes linger, overstaying their welcome for some artists, but embraced and repurposed by others.

American actor Matthew McConaughey was almost reduced to an amusing anecdote in 1999 when he was arrested while playing the bongos (or congas, depending on the version) while naked and high. Almost twenty years later, the story remains well known enough to conjure up an amusing image for the title of a *Vanity Fair* article by Joanna Robinson: "Matthew McConaughey Won't Back Away from His Drumming Past." The incident is now a metonym for the actor's quirkiness and slightly wild charm. Robinson quotes a 2013 *GQ* article in which the now seasoned, award-winning actor declares: "'*Of course* I still play the congas naked,' he says. 'I just close the windows.'"[25] Celebrity compounds celebrity when the famous do their best impression of the famous Texan. McConaughey's bongo scene is spoofed in a 2012 episode of *Saturday Night Live*, a sketch called "Getting Freaky with CeeLo" featuring Channing Tatum, known for his role as a stripper in *Magic Mike* (2012). Tatum's screen role builds anticipation for the McConaughey character to lose his clothing, and when he does, "McConaughey" shakes a pair of low-slung congas in a sexual healing–therapy session. 2020 saw the release of Matthew McConaughey's autobiography, *Greenlights*, replete with "personal yarns," according to a *New York Times* article on the book, and "filled with homespun wisdom that McConaughey has wrung from his toils, travels and that time he got arrested while playing bongos in the nude."[26] Anecdotes continue to confirm the idea of singularity among entertainers, whose uniqueness is a commodity, as can be seen by the way McConaughey has successfully integrated this anecdote into his personal celebrity and monetized it.

As in the long eighteenth century, contemporary anecdotes serve multiple purposes for their readership: they are a source of entertainment (particularly humor) and remain an integral part of celebrity life-writing, and not just in print. The anecdote's brevity and narrative self-containment have led it to thrive in social media platforms such as Twitter and TikTok. Twitter users engage in microblogging that, in its concision and tendency toward humor, resembles the anecdotal writing so constitutive of eighteenth-century theater biographies. Theatrical anecdotes, often resembling plays in miniature, can be compared productively to the media driven contemporary phenomenon of the TikTok: short, looping videos shared on this social media platform. On TikTok, amateur performers become celebrities when their videos go viral, and established celebrities also participate in these trends. Sharing with theatrical anecdotes the form of diminutive, often comic, performance, TikTok videos also possess the anecdote's quality of endless repetition: they capture and distill unusual moments; perpetuate individual celebrity; and are infinitely replicable. The consumption of TikTok videos is controlled by an algorithm (e.g., you watched a video of a cat in a box; here is a cat on a skateboard) reminiscent of the associative connections between eighteenth-century theatrical anecdotes. Especially in media like TikTok, stars and their stories elude fixity; likewise, anecdotes remain in flux hundreds of years after their first telling in print, endlessly reassembled, repackaged, and republished.

In print, the genre of anecdote remains commercially popular, accretive, and associative, as demonstrated by a recent publication, *The Oxford Book of Theatrical Anecdotes* (2020). The compiler, the politician and actor Gyles Brandreth, uses his own associative powers to move from one anecdote to another: "That story reminds me of the charming, wiry, one-armed Irish character actor David Kelly, who first came to notice playing the title role in Samuel Beckett's *Krapp's Last Tape* at the Abbey Theatre in Dublin in 1959. Later, when he played the part in New York he relished the review that appeared beneath the headline: 'At last the *Krapp* we have been waiting for.' And that reminds me of . . ."[27]. Brandreth's anecdote of Kelly is humorous, and shows his subject to be humorous too, but it is factually incorrect: although Kelly played a one-armed character in a televised serial, he himself had both arms.[28] Yet this slip is suggestive of one reason why celebrity and theatrical anecdotes have enjoyed consistent and lasting popular appeal. Anecdote's promise of access to secret histories of the green room and actors' essential characters is doubly appealing in the case of thespian celebrities who specialize in performing characters, and in evading public knowledge even as they court public attention. The justification for the inclusion of particular anecdotes has always been "*I* found them"; anecdotes are positioned as exchanges the editor witnessed, or that were told to them by a reputable source. As is the case with its many precursors, Brandreth's collection, advertised as "the ultimate anthology of theatrical anecdotes," promises prospective readers a history of the stage through anecdote, "covering every kind of theatrical story and experience."[29] As an extensive historical bibliography of theatrical anecdotes would show, there is no one definitive collection, however capacious its scope. Anecdotes continue to invite collection and defy containment.

In addition to these continuities in the genre of theatrical anecdotes, there are qualities distinct to the eighteenth-century theatrical anecdote worth briefly revisiting. Unlike contemporary celebrity gossip, with its global reach, theatrical anecdotes about the Restoration and eighteenth-century English stage granted readers access to a relatively closed, geographically specific community. Anecdotes are still important to the circulation of contemporary celebrity, but in the present, they circulate over a more diffuse and diverse body of cultural consumers. The emphasis on certain kinds of content and the interpretation of anecdotes has changed too. Stories about famous people are now much more likely to be presented as humorous infotainment than as offering serious historical insights. *People* magazine's online article of actor anecdotes, "Tom Cruise Crashed Kate Hudson's House and More Insanely Epic Celebrity Party Stories," invites readers to "live vicariously through these star tales of joy and mayhem."[30] Largely gone is the didactic quality discernible in many anecdotes published in the eighteenth and nineteenth centuries. Concern about anecdotal veracity is undeniably a stronger force among educated consumers, and this in turn has altered how anecdotes are deployed. Skepticism of anecdotes as historiographical fact has of course increased within scholarship; the ubiquitous opening anecdote of a conference paper is more often presented with a disclaimer that points to how anecdotes perpetuate interpretive injustices. In closing, and without diving too deeply into didacticism ourselves, we hope this book invigorates continued research on the theatrical anecdote and encourages the responsible use of anecdotal sources so carefully modeled by our contributors.

Notes

1. William Oxberrry, *Oxberry's Dramatic Biography and Histrionic Anecdotes*, 3 vols. (London: C. Baynes, for G. Virtue, 1826), 1:i.

2. Eve Tavor Bannet, "History of Reading: The Long Eighteenth Century," *Literature Compass* 10, no. 2 (February 2013): 122–133.

3. W. A. Hart, "Africans in Eighteenth-Century Ireland," *Irish Historical Studies* 33, no. 12 (May 2002): 19–32.

4. Quoted in Hart, "Africans in Eighteenth-Century Ireland," 30.

5. Peter Fryer, *Staying Power: The History of Black People in Britain* (London: Pluto Press, 1984).

6. See Vincent Carretta, ed., *Letters of the Late Ignatius Sancho, an African* (Peterborough, ON: Broadview Press, 2015).

7. A. Mott, "Ignatius Sancho," in *Biographical Sketches and Interesting Anecdotes of Persons of Color: To which is Added a Selection of Pieces in Poetry* (New York: W. Alexander & Son, 1826), 3–5.

8. A. Mott, preface to *Biographical Sketches*, v.

9. Marcos Balter, "His Name Is Joseph Boulogne, Not 'Black Mozart,'" *New York Times*, July 22, 2020, https://www.nytimes.com/2020/07/22/arts/music/black-mozart-joseph-boulogne.html.

10. Gabriel Banat, *The Chevalier de Saint-Georges: Virtuoso of the Sword and the Bow* (New York: Pendragon Press, 2006), 249.

11. Frederick James Crowest, *A Book of Musical Anecdotes: From Every Available Source*, 2 vols. (London: Richard Bentley and Son, 1878), 1:141.

12. Saint-Georges was the son of a Guadaloupe planter and his slave, Ninon. See Gabriel Banat, "Saint-Georges [Saint-George], Joseph Bologne, Chevalier de," *Grove Music Online*, 2001; accessed December 8, 2020.

13. Gunner Sjögan, "Ira Aldridge's Swedish Wife," in *Ira Aldridge, the African Roscius*, ed. Bernth Lindfors (Rochester, NY: University of Rochester Press, 2007), 64.

14. Quoted in Sjögan, "Ira Aldridge's Swedish Wife," 64.

15. Sjögan, "Ira Aldridge's Swedish Wife," 64.

16. Mrs. Matthews [Anne Jackson], *Anecdotes of Actors: With Other Desultory Recollections, Etc. Etc. Etc.* (London: T. C. Newby, 1844), 76.

17. Matthews [Anne Jackson], *Anecdotes of Actors*, 79, 78.

18. Tiffany Stern, *Rehearsal from Shakespeare to Sheridan* (Oxford: Clarendon Press, 2000), 259.

19. Quoted in Stern, *Rehearsal from Shakespeare to Sheridan*, 259.

20. *Orlando: Women's Writing in the British Isles from the Beginnings to the Present*, Cambridge University Press Online, 2006, http://orlando.cambridge.org/.

21. Ian Kelly, *Mr Foote's Other Leg* (London: NHB Modern Plays, 2015).

22. Quoted in Philip H. Highfill Jr., Kalman A. Burnim, and Edward A. Langhans, eds., *A Biographical Dictionary of Actors, Actresses, Musicians, Dancers, Managers & Other Stage Personnel in London, 1660–1800*, vol. 16, *West to Zwingman* (Carbondale: Southern Illinois University Press, 1993), 202.

23. See "Woffington, Margaret," in *A Biographical Dictionary*, 195–225.

24. See Act 2, Scene 6 of Kelly, *Mr Foote's Other Leg*: "The crew mistake you for a man, Mrs Woffington? AGAIN? Because there's an entire crew backstage and half the stalls her could swear on oath you're not" (87).

25. Joanna Robinson, "Matthew McConaughey Won't Back Away from His Drumming Past," *Vanity Fair*, January 27, 2017, https://www.vanityfair.com/style/2017/01/matthew-mcconaughey-drums-drumming-drummer-arrest.

26. Dave Itzkoff, "Matthew McConaughey Wrote the Book on Matthew McConaughey," *New York Times*, October 14, 2020, https://www.nytimes.com/2020/10/14/books/matthew-mcconaughey-memoir-greenlights.html.

27. Gyles Brandreth, prologue to *The Oxford Book of Theatrical Anecdotes* (Oxford: Oxford University Press, 2020).

28. Paul Donnelley, "*The Oxford Book of Theatrical Anecdotes*: Gyles Brandreth's Cracker of a Book," *The Sunday Express*, Sunday, November 15, 2020, https://www.express.co.uk/entertainment/books/1360509/Oxford-Book-of-Theatrical-Anecdotes-Gyles-Brandreth-theatre-showbiz. Donnelley's article includes a photograph of David Kelly with both arms.

29. "Description: *The Oxford Book of Theatrical Anecdotes*," Oxford University Press: Academic, https://global.oup.com/academic/product/the-oxford-book-of-theatrical-anecdotes-9780198749585?cc=ca&lang=en&#.

30. Lydia Price, "Tom Cruise Crashed Kate Hudson's House and More Insanely Epic Celebrity Party Stories," *People*, February 20, 2020, https://people.com/celebrity/epic-celebrity-party-stories/.

BIBLIOGRAPHY

"Account of Mr. James Quin." *The European Magazine, and London Review* 22 (1792): 50–51.

Adams, William Henry Davenport. *A Treasury of Modern Anecdote*. London: Simpkin, Marshall & Co., 1881.

Angelo, Henry. *Reminiscences of Henry Angelo: With Memoirs of his Late Father and Friends, Including Numerous Original Anecdotes and Curious Traits of the Most Celebrated Characters that have Flourished During the Past Eighty Years*. 2 vols. London: Colburn and Bentley, 1830.

Arbiter, Petronius. *Memoirs of the Present Countess of Derby, (Late Miss Farren); Including Anecdotes of Several Distinguished Persons*. London: H. D. Symonds, 1797.

Arbuthnot, John. *The Devil to Pay at St. James's: Or, a Full and True Account of a Most Horrid and Bloody Battle between Madam Faustina and Madam Cuzzoni*. London: A. Moore, 1727.

Arvine, Kazlitt. *The Cyclopedia of Anecdotes of Literature and the Fine Arts*. Boston: Gould and Lincoln, 1851.

Aspden, Suzanne. *The Rival Sirens: Performance and Identity on Handel's Operatic Stage*. Cambridge: Cambridge University Press, 2013.

Aston, Anthony. "Supplement to Cibber" (ca. 1747). In *An Apology for the Life of Mr. Colley Cibber, Written by Himself*, vol. 2, edited by Robert W. Lowe. London: John C. Nimmo, 1889.

Austin, J. L. *How to Do Things with Words*. Cambridge, MA: Harvard University Press, 1975.

Backscheider, Paula R. "Barry, Elizabeth." In *Oxford Dictionary of National Biography*. Oxford: Oxford University Press, 2004. https://doi-org.proxy.queensu.ca/10.1093/ref:odnb/1557.

———. "Frances Brooke: Becoming a Playwright." *Women's Writing*, 23, no. 3 (2016): 325–338.

Bailey, Joanne. *Unquiet Lives: Marriage and Marriage Breakdown in England 1660–1800*. Cambridge: Cambridge University Press, 2009.

Baine, Rodney. "Roxana's Georgian Setting." *Studies in English Literature* 15, no. 3 (1975): 459–471.

Baines, Paul, and Pat Rogers. *Edmund Curll, Bookseller*. Oxford: Oxford University Press, 2007.

Baldwin, Olive, and Thelma Wilson. "Fenton [*née* Besswick; *married name* Powlett or Paulet], Lavinia, Duchess of Bolton." In *The Oxford Dictionary of National Biography*, 60 vols, edited by H.C.G. Matthew and Brian Harrison, 19:310–312. Oxford: Oxford University Press, 2004.

Ballaster, Ros. *Fabulous Orients: Fictions of the East in England, 1662–1785*. New York: Oxford University Press, 2005.

———. "Performing Roxane: The Oriental Woman as the Sign of Luxury in Eighteenth-Century Fictions." In *Luxury in the Eighteenth Century: Debates, Desires and Delectable Goods*, edited by Maxine Berg and Elizabeth Eger, 165–177. New York: Palgrave MacMillan, 2003.

Balter, Marcos. "His Name Is Joseph Boulogne, Not 'Black Mozart.'" *New York Times*, July 22, 2020. https://www.nytimes.com/2020/07/22/arts/music/black-mozart-joseph-boulogne.html.

Banat, Gabriel. *The Chevalier de Saint-Georges: Virtuoso of the Sword and the Bow*. New York: Pendragon Press, 2006.

———."Saint-Georges [Saint-George] Joseph Bologne, Chevalier de." *Grove Music* online, 2001. Accessed December 8, 2020. https://www-oxfordmusiconline-com.proxy.queensu.ca/grovemusic/view/10.1093/gmo/9781561592630.001.0001/omo-9781561592630-e-0000024316.

Bannet, Eve Tavor. "History of Reading: The Long Eighteenth Century." *Literature Compass* 10, no. 2 (February 2013): 122–133.

Barlow, Frederic. *The Complete English Peerage: or, A Genealogical and Historical Account of the Peers and Peeresses of this Realm, To the Year 1772, inclusive . . . in Two Volumes*. London: Printed for the author and sold by T. Evans, 1773.

Barnes, Celia. "'A Morbid Oblivion': Samuel Johnson, James Boswell, and Remembering Not to Forget." *The Age of Johnson* 23 (2015): 1–19.

Bate, Johnathan. "A Life of Anecdote." In *The Genius of Shakespeare*, 3–33. London: Picador, 1997.

Bedford, Arthur. *The Great Abuses of Music*. London: John Wyatt, 1711.

Bee, Jon. "Essay on the Life, Genius, and Writings, of Samuel Foote, Esq." In *Samuel Foote: The Works*, vol. 1, 3–33. London: Sherwood, Gilbert, and Piper, 1830.

Bell, Alan. "Joseph Haslewood." In *The Oxford Dictionary of National Biography*, edited by H.C.G. Matthew and Brian Harrison, 60 vols. 25:174–175. Oxford: Oxford University Press, 2004.

Bellamy, George Anne. *An Apology for the Life of George Anne Bellamy. Late of Covent-Garden Theatre*. Vol. 1. London: J. Bell, 1785.

Bellchamber, Edmund. "Memoirs of the Actors and Actresses." In *An Apology for the Life of Mr. Colley Cibber, Written by Himself*, vol. 2, edited by Robert W. Lowe, 279–318. London: John C. Nimmo, 1889.

Benedetti, Jean. *David Garrick and the Birth of Modern Theatre*. London: Methuen, 2001.

Bent, S. Arthur. "The Illuminating Power of Anecdote." *The North American Review* 55, no. 430 (1892): 347–354.

Bloxam, Suzanne. *Walpole's Queen of Comedy: A Biography of Elizabeth Farren, Countess of Derby*. Ashford, UK: Published privately by the author, Suzanne Bloxam, 1988.

Boaden, James. *The Life of Mrs. Jordan: Including Original Private Correspondence, and Numerous Anecdotes of Her Contemporaries*. London: E. Bull, 1831.

Bobker, Danielle. *The Closet: The Eighteenth-Century Architecture of Intimacy*. Princeton, NJ: Princeton University Press, 2020.

Bon-mots of Samuel Foote and Theodore Hook. London: J. M. Dent and Company, 1894.

Boschereccio [pseud.]. *An Elegy on the Death of Samuel Foote, Esquire*. London: G. Kearsley, 1778.

Boswell, James. *The Journal of a Tour to the Hebrides*. London: Henry Baldwin, 1785.

———. *Life of Johnson*. Edited by R. W. Chapman. Oxford: Oxford University Press, 1980.

Brandreth, Gyles. *The Oxford Book of Theatrical Anecdotes*. Oxford: Oxford University Press, 2020.

Bratton, Jacky. "Anecdote and Mimicry as History." In *New Readings in Theatre History*, edited by Jacky Bratton, 95–132. Cambridge: Cambridge University Press, 2003.

———. *New Readings in Theatre History*. Cambridge: Cambridge University Press, 2003.

Broadbent, R. J. "Annals of the Manchester Stage, 1735–1845." 3 vols. Unpublished Manuscript. Manchester Library Theatre Collection.

———. "Elizabeth Farren, Countess of Derby." *Transactions of the Historic Society of Lancashire and Cheshire*, n.s., 25 (1910): 83–96.

B[rooke], F[rances]. "Authentic Memoirs of Mrs. Yates." *Gentleman's Magazine* (July 1787): 585–589.

———. *The British Magazine and Review* (April 1783): 250–255.

———. *The Excursion*. 1777. Edited by Paula R. Backscheider. Lexington: University Press of Kentucky, 2015.

Brooks, Helen E. M. *Actresses, Gender, and the Eighteenth-Century Stage: Playing Women*. London: Palgrave Macmillan, 2015.

Brown, Thomas. *The Second Volume of the Works of Mr. Tho. Brown, containing Letters from the Dead to the Living, Both Serious and Comical*. London: B. Bragg, 1707.

———. *The Third Volume of the Works of Mr. Thomas Brown*. London: B. Bragg, 1708.

Buchanan, Lindal. "Angels in the (Theatrical) House: Pregnancy, Rhetorical Access, and the London Stage." *Rhetorica: A Journal of the History of Rhetoric* 30, no. 3 (Summer 2012): 277–305.

Burden, Michael. "Casting Issues in Purcell's Opera *The Fairy-Queen*." *Music and Letters* 74, no. 4 (2003): 596–607.

———. "Gertrud Mara." In *The Oxford Dictionary of National Biography*, 60 vols., edited by H.C.G. Matthew and Brian Harrison, 36:594–596. Oxford: Oxford University Press, 2004.

Burkert, Mattie, Will Daland, Emma Hallock, Todd Hugie, Lauren Liebe, Derek Miller, Dustin Olson, and Ben R. Schneider, Jr., eds. *The London Stage Database*. https://londonstagedatabase.usu.edu/.

Burling, William J. *Summer Theatre in London, 1661–1820, and the Rise of the Haymarket Theatre*. Madison, NJ: Fairleigh Dickinson University Press, 2000.

Burney, Charles. "Burney Collection, the Life and Work of David Garrick." 1741–1747. Microfilm 939.D.1–9, British Library.

Burney, Frances. *Evelina: or, A Young Lady's Entrance into the World. In a Series of Letters*. 1778. Edited by Susan Kubica Howard. Peterborough, ON: Broadview Press, 2000.

Bush-Bailey, Gilli. *Treading the Bawds: Actresses and Playwrights on the Late Stuart Stage*. New York: Palgrave, 2006.

Byrn, M. Lafayette. *Repository of Wit and Humor: Comprising More Than One Thousand Anecdotes, Odd Scraps, Off-hand Hits, and Humorous Sketches*. Boston: J. P. Jewett & Company, 1853.

Carnell, Rachel K. *The Secret History in Literature, 1660–1820*. Cambridge: Cambridge University Press, 2017.

Castle, Terry. "'To Amy who knew my Disease.'" In *The Female Thermometer: Eighteenth-Century Culture and the Invention of the Uncanny*, 44–55. New York: Oxford University Press, 1995.

Characters of the Present Most Celebrated Courtezans. London: M. James, 1780.

Charles, Katherine. "Staging Sociability in *The Excursion*: Frances Brooke, David Garrick, and the King's Theatre Coterie." *Eighteenth-Century Fiction* 27, no. 2 (2014–2015): 257–284.

Chetwood, W. R. *A General History of the Stage; (More Particularly the Irish Theatre) from Its Origin in Greece Down to the Present Time*. Dublin: E. Rider, 1749.

Cibber, Colley. *An Apology for the Life of Mr. Colley Cibber, Comedian*. London: John Watts, 1740.

[Cibber, Theophilus]. *An Apology for the Life of Mr. The' Cibber, Comedian. Being a Proper Sequel to the Apology for the Life of Mr. Colley Cibber, Comedian, with an Historical View of the Stage to the Present Year*. Dublin: George Faulkner, 1741.

Clark, Ruth. *Anthony Hamilton: His Life and Works*. London: John Lane, 1921.

Collier, Jeremy. *A Short View of the Immorality and Profaneness of the English Stage*. 4th ed. London: S. Keble, R. Sare, and H. Hindmarch, 1699.

A Comparison Between the Two Stages, with an Examen of "The Generous Conqueror"; and Some Critical Remarks on "The Funeral, or Grief Alamode," "The False Friend," "Tamerlane" and Others. In Dialogue. London: n.p., 1702.

A Compleat Collection of Remarkable Tryals of the Most Notorious Malefactors, at the Sessions-House in the Old Baily. London: J. Philips, 1718–1721.

The Complete London Jester, or Wit's Companion. 2nd ed. London: T. Lownds, 1765.

Congreve, Francis Aspry. *Authentic Memoirs of the Late Mr. Charles Macklin, Comedian*. London: J. Barker, 1798.

Congreve, William. "The Way of the World." 1700. In *The Broadview Anthology of Restoration and Eighteenth-Century Drama*, edited by J. Douglas Canfield, 541–590. Toronto: Broadview Press, 2005.

The Contre Temps; or, Rival Queans: A Small Farce. London: A. Moore, [1727].

Cooke, William. "Anecdotes of Charles Macklin." *The Cabinet* 4 (September 1808): 191–192.

———. *Memoirs of Charles Macklin, Comedian*. London: Printed for J. Asperne by T. Maiden, 1804.

———. *Memoirs of Samuel Foote, Esq: With a Collection of His Genuine Bon-mots, Anecdotes, Opinions, &c. Mostly Original. And Three of His Dramatic Pieces, Not Published in His Works*. London: Richard Phillips, 1805.

Cope, Kevin L. "The Glory That Was Rome—and Grenada, and Rhodes, and Tenochtitlan: Pleasurable Conquests, Supernatural Liaisons, and Apparitional Drama in Interregnum Entertainments." *Studies in the Literary Imagination* 32, no. 2 (Fall 1999): 1–18.

———. "Raising a Risible Nation: Merry Mentoring and the Art (and Sometimes Science) of Joking Greatness." In *Mentoring in Eighteenth-Century*

British Literature and Culture, edited by Anthony W. Lee, 131–148. Burlington: Ashgate, 2013.

The County Magazine [. . .]; Particularly Dedicated to the Inhabitants of Berkshire, Dorsetshire, Hampshire, Somersetshire, and Wiltshire. Containing a Copious Selection of Whatever is Valuable in Literature, Politics, and History, and the Greatest Variety of Miscellaneous and Original Pieces in Prose and Verse. Salisbury: B. C. Collins, 1787.

Cradock, Joseph. *Literary & Miscellaneous Memoirs*. 4 vols. London: J. Nichols, 1826.

Crowest, Frederick James. *A Book of Musical Anecdotes: From Every Available Source*. 2 vols. London: Richard Bentley and Son, 1878.

Cunningham, Vanessa. *Shakespeare and Garrick*. Cambridge: Cambridge University Press, 2008.

[Curll, Edmund]. *Authentic Memoirs of the Life of that Justly Celebrated Actress, Mrs. Ann Oldfield*. London: Printed, and sold by the booksellers and pamphleteers of London and Westminster, 1731.

———. *The History of the English Stage, from the Restauration to the Present Time*. London: E. Curll, 1741.

D'Aulnoy, Marie-Catherine. *Memoirs of the Court of England*. London: B. Bragg, 1707.

Davenant, William. *The Siege of Rhodes, Parts 1 & 2*. 1656. Edited by Ann-Mari Hedbäck. Stockholm: Uppsala, 1973.

Davies, Thomas. "Anecdotes of the Late David Garrick" (I). *Universal Magazine* 66 (June 1780): 252–256.

———. *Dramatic Miscellanies: Consisting of Critical Observations on Several Plays of Shakspeare: With a Review of His Principal Characters, and Those of Various Eminent Writers, as Represented by Mr. Garrick, and Other Celebrated Comedians*. 3 vols. London: Printed for the author, 1783–1784.

———. *Memoirs of the Life of David Garrick*. 2 Vols. London: Printed for the author, 1780.

Dean, Winton. "Clive, Kitty [Catherine]." In *The New Grove Dictionary of Music and Musicians*, 29 vols, edited by Stanley Sadie, 7:856–858. London: Macmillan, 2001.

Defoe, Daniel. *Roxana*. 1724. Edited by Melissa Mowry. Peterborough, ON: Broadview Press, 2009.

"Description: *The Oxford Book of Theatrical Anecdotes*," *Oxford University Press: Academic*. https://global.oup.com/academic/product/the-oxford-book-of-theatrical-anecdotes-9780198749585?cc=ca&lang=en&#.

Deutsch, Helen. *Loving Dr. Johnson*. Chicago: University of Chicago Press, 2005.

———. "Oranges, Anecdote and the Nature of Things." *SubStance* 38, no. 1 (2009): 31–55.

Dibdin, Charles. *A Complete History of the Stage*. Vol. 5. London: C. Dibdin, [1800].

Dickie, Simon. *Cruelty and Laughter: Forgotten Comic Literature and the Unsentimental Eighteenth Century*. Chicago: University of Chicago Press, 2011.

Donnelley, Paul. "*The Oxford Book of Theatrical Anecdotes*: Gyles Brandreth's Cracker of a Book." *The Sunday Express*, Sunday, November 15, 2020.

Doran, John. "Lizzy Farren's Christmas Eves." *Gentleman's Magazine and Historical Review* (March 1855): 241–247.

———. "Their Majesties' Servants." *Annals of the English Stage from Thomas Betterton to Edmund Kean*. Vol. 1. Philadelphia: David McKay, 1890.

Downer, Alan S. "Nature to Advantage Dressed: Eighteenth-Century Acting." *PMLA* 58, no. 4 (December 1943): 1002–1037.

The Drama: Or, Theatrical Pocket Magazine. No. 3, 70–71. London: T. and J. Elvey, 1822.

Dugaw, Dianne. "Theorizing Orality and Performance in Literary Anecdote and History: Boswell's Diaries." *Oral Tradition* 24, no, 2 (2009): 415–428.

D'Urfey, Thomas. *Wit and Mirth; or, Tom D'Urfey's Pills to Purge Melancholy: A Selection of his Best Songs into One Volume. With an Account of the Author's Life*. London: William Holland, 1791.

Ebers, John. *Seven Years of the King's Theatre*. London: William Harrison Ainsworth, 1828.

The Encyclopaedia of Anecdote. Dublin: Printed by T. Jackson, [1800?].

Engel, Laura. "Notorious Celebrity: Mary Wells, Madness and Theatricality." In *The English Malady: Enabling and Disabling Fictions*, edited by Glen Colburn, 276–277. Cambridge: Cambridge Scholars Publishing, 2009.

Engelbach, Arthur Harold. *Anecdotes of the Theatre*. London: Grant Richards, 1914.

English Jests and Anecdotes (Nuggets for Travelers). Edinburgh: William Paterson, 1886.

The Festival of Wit: or, the Small Talker, Consisting of Anecdotes, Epigrammatic Flashes, Bon Mots, Repartees, and Puns, Royal, Noble, Naval, Military, Clerical, &c. London: M. A. Holland, 1782.

Fineman, Joel. "The History of the Anecdote: Fiction and Fiction." In *The New Historicism*, edited by H. Aram Veeser, 49–76. New York: Routledge, 1989.

———. "The History of the Anecdote." In *The Subjectivity Effect in Western Literary Tradition: Essays toward the Release of Shakespeare's Will*, 59–87. Cambridge, MA: MIT Press, 1991.

Fisher, Judith W. "Creating Another Identity: Aging Actresses in the Eighteenth Century." *Journal of Aging and Identity* 4, no. 2 (1999): 57–77.

Fisk, Deborah Payne. "Weaver [née Farley], Elizabeth (fl. 1661–1678), actress." *Oxford Dictionary of National Biography*. Oxford: Oxford University Press, 2008. https://doi.org/10.1093/ref:odnb/67770.

Fleming, Victor, dir. *Gone With the Wind*. Based on the novel by Margaret Mitchell. Los Angeles: Metro-Goldwyn-Mayer, 1939.

Foote, Samuel. *A Letter From Mr. Foote to the Reverend Author of the Remarks, Critical and Christian, on "The Minor"*. London: T. Davies, T. Becket, and J. Coote, 1760.

Foote, S[amuel]. *Memoirs of the Life of Sir John Dineley Goodere, Baronet, who was Murdered by the Contrivance of His Own Brother, on Board the Ruby Man of War, in King's Road, Near Bristol, Jan. 19, 1740–1. Together Wtth [sic] the Life, History, Trial, and Last Dying Words of His Brother Captain Samuel Goodere*. Worcester: J. Butler and James Grundy, 1785.

Foote, Samuel, Esq. *The Roman and English Comedy Consider'd and Compar'd. With Remarks on "The Suspicious Husband"*. London: T. Waller, [1747].

Foyster, Elizabeth. "Boys Will Be Boys? Manhood and Aggression, 1660–1800." In *English Masculinities, 1660–1800*, edited by Tim Hitchcock and Michele Cohen, 151–166. London: Longman, 1999.

Frye, Northrop. Marginalia in *Memoirs of the Court of Charles the Second*, edited by Walter Scott. London: Henry G. Bohn, 1859. Annotated no. 121: E. J. Pratt Library, Victoria University, University of Toronto.

Fryer, Peter. *Staying Power: The History of Black People in Britain*. London: Pluto Press, 1984.

Fyvie, John. *Tragedy Queens of the Georgian Era*. New York: E. P. Dutton and Company, 1909.

Gabble, Gridiron [pseud. Joseph Haslewood]. *Green Room Gossip*. London: J. Barker, 1809.

Gallagher, Catherine, and Stephen Greenblatt. "The Touch of the Real." In *Practicing New Historicism*, 20–48. Chicago: University of Chicago Press, 2000.

Galt, John. *The Lives of the Players*. London: Henry Colburn and Richard Bentley, 1831.

Garrick, David. *The Letters of David Garrick*. Edited by David M. Little, George M. Kahrl, and Phoebe deK. Wilson. 3 vols. Cambridge, MA: Harvard University Press, 1963.

Garrick, David, and George Colman, the Elder. *The Clandestine Marriage*. 1766. Peterborough, ON: Broadview Press, 1995.

Genest, John, ed. *Some Account of the English Stage, from the Restoration in 1660 to 1830*. 10 vols. New York: Burt Franklin, 1832; 1965.

———. *Some Account of the English Stage, from the Restoration in 1660 to 1830*. 10 vols. Bath: Printed by H. E. Carrington, 1832.

A Gentleman. *Aristophanes: Being a Classic Collection of True Attic Wit, Containing the Jests, Gibes, Bon-mots, Witticisms, and Most Extraordinary Anecdotes of Samuel Foote, Esq. the Lords Chesterfield, Tyrawley, Messrs. Churchill, Thornton, Cox, Lloyd, and Their Cotemporaries [sic]; . . . Collected, During the Course of Twenty Years, by a Gentleman, . . . With an Engraved Head of Samuel Foote, Esq.* London: Robert Baldwin, 1778.

"Genuine Biographical Anecdotes of David Garrick" (1). *The Gentleman's Magazine* 49 (March 1779): 117–119.

"Genuine Biographical Anecdotes of David Garrick" (2). *The Gentleman's Magazine* 49 (April 1779): 171–173.

"Genuine Biographical Anecdotes of David Garrick" (3). *The Gentleman's Magazine* 49 (May 1779): 226–228.

George, Mary Dorothy. *Catalogue of Political and Personal Satires Preserved in the Department of Prints and Drawings in The British Museum*. Vol. 5, *1771–1783*. London: Printed by order of the trustees, 1935.

———. *Catalogue of Political and Personal Satires Preserved in the Department of Prints and Drawings in The British Museum*. Vol. 6, *1784–1792*. London: Printed by order of the trustees, 1938.

Gibbons, Orlando. *First Set of Madrigals and Mottets*. London: Thomas Snodham, 1612.

Gilder, Rosamund. *Enter the Actress: The First Women in the Theatre*. Boston: Houghton Mifflin Company, 1931.

Giles, David. *Illusions of Immortality: A Psychology of Fame and Celebrity*. London: Macmillan, 2000.

Glasson, Francis T. "The Place of the Anecdote: A Note on Form Criticism." *The Journal of Theological Studies*, 32, no. 1 (1981): 142–150.

Goring, Paul. *The Rhetoric of Sensibility in Eighteenth-Century Culture*. Cambridge: Cambridge University Press, 2004.

Gossman, Lionel. "Anecdote and History." *History and Theory* 42 (May 2003): 143–168.

Granger, William. *The New Wonderful Museum, and Extraordinary Magazine: Being a Complete Repository of All the Wonders, Curiosities, and Rarities of Nature and Art, from the Beginning of the World to the Present Year*. London: Alex Hogg, 1807.

Grize, Justin. "Singing Beasts: Opera and the Animal." PhD diss., University of Sussex, 2017. ProQuest. https://www.proquest.com/dissertations-theses/singing-beasts-opera-animal/docview/2230917069/se-2?acccountid=6180.

Hamilton, Anthony. *Memoirs of the Court of Charles the Second*. 1714. Edited by Walter Scott. London: Henry G. Bohn, 1859.

Hamilton, Kate C. "The 'Famous Mrs. Barry': Elizabeth Barry and Restoration Celebrity." *Studies in Eighteenth-Century Culture* 42 (2013): 291–320.

Hare, Arnold. *The Georgian Theatre in Wessex*. London: Phoenix House, 1958.

———, ed. *Theatre Royal Bath: A Calendar of Performances at the Orchard Street Theatre 1750–1805*. Compiled by Heather Bryant, Arnold Hare, Peter Hibbard, Margaret Jarrett, Raymond Meddick, Phyllis Parnell, Mary Sanderson, Audrey Shaw, Denise Tett, Jean Watson, and Gordon Woodward. Bath: Kingsmead Press, 1977.

Harral, T[homas]. *A Monody on the Death of John Palmer, The Comedian, to Which Is Prefixed a Review of His Theatrical Powers: With Observations on the Most Eminent Performers on the London Stage*. London: George Cawthorn, 1798.

Hart, W. A. "Africans in Eighteenth-Century Ireland." *Irish Historical Studies* 33, no. 129 (May 2002): 19–32.

[Haslewood, Joseph.] *The Secret History of the Green Room: Containing Authentic and Entertaining Memoirs of the Actors and Actresses in the Three Theatres Royal*. 2nd ed. 3 vols. London: H. D. Symonds, 1792.

Hawkins, John. *A General History of the Science and Practice of Music: Volume the Fifth*. London: T. Payne and Son, 1776.

Herring, Thomas. *Seven Sermons on Public Occasions*. London: printed for the editor, 1763.

Highfill, Philip H., Jr., Kalman A. Burnim, and Edward A. Langhans, eds. *A Biographical Dictionary of Actors, Actresses, Musicians, Dancers, Managers & Other Stage Personnel in London, 1660–1800*. 16 vols. Carbondale: Southern Illinois University Press, 1973–1993.

Hill, John. *The Actor: Or, a Treatise on the Art of Playing*. London: R. Griffiths, 1755.

Hobson, Harold. *Theatre*. London: Burke Publishing Co., 1953.

Hope, William. *A Vindication of the True Art of Self-Defence*. Edinburgh: William Brown and Company, 1724.

Howe, Elizabeth. *The First English Actresses: Women and Drama, 1660–1700*. Cambridge: Cambridge University Press, 1992.

Hudson, Hannah. "'This Lady Is Descended from a Good Family': Women and Biography in British Magazines, 1770–1798." In *Women's Periodicals and Print Culture in Britain, 1820s: The Long Eighteenth Century*, edited by Jennie Batchelor and Manushag N. Powell, 278–294. Edinburgh: University of Edinburgh Press, 2018.

Hume, Robert D. "Elizabeth Barry's First Roles and the Cast of *The Man of Mode*." *Theatre History Studies* 5 (January 1985): 16–19.

———. "Garrick in Dublin in 1745–46." *Philological Quarterly* (2015): 507–540.

———. "John Rich as Manager and Entrepreneur." In *The Stage's Glory: John Rich (1692–1761)*, edited by Berta Joncus and Jeremy Barlow, 29–60. Newark: University of Delaware Press, 2011.

Hume, Robert D., and Judith Milhous. "Murder in Elizabeth Barry's Dressing Room." *The Yale University Library Gazette* 79, no. 3/4 (April 2005): 149–174.

———. "Theatre History 1660–1800: Aims, Materials, Methodology." In *Players, Playwrights, Playhouses: Investigating Performance, 1660–1800*, edited by Michael Cordner and Peter Holland, 9–44. London: Palgrave Macmillan, 2007.

Hutcheon, Linda. *A Theory of Parody: The Teachings of Twentieth-Century Art Forms*. Urbana: University of Illinois Press, 1985; 2000.

Including Anecdotes of Several Distinguished Persons [. . .]. With a Post-script Extraordinary! 7th ed. London: H. D. Symonds, [1797].

Itzkoff, Dave. "Matthew McConaughey Wrote the Book on Matthew McConaughey." *New York Times*, October 14, 2020. https://www.nytimes.com/2020/10/14/books/matthew-mcconaughey-memoir-greenlights.html.

Johnson, James William. *A Profane Wit: The Life of John Wilmot, Earl of Rochester*. Rochester, NY: University of Rochester Press, 2004.

Johnson, Samuel, ed. *A Dictionary of the English Language: In which The Words are deduced from their Originals, and Illustrated in their Different Significations by Examples from the best Writers*. 2nd ed. 2 vols. London: W. Strahan, for J. Knapton; C. Hitch and L. Hawes; A. Millar; R. and J. Dodsley; and M. and T. Longman, 1756.

———. "Life of Waller." In *The Lives of the English Poets*, vol. 1, 228–283. London: Thomas Tegg, 1824.

———. *The Major Works*. Edited by Donald Greene. Oxford: Oxford University Press, 2000.

Joncus, Berta. *Kitty Clive, or The Fair Songster*. Woodbridge: Boydell Press, 2019.

Jones, Emrys D., and Victoria Joule, eds. *Intimacy and Celebrity in Eighteenth-Century Literary Culture: Public Interiors*. Basingstoke, UK: Palgrave Macmillan, 2018.

Jones, Henry. *Poems on Several Occasions*. London: R. Dodsley, 1749.

Kelly, Ian. *Mr Foote's Other Leg*. London: Picador, 2012.

———. *Mr Foote's Other Leg*. London: NHB Modern Plays, 2015.

Kendall, Alan. *David Garrick: A Biography*. London: Harrap, 1985.

Kinservik, Matthew. *Disciplining Satire: The Censorship of Satiric Comedy on the Eighteenth-Century London Stage*. Lewisburg, PA: Bucknell University Press, 2002.

———. *Sex, Scandal, and Celebrity in Late Eighteenth-Century England.* Basingstoke, UK: Palgrave Macmillan, 2007.

Kirkman, James. "Anecdotes of Charles Macklin, from his Life, by Kirkman." *Universal Magazine* 104 (May 1799): 317–324.

———. *Memoirs of the Life of Charles Macklin, Esq.* 2 vols. London: Allen Lackington, 1799.

Knight, John Joseph. "Foote, Samuel." *Dictionary of National Biography, 1885–1900.* Vol. 19, 370–375. London: Smith, Elder, 1889.

Knolles, Richard. *Generall Historie of the Turkes.* London: A. Islip, 1603.

Ladd, Heather. "Theatre, Celebrity, and Contagion: David Garrick's 1742 Dublin Visit and James R. Planché's *Garrick Fever.*" *Theatre Notebook* 72, no. 2 (2018): 78–99.

Lamb, Jeremy. *So Idle a Rogue: The Life and Death of Lord Rochester.* London: Allison & Busby, 1993.

Lanier, Henry Wysham. *The First English Actresses from the Initial Appearance of Women on the Stage in 1660 Till 1700.* New York: Players, 1930.

Lanser, Susan. *The Sexuality of History.* Chicago: University of Chicago Press, 2014.

Larwood, Jacob. *Theatrical Anecdotes: Or Fun and Curiosities of the Play, the Playhouse, and the Players.* London: Chatto & Windus, 1882.

Law, Jonathan. *Methuen Drama Dictionary of the Theatre.* London: Methuen, 2013.

Lee, Nathaniel. *The Rival Queens; or, the Death of Alexander the Great.* 1677. Edited by P. F. Vernon. Lincoln: University of Nebraska Press, 1970.

———. *The Rival Queens: Or, the Death of Alexander the Great.* London: W. Feales, 1677; 1736.

Leonato [Thomas Davies]. "Eulogium on Mr. Garrick's Leaving the Stage." *Gentleman's Magazine* 46 (1776): 304–306.

"A Letter to Mr. Garrick on the Opening of the Theatre, with Observations on the Conduct of Managers, to Actors, Authors, and Audiences: And Particularly to New-Performers." London: J. Coote, 1758.

The Life of Lavinia Beswick, alias Fenton, alias Polly Peachum. London: A. Moore, 1728.

The Life of Mr. James Quin, Comedian. London: S. Bladon, 1766.

"Liverpool Playbills: Drury Lane 1767–71, Theatre Royal 1773–77." Liverpool Record Office.

Loselle, Andrea. "Introduction." *SubStance* 38, no. 1 (2009): 3–4.

Luckhurst, Mary, and Jane Moody, eds. *Theatre and Celebrity in Britain, 1660–2000.* New York: Palgrave Macmillan, 2005.

Mackie, Erin. "Boys Will Be Boys: Masculinity, Criminality, and the Restoration Rake." *The Eighteenth Century* 46, no. 2 (2005): 129–149.

Mainwaring, John. *Memoirs of the Life of the Late George Frederic Handel.* London: R. and J. Dodsley, 1760.

[Manley, Delarivier]. *Secret Memoirs and Manners Of several Persons of Quality of Both Sexes. From the New Atalantis, an Island in the Mediterranean.* 6th ed. 4 vols. London: John Morphew, 1720.

Marcus, Sharon. *Between Women: Friendship, Desire, and Marriage in Victorian England.* Princeton, NJ: Princeton University Press, 2007.

Marsden, Jean. "Affect and the Problem of Theatre." *The Eighteenth Century* 58, no. 3 (2017): 297–307.

Martin, Susan M. "Actresses on the London Stage, 1670–1755: A Prosopographical Study." PhD diss., Pennsylvania State University, 2008.

———. *Fatal Desire: Women, Sexuality, and the English Stage, 1660–1720.* Ithaca, NY: Cornell University Press, 2006.

Martinez, Marc. "The Tricks of Lun: Mimesis and Mimicry in John Rich's Performance and Conception of Pantomimes." *Theatre History Studies* 29 (2009): 148–170.

Mathews, Mrs. [Anne Jackson]. *Anecdotes of Actors: With Other Desultory Recollections, Etc. Etc. Etc.* London: T. C. Newby, 1844.

McDowell, Paula. "Defoe and the Contagion of the Oral: Modeling Media Shift in *A Journal of the Plague Year.*" *PMLA* 121, no. 1 (2006): 87–106.

McGirr, Elaine. "Nell Gwyn's Breasts and Colley Cibber's Shirts: Celebrity Actors and Their Famous 'Parts.'" In *Intimacy and Celebrity in Eighteenth-Century Literary Culture: Public Interiors*, edited by Emrys D. Jones and Victoria Joule, 3–34. Basingstoke, UK: Palgrave Macmillan, 2018.

———. "New Lines: Mary Ann Yates, *The Orphan of China*, and the New She-Tragedy." *ABO: Interactive Journal for Women in the Arts, 1640–1830* 8: no. 2 https://doi.org/10.5038/2157-7129.8.2.1198.

———. "'What's in a Name?': *Romeo and Juliet* and the Cibber Brand." *Shakespeare* 14, no. 4 (October 2, 2018): 399–412.

McKeon, Michael. *The Secret History of Domesticity: Private, Public, and the Division of Knowledge.* Baltimore: Johns Hopkins University Press, 2005.

Melville, Lewis. *Stage Favourites of the Eighteenth Century.* London: Hutchinson & Co., 1928.

Menzer, Paul. *Anecdotal Shakespeare: A New Performance History.* London: Bloomsbury Arden Shakespeare, 2015.

Mieder, Wolfgang, Fred R. Shapiro, and Charles Clay Doyle. *The Dictionary of Modern Proverbs.* New Haven, CT: Yale University Press, 2012.

Milhous, Judith, and Robert D. Hume. "Construing and Misconstruing Farinelli in London." *British Journal of Eighteenth-Century Studies* 28, no. 3 (2005): 361–385.

Mock, Roberta. "Dennis Delane [Delany]." In *Oxford Dictionary of National Biography*. Oxford University Press, 2004. https://doi.org/10.1093/ref:odnb/7439.

Monks, Aoife. "Collecting Ghosts: Actors, Anecdotes and Objects at the Theatre." *Contemporary Theatre Review* 23, no. 2 (2013): 146–152.

The Monthly Mirror: Reflecting Men and Manners. With Strictures on their Epitome, the Stage. September 1799, July 1801.

Moody, Jane. "Stolen Identities: Character Mimicry and the Invention of Samuel Foote." In *Theatre and Celebrity in Britain, 1660–2000*, edited by Mary Luckhurst and Jane Moody, 65–86. New York: Palgrave Macmillan, 2005.

Mott, A. *Biographical Sketches and Interesting Anecdotes of Persons of Color: To which is Added a Selection of Pieces in Poetry*. New York: W. Alexander & Son, 1826.

Mounsey, Chris. "Thomas Sheridan and the Second Smock Alley Theatre Riot, 1754." *New Hibernia Review / Iris Éireannach Nua* 4, no. 3 (2000): 65–77.

"Mrs. Yates." *Theatrical Biography; or, Memoirs of the Principal Performers of the Three Theatres Royal*. 2 vols. Vol 2. Dublin, 1772.

Munns, Jessica. "Otway, Thomas." In *Oxford Dictionary of National Biography*. Oxford University Press, 2004. https://doi.org/10.1093/ref:odnb/20944.

Murphy, Arthur. *The Life of David Garrick, Esq*. 2 vols. London: J. Wright, J. F. Foot, 1801.

Nicholson, Helen. "Emotion." *CTR* 23, no 1 (2013): 20–22.

Nicoll, Allardyce. *A History of English Drama, 1660–1900, Volume 1*. 4th ed. Cambridge: Cambridge University Press, 1967.

Nipclose, Sir Nicholas [Francis Gentleman]. *The Theatres. A Poetical Dissection*. London: John Bell and C. Etherington, 1772.

Norman, N. D. "From a Record of Death to a Memory of Life: The Rise of the Biographical Obituary in the *Gentleman's Magazine*." Master's thesis, Virginia Tech, 2008.

Notes and Queries. Vol. 10, no. 249 (October 4, 1884): 268.

Notes and Queries. Vol. 10, no. 254 (November 8, 1884): 371.

Nussbaum, Felicity. *Rival Queens: Actresses, Performance, and the Eighteenth-Century British Theater*. Philadelphia: University of Pennsylvania Press, 2010.

———. *Torrid Zones: Maternity, Sexuality, and Empire in Eighteenth-Century English Narratives*. Baltimore: Johns Hopkins University Press, 1995.

O'Bryan, Daniel. *Authentic Memoirs or, the Life and Character Of that most Celebrated Comedian, Mr. Robert Wilks*. London: S. Slow, 1732.

O'Keeffe, John. *Recollections of the Life of John O'Keeffe, Written by Himself*. 2 vols. London: Henry Colburn, 1826.

Orlando: Women's Writing in the British Isles from the Beginnings to the Present. Cambridge University Press online, 2006. https://orlando.cambridge.org/.

Oxberry, William, ed. *Oxberry's Anecdotes of the Stage, &c. &c.* London: G. Virtue, 1827.

———. *Oxberry's Dramatic Biography and Histrionic Anecdotes*. 3 vols. London: C. Baynes, for G. Virtue, 1826.

Oxford English Dictionary online. December 2019. Oxford University Press.

Payne, Deborah C. "Reified Object or Emergent Professional? Retheorizing the Restoration Actress." In *Cultural Readings of Restoration and Eighteenth-Century English Theatre*, edited by J. Douglas Canfield and Deborah C. Payne, 13–38. Athens: University of Georgia Press, 2005.

Pepys, Samuel. *The Diary of Samuel Pepys, M.A., F.R.S.*, edited by Henry B. Wheatley. 10 vols. London: George Bell & Sons, 1893.

Philips, Ambrose. *Pastorals, Epistles, Odes, and Other Original Poems, With Translations from Pindar, Anacreon, and Sappho*. London: Tonson and Draper, 1748.

Phillips, Lesley. *The Eccentric Mr Whitley*. N.p.: Independently published, 2017.

Picard, Liza. *Restoration London: Engaging Anecdotes and Tantalizing Trivia from the Most Magnificent and Renowned City of Europe*. London: Harper Perennial, 2000.

Pooley, Julian, and Robin Myser. "Nichols Family." In *Oxford Dictionary of National Biography*. Oxford University Press, 2004. https://doi.org/10.1093/ref:odnb/63494.

Postlewait, Thomas. "The Criteria for Evidence: Anecdotes in Shakespearean Biography, 1709–2000." In *Theorizing Practice: Redefining Theatre History*, edited by W. B. Worthen and Peter Holland, 47–70. Basingstoke, UK: Palgrave Macmillan, 2003.

Price, Lydia. "Tom Cruise Crashed Kate Hudson's House and More Insanely Epic Celebrity Party Stories." *People*, February 20, 2020. https://people.com/celebrity/epic-celebrity-party-stories/.

Pritchard, R. E. *Passion for Living: John Wilmot, Earl of Rochester*. Cambridge: Lutterworth Press, 2012.

Price, Victor J. *Birmingham Theatres: Concert and Music Halls, 1740–1988*. Studley, Warwickshire: Brewin Books, 1988.

Procopius. *The Secret History*. Translated by Richard Atwater. New York: Cosimo, 2007.

Pullen, Kirsten. *Actresses and Whores: On Stage and in Society*. Cambridge: Cambridge University Press, 2005.

Raleigh, Walter. "'What is our life? The play of passion.'" In *Elizabethan Poetry: An Anthology*, edited by Bob Blaisdell, 122. Mineola, NY: Dover Publications, 2005.

Rawson, Claude. "Fielding's Style." In *The Cambridge Companion to Henry Fielding*, edited by Claude Julien Rawson, 153–174. Cambridge: Cambridge University Press, 2007.

Rees, Nigel, ed. *Brewer's Quotations*. London: Cassell, 1994.

Reeve, Matthew M. "Gothic Architecture, Sexuality, and License at Horace Walpole's Strawberry Hill." *The Art Bulletin* 95, no. 3 (2013): 411–439.

Richardson, Samuel. *Pamela; or, Virtue Rewarded*. 1741. Edited by Thomas Keymer and Alice Wakely. New York: Oxford University Press, 2001.

Ritchie, Leslie. *David Garrick and the Mediation of Celebrity*. Cambridge: Cambridge University Press, 2019.

———. "Pox on Both Your Houses: The Battle of the Romeos." *Eighteenth-Century Fiction* 27, no. 3 (2015): 373–393.

Roach, Joseph. *It*. Ann Arbor: University of Michigan Press, 2007.

———. *The Player's Passion: Studies in the Science of Acting*. Newark: University of Delaware Press, 1985.

———. "Power's Body: The Inscription of Morality as Style." In *Interpreting the Theatrical Past: Essays in the Historiography of Performance*, edited by Thomas Postlewait and Bruce A. McConachie, 99–118. Iowa City: University of Iowa Press, 1989.

Robinson, Joanna. "Matthew McConaughey Won't Back Away from His Drumming Past." *Vanity Fair*, January 27, 2017. https://www.vanityfair.com/style/2017/01/matthew-mcconaughey-drums-drumming-drummer-arrest.

Rojek, Chris. *Celebrity*. London: Reaktion Books, 2001.

Roose-Evans, James. *London Theatre: From the Globe to the National*. Oxford: Phaidon, 1977.

Rosenthal, Laura J. "'Counterfeit Scrubbado': Women Actors in the Restoration." *Eighteenth Century: Theory and Interpretation* 34, no. 1 (Spring 1993): 3–22.

Rowlandson, Thomas. *The Prospect Before Us*. 1791. Etching. Published by Samuel William Fores, January 13, 1791. London, British Museum, J,2.86.

———. *The Prospect Before Us*. 1791. Etching. Inscribed: "Humanely incrib'd to all those Professors of Music and Dancing whom the cap may fit." Published by Samuel William Fores, January 13, 1791. Preparatory watercolor. London, British Museum, 1985,0608.31.

Russell, William Clark. *Representative Actors*. London: Frederick Warne and Co., 1888.

Rycaut, Paul. *Present State of the Ottoman Empire*. 1686. Reprint, New York: Arno Press and the New York Times, 1971.

Sambrook, James. "Williams, John [pseud. Anthony Pasquin]." In *Oxford Dictionary of National Biography*. Oxford University Press, 2004. https://doi.org/10.1093/ref:odnb/29520.

"Samuel Foote." *The Living Age*. Vol. 43, 387–430. Boston: Littell, Son and Company, 1854.

Sancho, Ignatius. *Letters of the Late Ignatius Sancho, an African*. Edited by Vincent Carretta. Peterborough, ON: Broadview Press, 2015.

Savage, Elizabeth. "Making Mary: Imitation and Infamy in the Eighteenth-Century Theater." *Restoration and Eighteenth-Century Theatre Research* 30, no. 1–2 (Summer 2015): 73–87.

Scobie, Ruth. "Foote, Fox, and the Mysterious Mrs. Grieve." In *Intimacy and Celebrity in Eighteenth-Century Literary Culture: Public Interiors*, edited by Emrys D. Jones and Victoria Joule, 233–256. Basingstoke, UK: Palgrave Macmillan, 2018.

Scott, Virginia. *Women on the Stage in Early Modern France, 1540–1750*. Cambridge: Cambridge University Press, 2010.

Scouten, Arthur Hawley, ed. *The London Stage 1660–1800; A Calendar of Plays, Entertainments & Afterpieces, Together with Casts, Box-Receipts and Contemporary Comment Compiled from the Playbills, Newspapers and Theatrical Diaries of the Period, Part 3: 1729–1747*. 2 vols. Carbondale: Southern Illinois University Press, 1961.

Sedgwick, Eve Kosofsky. *Between Men: English Literature and Male Homosocial Desire*. New York: Columbia University Press, 1992.

Shoemaker, Robert. *The London Mob: Violence and Disorder in Eighteenth-Century England*. London: A&C Black, 2004.

———. "The Taming of the Duel: Masculinity, Honour and Ritual Violence in London, 1660–1800." *The Historical Journal* 45, no. 3 (September 2002): 525–545.

Sjögan, Gunner. "Ira Aldridge's Swedish Wife." In *Ira Aldridge, the African Roscius*, edited by Bernth Lindfors, 68–72. Rochester, NY: University of Rochester Press, 2007.

Smith, Geoffrey. "'A Gentleman of Great Esteem with the King': The Restoration Roles and Reputations of Thomas Killigrew." In *Thomas Killigrew and the Seventeenth-Century English Stage*, 151–174. Burlington, VT: Ashgate, 2013.

Solinger, Jason. *Becoming the Gentleman: British Literature and the Invention of Modern Masculinity, 1660–1815*. New York: Palgrave Macmillan, 2012.

Solomon, Diana. "Anecdotes and Restoration Actresses: The Cases of Elizabeth Barry and Anne Bracegirdle." *Restoration and Eighteenth-Century Theatre Research* 31, no. 2 (2016): 19–36.

———. *Prologues and Epilogues of Restoration Theater: Gender and Comedy, Performance and Print*. Newark: University of Delaware Press, 2013.

Songs, Chorusses, &c. Which Are Introduced in the New Entertainment of the Jubilee, at the Theatre Royal, in Drury Lane. London: T. Becket and P. A. De Hondt, 1769.

The Sporting Magazine: Or, Monthly Calendar of the Transactions of the Turf, the Chase, and Every Other Diversion Interesting to the Man of Pleasure, Enterprize, and Spirit. April 1797.

Spratt, Danielle. "'Genius Thus Munificently Employed!!!': Philanthropy and Celebrity in the Theaters of Garrick and Siddons." *Eighteenth-Century Life* 37, no. 3 (2013): 55–84.

State Papers Online: The Government of Britain, 1509–1714. Gale Cengage Learning, 2019.

Steele, Elizabeth. "The Memoirs of Mrs. Sophia Baddeley." In *Women's Theatrical Memoirs*, edited by Sue McPherson and Julia Swindells, vols. 6–8. London: Pickering & Chatto, 2008.

Stefanovska, Malina. "Exemplary or Singular? The Anecdote in Historical Narrative." *SubStance: A Review of Theory and Literary Criticism* 118, vol. 38, no. 1 (January 2009): 16–30.

Stephenson, Judy Z. "'Real' Wages? Contractors, Workers, and Pay in London Building Trades, 1650–1800." *The Economic History Review* 71, no. 1 (February 2018): 106–132.

Stern, Tiffany. *Rehearsal from Shakespeare to Sheridan.* Oxford: Oxford University Press, 2000.

Stoddard, Richard Henry, ed. *Personal Reminiscences: By O'Keefe, Kelly, and Taylor.* New York: Scribner, Armstrong, & Company, 1875.

Stone, George Winchester, Jr., ed. *The London Stage 1660–1800; A Calendar of Plays, Entertainments & Afterpieces, Together with Casts, Box-Receipts and Contemporary Comment Compiled from the Playbills, Newspapers and Theatrical Diaries of the Period. Part 4: 1747–1776.* 3 vols. Carbondale: Southern Illinois University Press, 1962.

Straub, Kristina. *Sexual Suspects.* Princeton, NJ: Princeton University Press, 1992.

Tague, Ingrid H. *Animal Companions: Pets and Social Change in Eighteenth-Century Britain.* University Park: Pennsylvania State University Press, 2015.

The Testimony of Truth to Exalted Merit: Or, A Biographical Sketch of the Right Honourable The Countess of Derby; in Refutation of a False and Scandalous Libel. London: George Cawthorn, 1797.

The Theatrical Olio; or, Thespian Jester. Being an Entertaining Selection of Droll Anecdotes, Pleasing Stories, Funny Jokes, Bon Mots, Epigrams, Whimsical Adventures, &c. &c. Related by Several Eminent Performers. Southwark: W. Kemmish, [1798].

Thomson, Peter. "Celebrity and Rivalry: David [Garrick] and Goliath [Quin]." In *Theatre and Celebrity in Britain, 1660–2000*, edited by Mary Luckhurst and Jane Moody, 127–147. Basingstoke, UK: Palgrave Macmillan, 2005.

———. "Farren [Farran], Elizabeth [married name Elizabeth Smith Stanley, Countess of Derby]." In *Oxford Dictionary of National Biography*. Oxford University Press, 2004. https://doi.org/10.1093/ref:odnb/9191.

———. "Yates [nee Graham], Mary Ann." In *Oxford Dictionary of National Biography*. Oxford University Press, 2004. https://doi.org.proxy.queensu.ca/10.1093/ref:odnb/30196.

Threadgold, Terry. *Feminist Poetics: Poiesis, Performance, Histories*. London: Routledge, 1997.

Timbs, John. *Lives of Wits and Humourists*. 2 vols. London: Richard Bentley, 1862.

Tooke, William, Robert Nares, and William Beloe, eds. *A New and General Biographical Dictionary*. 15 vols. London: G. G. and J. Robinson et al., 1798.

Trumpener, Katie. "Rewriting Roxane: Orientalism and Intertextuality in Montesquieu's *Lettres persanes* and Defoe's *The Fortunate Mistress*." *Stanford French Review* 11 (1987): 177–191.

Twigg, Julia. *Fashion and Age: Dress, the Body and Later Life*. London: Bloomsbury, 2013.

Van Lennep, William, Emmett L. Avery, and Arthur H. Scouten, eds. *The London Stage 1660–1800: A Calendar of Plays, Entertainments & Afterpieces, Together with Casts, Box-receipts and Contemporary Comment: Compiled from the Playbills, Newspapers and Theatrical Diaries of the Period. Part I: 1660–1700*. Carbondale: Southern Illinois University Press, 1965.

Veritatis, Scriptor. *The Memoirs of the Present Countess of Derby, Rescued by Truth from the Assassinating Pen of Petronius Arbiter; and Proving the Stage, from the Patronage of the Most Exalted Personages, to Have Been Always Considered as a School for Morality*. London: Printed for the author, 1797.

Victor, Benjamin. *The History of the Theatres of London and Dublin, From the Year 1730 to the Present Time. To Which Is Added, An annual Register of All the Plays, &c. Performed at the Theatres-Royal in London, From the Year 1712*. London: Printed for T. Davies, 1761.

[Villiers,] George, Duke of Buckingham. *The Rehearsal: As It Is Now Acted at the Theatre-Royal. To Which Is Added, a Key, or Critical View of the Authors, and Their Writings, Expos'd in This Play*. 13th ed. London: W. Feales, R. Wellington, J. Wellington, A. Bettesworth, and F. Clay, 1735.

Walker's Hibernian Magazine: Or, Compendium of Entertaining Knowledge. July 1794.

Wanko, Cheryl. *Roles of Authority: Thespian Biography and Celebrity in Eighteenth-Century Britain*. Lubbock: Texas Tech University Press, 2003.

———. "Three Stories of Celebrity: *The Beggar's Opera* 'Biographies.'" *Studies in English Literature, 1500–1900, Restoration and Eighteenth Century* 38, no. 3 (1998): 481–498.

Weber, William. *The Rise of Musical Classics in Eighteenth-Century England.* Oxford: Oxford University Press, 1992.

Weldy Boyd, Amanda. *Staging Memory and Materiality in Eighteenth-Century Theatrical Biography*. London: Anthem Press, 2017.

Wessel, Jane. "Mimicry, Property, and the Reproduction of Celebrity in Eighteenth-Century England." *The Eighteenth Century: Theory and Interpretation* 60, no. 1 (2019): 65–86.

West, Shearer. *Portraiture.* Oxford: Oxford University Press, 2004.

———. "Siddons, Celebrity and Regality: Portraiture and the Body of the Ageing Actress." In *Theatre and Celebrity in Britain: 1660–2000*, edited by Mary Luckhurst and Jane Moody, 191–213. Basingstoke, UK: Palgrave Macmillan, 2005.

Wilkinson, Tate. *Memoirs of His Own Life, by Tate Wilkinson, Patentee of the Theatres-Royal, York & Hull.* 4 vols. York: Printed for the author by Wilson, Spence, and Mawman, 1790.

———. *Original Anecdotes Respecting the Stage, and the Actors of the Old School, with Remarks on Mr. Murphy's "Life of Garrick."* London: J. Wright, [1805].

———. *The Wandering Patentee; or, A History of the Yorkshire Theatres, from 1770 to the Present Time: Interspersed with Anecdotes Respecting Most of the Performers in the Three Kingdoms from 1765 to 1795.* 4 vols. York: Printed for the author, by Wilson, Spence, and Mawman, 1795.

[Williams, David]. *A Letter to David Garrick, Esq. On His Conduct as Principal Manager and Actor at Drury-Lane*. London: S. Bladon, 1772.

Wilmot, John. *The Letters of John Wilmot, Earl of Rochester.* Edited by Jeremy Treglown. Chicago: University of Chicago Press, 1980.

Wilson, Henry. *Wonderful Characters: Comprising Memoirs and Anecdotes of the Most Remarkable Persons of Every Age and Nation*. London: J. Robins and Company, Albion Press, 1826.

Wilson, John H. *All the King's Ladies: Actresses of the Restoration.* Chicago: University of Chicago Press, 1958.

———. "Lord Oxford's 'Roxolana.'" *Theatre Notebook* 12, no. 1 (Autumn 1957): 14.

———. "Rant, Cant, and Tone on the Restoration Stage." *Studies in Philology* 52 (October 1955): 592–598.

Wilson, Kathleen. *The Island Race: Englishness, Empire, and Gender in the Eighteenth Century*. New York: Routledge, 2003.

Winston, James. *The Theatric Tourist.* Facsimile of the 1st edition of 1805, edited by Iain Mackintosh, with an introduction by Marcus Risdell. London: Society for Theatre Research and the British Library, 2008.

Wood, James Robert. "Mr. Spectator's Anecdotes and the Science of Human Nature." *Eighteenth-Century Life* 38, no. 1 (Winter 2014): 63–92.

Woodfield, Ian. *Opera and Drama in Eighteenth-Century London*. Cambridge: Cambridge University Press, 2001.

Wycherley, William. *The Country Wife*. 1675. In *The Broadview Anthology of Restoration and Eighteenth-Century Drama*, edited by J. Douglas Canfield, 92–154. Toronto: Broadview Press, 2005.

NOTES ON CONTRIBUTORS

Danielle Bobker is associate professor of English at Concordia University in Montreal. Her book, *The Closet: The Eighteenth-Century Architecture of Intimacy*, was a finalist for the Quebec Writers' Federation's Mavis Gallant Prize for Non-Fiction. Her new project, "Flayed," unravels conceptual and linguistic entanglements of humor, sex, and violence in eighteenth-century satire and twenty-first-century comedy and comedy criticism. On one long summer night in 1994, she worked alongside Nicole Kidman and Joaquin Phoenix as an extra in *To Die For*, but you'll have to take her word for it because her scene was cut.

Michael Burden is professor of opera studies at the University of Oxford, and fellow in Music at New College, where he is also dean. His research is on music, dance, and staging opera in the eighteenth- and nineteenth-century theater. His latest project is the online calendar *The London Stage 1800–1844*. He first became interested in the eighteenth century when he discovered that life's true proportions found in the golden ratio were those of late Georgian sash windows.

Heather Ladd is a former associate professor in the Department of English at the University of Lethbridge. She is the coeditor of this collection and has published on many eighteenth-century writers, including Charlotte Smith, Ann Radcliffe, John Gay, Thomas D'Urfey, and Elizabeth Craven. She is now located in Vancouver, British Columbia, and currently teaches at Kwantlen Polytechnic University in the Department of English. While living in southern Alberta, she occasionally performed as a drag king under the drag name Dick Hazard, taken from the anonymously written novel *The Adventures of Dick Hazard* (1755).

Máire MacNeill received her PhD from Royal Holloway, University of London. She is an independent scholar who works on masculinity and violence in eighteenth-century theater and culture, and has previously published work on theatrical duels, satires on military figures, and Defoe's *Memoirs of a Cavalier*. She is currently working on a project that examines legacies of violence in the long eighteenth century. She studied fencing for two years before the many bruises she sustained convinced her that she'd much prefer writing about sword-fighting than doing it.

Nevena Martinović received her PhD from Queen's University. She works in the fields of eighteenth-century studies, theater and performance studies, and age studies. Her dissertation "Aging Ungracefully: Transgressive Femininity on the 18th Century Stage" argued that ageist rhetoric was used against eighteenth-century actresses when they behaved in ways that were considered socially transgressive. Her work has been published in *Lumen* and *Theatre Research in Canada*. On a country music-inspired Tennessee road trip, Nevena met Joanne Cash at the Nashville Cowboy Church and was delighted to discover they had the same half-black, half-white hairstyle reminiscent of Cruella de Vil.

Elaine McGirr is professor of eighteenth-century studies and head of theater at the University of Bristol. She has published widely on celebrity, genre, comedies, adaptation, and performers as authors. Recent publications include *Partial Histories: A Reappraisal of Colley Cibber*, *Stage Mothers: Women, Work and the Theatre 1660–1830* (coedited with Laura Engel), and articles on Richardson, Aphra Behn, Shakespearean adaptation, eighteenth-century comedies, private theatricals, celebrity, and the authority of actresses. McGirr once taught the Fonz's son how to work a washing machine.

Chelsea Phillips fell off a stage in a fish costume when she was four. She went on to earn an MFA from Mary Baldwin University/American Shakespeare Center and a PhD from Ohio State University, and is now assistant professor at Villanova University. This leads her to conclude that there was no permanent damage from this early piscine mishap. Her monograph, *Carrying All Before Her: Celebrity Pregnancy and the London Stage, 1689–1800*, was published by the University of Delaware Press; her most recent article, "Bodies in Play: Maternity, Repertory, and the Rival Romeo and Juliets," can be found in *Theatre Survey*.

Fiona Ritchie is associate professor of drama and theater in the Department of English at McGill University, Montreal. Her research focuses on gender and theater history in the long eighteenth century, and she is currently working on a study of women and regional theater in Britain and Ireland. She has also published widely in the field of eighteenth-century Shakespeare, including the monograph *Women and Shakespeare in the Eighteenth Century* and the essay collection (coedited with Peter Sabor) *Shakespeare in the Eighteenth Century*. When employed as the deputy curator of Dr. Johnson's House, London, she enjoyed polishing the statue of Johnson's cat, Hodge.

Leslie Ritchie is professor of English at Queen's University in Kingston, Ontario. Her research concerns the intersections of literature, media, and performance in eighteenth-century Britain. She is the coeditor of this collection, and the author of *David Garrick and the Mediation of Celebrity* and *Women Writing Music in Late Eighteenth-Century England: Social Harmony in Literature and Performance*. She first became interested in the eighteenth century while working at a living history site as a professional canoeist, and is (probably) the only contributor to this volume who has fired a cannon.

Amanda Weldy Boyd is the author of *Staging Memory and Materiality in Eighteenth-Century Theatrical Biography*. Formerly adjunct associate professor of English at Hope International University, Weldy Boyd is working on a historical fiction piece about Charles Macklin and his many outlandish doings. Like Macklin himself,

Amanda loves the robust exchange of ideas: it is said that once, as a toddler on a long car ride, she carried on all parts of a conversation by herself, not stopping her dissertation on whatever three-year-olds talk about even as her parents got out of the car, shut the door, and came round to unbuckle her from her car seat. Thirty years later, some say she is still in the middle of a very extended monologue, though the subject has changed periodically across the decades.

Seth Wilson holds a PhD in theater and performance studies from the University of Georgia, where his dissertation focused on the performance of gender in the Atlantic world during the long eighteenth century. His research interests include eighteenth-century European theater history, particularly British actresses, philosophical aesthetics and performance, and sports as performance. In addition to his scholarly work, he is also a professional director, dramaturg, and actor. Anecdotally, he is also among the winningest contestants in the history of the game show *Jeopardy!*, having won twelve episodes of the show in the fall of 2016.

INDEX

Italic page numbers indicate figures.